AF584537

Essays on Jane Jacobs

Essays on Jane Jacobs

EDITED BY

JESPER MEIJLING

TIGRAN HAAS

Translation: Julie Martin

BOKFÖRLAGET STOLPE AXEL AND MARGARET AX:SON JOHNSON FOUNDATION FOR PUBLIC BENEFIT

Contents

Preface

Jesper Meijling & Tigran Haas

THIS IS A book about the writer Jane Jacobs. We hope it will raise new interest in her thinking about people, societies, cities and economies, and show its relevance for the contemporary world. We also hope that it will provide inspiration and act as an aid to testing Jacobs' ideas in a wider, modern context, and to assist in delivering what she herself was striving for: a deeper understanding of the complex connections that lie behind how we build our societies and our cities – and how we live together within them. We believe that Jacobs' thoughts are very pertinent to the present and in certain regards more so than in her lifetime, or even just a few years ago. In the politically unstable reality that we now inhabit, she may have important things to say to us that are perhaps no longer self-evident and may have been forgotten, concerning how we create better living environments for all present, taking into account the big questions about how societies and their values are shaped and made sustainable.

This book came into being through a desire to draw wider attention to her writing and her ideas, with all its clarifying as well as complex and contradictory aspects. In November 2016, we held an international conference on Jacobs to mark the occasion of the centenary of her birth. It took place at the Royal Institute of Technology (KTH) in Stockholm and was hosted by the Centre for the Future of Places (CFP). We had three main speakers – Peter L. Laurence, Michael W. Mehaffy and Eva Minoura – and our ambition was to put the commonly held perceptions of Jacobs under deeper scrutiny over the course of the day-long conference. We did of course want to pay due attention to her most famous book, *The Death and Life of Great American Cities*, but the aim was to go further and shed a broader light on her wider-ranging works.

For Jacobs' highly original catalogue also includes such volumes as *The Economy of Cities*, *Systems of Survival* and *Dark Age Ahead*, each of which exhibits that distinctive methodical way of tackling the really big questions facing all modern human settlements. Perhaps it was this characteristically persistent curiosity about society's mysteries that drove her to chart area after area: the economic frameworks of cities, the origins of urban civilisation and the morality of public and civic life, to name a few. And that is not to mention the considerable written output, alluded to in these pages, which she produced before her critical breakthrough publication.

There was obviously neither time nor space for a consideration of all things Jacobian at our one-day conference, so we decided to press ahead and make the book that you have now before you. It came out in its original Swedish version in 2018, published by Nordic Academic Press in Lund. Naturally, we and the volume's contributing authors have not been able to capture the entirety of Jacobs' life's work, but we have tried to cover her achievement from a greater number of angles and furnish it with a fuller assessment than earlier books and anthologies may have attempted. If we are lucky, it will not only be a good read but it will also serve as an inspiration for a more active interest in her work, encouraging new research and further inquiries into her ideas, legacy and influence.

This book has been made possible by contributions to the Centre for the Future of Places from the Ax:son Johnson Foundation. We would like to express our grateful thanks to the foundation and in particular to Kurt Almqvist and Viveca Ax:son Johnson for that support.

Warm thanks are also due to the contributing writers whose commitment has helped the book come to fruition, to Nordic Academic Press, and in particular to Peter L. Laurence for his extra efforts with both text and illustrations, and to the ArkDes library staff for their exemplary assistance.

Last but not least we would like to thank our publisher with Marika Stolpe at the helm, Jennifer Paterson at her side and in particular Nils Johan Tjärnlund for his meticulous work on the book and the great cooperation accomplished along the way.

Quebec and the Struggle over Sovereignty
THE QUESTION OF SEPARATISM
Jane Jacobs
THE QUESTION OF SEPARATISM
Jane Jacobs

Introduction

Towards a Larger Jacobs

Jesper Meijling and Tigran Haas

FACED WITH A contemporary environment that is difficult to interpret, we need assistance. There are writers who offer us keys to a better understanding of major changes and shifts in society, and who have the ability to put them into words. They help us to see things that we are subconsciously wrapped up in, and that have become almost invisible to us. They also enable us to perceive the breadth and consequences of things we haven't previously seen or grasped. Perhaps we are looking for more such signposts and interpretations today, when it no longer seems at all clear where our digitalised and globalised society is heading. On the other hand, we cannot be sure if we have read enough or in the right way. When a digitalised and globalised society began to be described by such thinkers as Saskia Sassen, William Mitchell and Manuel Castells, we could not know that many other things which we were perhaps not willing to read into their conjectures would also begin to fill our existence.[1] The direction seems far from utopian and the bad old economic and social ghosts are walking again, as Thomas Piketty demonstrated a few years ago in *Capital in the 21st Century*, his great work on the economic inequalities of the world.

Instead of just waiting for further new voices, we have a great opportunity to revisit the ones we thought we had finished with, to see whether they have a point that did not previously get through. Some writings and analyses live longer than others – we can never be sure whether we have emptied them out or even understood them in depth, nor can we definitively assess how much they have to tell us about our society. The kind of text we are pointing to here is a combination of vast quantities of minor observations and data and the audacity to actually claim something – and moreover get it right – about the material development of society, about the formation of social and economic life,

Portrait of Jane Jacobs at 64 in her home in Toronto, taken on the occasion of the publication of *The Question of Separatism.*

about the consequences of our accumulated patterns of behaviour. This genre could be said to begin around the time of Marx and De Tocqueville, with the discovery of "society" as an object of study, and so we can see it offers us the possibility of turning back to authors of interest without haste. Time will tell which of the ones we mention above will be a part of it.

One writer we suggest should be included here is Jane Jacobs, and we will shortly explain why. We think that she may have even more to say to us today than she did just a few years ago. Her approach seems to reflect precisely those concerns that characterise the time we are living in now: on the one hand a broad interest in the sustainability of social structures, on the other hand social life and democratic norms that are under attack. It is precisely this demarcation area that Jacobs was operating in, the conditions of society and civilisation, from local life to a whole country, and the threats they face.

Jacobs has never been forgotten since she hit the headlines when her major work *The Death and Life of Great American Cities* came out in 1961. Public attention shifted somewhat thereafter but since about 1990 interest has grown constantly, marked among other things by an important conference held in Toronto in 1997.[2]

In conjunction with the 50th anniversary, in 2011, of her breakthrough book, and her centenary in 2016, several new titles were published on the subject of Jacobs that were able to ride the wave of that growing interest. There were several anthologies that endeavoured to place Jacobs in the current context of issues relating to urban development and societal planning. In *Reconsidering Jane Jacobs* (edited by Max Page & Timothy Mennel, 2011), the collaborating writers base their work largely on *The Death and Life of Great American Cities* and try to relate it to current town planning contexts around the world. *The Urban Wisdom of Jane Jacobs* (edited by Sonia Hirt & Diane Zahm, 2012) is somewhat more mixed in its perspective, whilst *Contemporary Perspectives on Jane Jacobs: Reassessing the Impacts of an Urban Visionary* (edited by Dirk Schubert, 2014) is entirely about her influence on town planning practice and thinking. Taken together, these books all clearly place her in the frame of an established discussion about 'the urban': town planning, urban sociology and urban design. It is of course exciting that Jacobs has been noticed and become such a rich source to draw on in this field – but there are still problems. The question of what Jacobs can be used for has been rendered a little too simple to answer in our opinion. She has been confined to a role that has suited others but which she did not seek herself, and which does not actually correspond to her work.

How useful and influential Jacobs has been is also reflected in the fact that, in recent decades, some areas of her thinking have become an established starting point in a number of American authors' theories. The American sociologist Sharon Zukin has used it for a critical sociological perspective, with Jacobs-inspired topics such as genuine city life and popular influence versus gentrification, commercial levelling out and the arrogance of the powers that be.[3] Both Edward Glaeser (*Triumph of the City*, 2011) and Richard Florida (*Cities and the Creative Class*, 2005), two well-established socio-economic strategists, have drawn much on Jacobs for their analyses. Above all they have found a basis for their development ideas with more modern terms such as "creative cities" and their advantages in global competition. The New Urbanism movement has cultivated ideas that draw on Jacobs, with many publications from the 1980s onwards, however disputed they may be in their application of her thinking. Even more rooted in a classic town-planning theory tradition with broad influence is Michael Mehaffy, who in his writings highlights Jacobs' theoretical sources and her specific knowledge model as a basis for a better planning approach.[4] (Mehaffy has contributed his own chapter to this anthology.) Many urban sociologists have been interested in Jacobs during the same period but without using her as a starting point. Among those with an American connection are Saskia Sassen (*The Global City: New York, London, Tokyo*, 1991) and Richard Sennett (*Flesh and Stone: The Body and the City in Western Civilization*, 1994), with their focus on city life as an observation point for the development of society and culture – something that Sassen comments on in his chapter in this book.

In summary, interest in Jacobs has hitherto largely been about incorporating her in a given discourse or using her for a certain idea. But what if you turn that round and try to start with Jacobs herself? She is a more wide-ranging writer than any we have named in the introduction. Not more complete, not more productive – but she developed many more comprehensive ideas than those with whom she has generally been associated. She did not cut things up into small pieces but took on the whole mystery of the structure of society.

In spite of all the attention, Jacobs is still largely unknown, however odd that may sound. Her persona is known to many (an activist with cat glasses) and a lot of people have read her most famous book, *Death and Life*, or at any rate some extracts from it – or at least have an idea of what it is about. But what many do not know is that the book is not the sum of Jacobs' writing: it was published in the middle of her professional life so to speak. She had written much in the preceding decades, had already published her first book, and most of the books she wrote came in the ensuing decades. It was only then that she could further develop the ideas that had been maturing over a long period of activity, and formulate completely new ones.

Jane Jacobs came from the provinces, more specifically from a middle-class family in the industrial coal town of Scranton, Pennsylvania. She moved to New York in the Great Depression, sharing rooms with her sister as she began to explore the big city as a freelance journalist. The fact that she began her development as a writer in the 1930s possibly left its mark: there is something of the "functionalist" in everything she wrote, in the sense of someone who wanted to understand and describe how things work. Throughout her life's work she also retained a strong feeling for what made up the vital cultural and political spirit of the 1930s, namely the ordinary citizens, the people: how they were governed or governed themselves, what society and its individuals could achieve together, plus the possibilities of democracy and its need for an active defence. But this did not lead Jacobs into any new ideology or school, as it did for many of her generation. It is the way she went further, how she pushed on and developed both professionally and intellectually that has, by and large, remained unknown, contributing to the idea that *Death and Life* came as if from nowhere. That may explain in large part why she has become so confined within the narrow context of particular debates, and why her authorship and career have not received a broader appraisal.

This distinction also marked the very first biographies, that came out in conjunction with the growing interest in Jacobs. Their writers helped to confirm the role that has been ascribed to Jacobs, like Alice

On the press pages in *Architectural Forum* an editorial staff colleague Walter McQuade comments on Jane Jacobs cycling under the headline "get a bike!" Over the years that Jane Jacobs cycled past traffic jams along Fifth Avenue on her way to or from her home in Greenwich Village the typical catcall changed from "Get a horse!" to "That's a good idea!" and "Take me with you!" Jacobs on her bike is seen in the righthand column. *Architectural Forum*, April 1956.

man. On exhibit at the Museum of tural History in New York City is a ze pigeon nest from the stern neigh-hood of Wall St. This one is made irely of paper clips and hairpins bor-ved without interest from J. P. Morgan l the other downtown neighbors.

(HOIST)

e elaborate glass trucks which trundle derly around our cities have an air-rne branch now. Recently, in Chicago, en a 300-lb. sheet of glass, 7' x 8', d to be transported to the twenty-third or of an apartment house, the Hamilton ass Co. used a helicopter to do the job.

ys Hamilton's president: "It was no nt. It was the only practical way we ld deliver it without severe technical oblems and extreme high cost. Since the ass would not fit into the building eleva-, it would have been necessary to erect scaffolding up the side of the building, ng twelve men at a prohibitive cost." e estimate was that a boom and hoist rangement would have cost between $800 d $1,000. The helicopter delivery cost 00.

(GET A BIKE!)

eryone talks about the traffic in our ies, but few individuals do anything out it. It is a pleasure to know one of se who does; this lady, who shall be meless, gets on a bicycle in Rockefeller nter every day at close of work and dals down Fifth Ave., south through crowded department store district, utheast through the impossible press of garment district, on through the fallen tals and broken blossoms of the whole-

continued on p. 51

(PARENTHESES)

cont'd.

sale flower zone, and then down through wicked Greenwich Village until she reaches home, her house on Hudson St.

This cyclist knows a lot about NYC traffic. Lewis Mumford might learn a good deal on the handlebars of her bike, mornings and evenings when the weather is good and the wind holds fair to and from the office. (During the working day, she wedges her bike in among the ranks of

Cadillacs in the Rockefeller Center garage down the block.)

This bicycle-riding to the office in New York is nothing new for her; her estimate of New York traffic? . . . "Bad, getting worse, but not for bicycles."

As automobile traffic has worsened in recent years there has also been a change in drivers' attitudes toward the lonely bike rider slipping past, she reports. To illustrate, she has compiled two comparative lists—what the lady bicyclist heard two years ago, and what she hears these days. The remarks, and their frequency per trip:

Back in 1954—

"Get a horse"—10 ("Very tiresome.")
"Want a lift?"—5
"Ho, ho, ho, look at that! Yak, yak!"—5
"Whyn't you stay in the park?"—2
"Watch out girlie, you'll get hurt."—2
"Hang on and I'll pull you."—1
"Your back wheel's spinning."—1

But now, in the past year—

"That's a good idea!"—3
"Hurry, you'll miss the light."—1
"Good for you!"—3
"Your back wheel's spinning."—2
("Those back wheel people are very reliable, year after year.")
"I envy your energy."—1
"There's the life of Riley."—1
"Fastest thing going."—1
"Take me with you."—2
"Hello, Hon!"—1

The wheel of transportation obviously is turning backward. In 1956 she has not heard a single *"Get a horse!"*—W. McQ.

Alexiou with *Jane Jacobs: Urban Visionary* from 2006, and Anthony Flint with his *Wrestling with Moses: How Jane Jacobs took on New York's Master Builder and Transformed the American City*, from 2011. Robert Kanigel's *Eyes on the Street: the Life of Jane Jacobs*, from 2016, is the first more comprehensive biography, which actually starts from Jacobs herself and her life, but it has some major shortcomings. A marked change occurs with the publication of historian Peter Laurence's book *Becoming Jane Jacobs*, also from 2016, which was the fruit of long research, and in which he digs deep to find primary sources and uncovers a whole, largely new picture of Jacobs' intellectual and professional life before 1961. Laurence reflects again on important parts of that history in his two chapters in our anthology. In later years two books of collected works have also been published, *Ideas That Matter: The Worlds of Jane Jacobs* (ed. Max Allen, 2011) and *Vital Little Plans: The Short Works of Jane Jacobs* (ed. Samuel Zipp & Nathan Storring, 2016), both with ambitious compilations of such texts as have previously been inaccessible for various reasons, published as well as unpublished, ranging from her reporting for American *Vogue* in the mid-1930s to an extract from a final planned book that was never completed.

There remains much still to discover about Jacobs' writings and thinking. An attempt to capture that breadth is the basis for the present book. The authors' learned and critical contributions can thus form a kind of guide, an overview. Their texts deal among other things with how she has been confined and made famous for things she did not represent, committed to views and agendas that she herself never supported or worked for.

In terms of her writing, there are several contexts that can be elucidated. Jacobs' apparently contradictory traits as an author have made her hard to place – hence she has also been embraced by different groups and trends. Peter Laurence notes in the first of his two chapters, on the basis of his comprehensive research, how she actually refused to collaborate in her own biography or in any attempt to present a uniform picture of herself. This has contributed to the difficulties of charting her early writing to its full extent, highlighting the effort needed to attempt it, as seen in *Becoming Jane Jacobs*. Her full authorship extends from the depression of the 1930s to the time after the attacks of 9/11 in 2001, but the blank patch on the map that represents her long, dogged writing career up to her big breakthrough in 1961 was precisely that part of her life as an author when she gradually built up the knowledge and maturity that ultimately prepared her to break away, in a well-considered fashion, from many of the ideas she had previously defended.

Another context that tends to disappear in a strictly subject-limited presentation of Jacobs is the one found in the cultural and political environment that existed in the early 1960s when her breakthrough work, *Death and Life*, joined the social debate. We can see that the book was not an isolated moment significant only for a subsequent exegesis within a certain group: it was a literary event when it came out, but it was accompanied by other literary events. Of all Jacobs' books, it is the one that has had the greatest influence, but it would not have done so without its cultural and contemporary context. Jacobs had observed, built up knowledge and worked in depth on town planning issues over many years. When her big contributions came and broke new ground in the debate at the beginning of the Sixties, this took place in parallel with what a number of other authors had observed, built up and presented to their readers in other areas of society and in a similar way. Several epoch-making books were presented in those years. Most closely comparable with Jacobs' breakthrough book in the wider American society debate are the marine biologist and environmental debater Rachel Carson's *Silent Spring* (1962) and the feminist writer Betty Friedan's *The Feminine Mystique* (1963), which Catharina Thörn also comments on in her chapter in this anthology. A couple of years later came *Unsafe at Any Speed* (1965) by Ralph Nader, the lawyer and consumer rights activist, which dealt with the human costs of the car. What unites them is that in select but central and far-reaching areas of society they formulate a break from and a showdown with certain established truths underpinning society that turned out to be enormous blind spots entailing great risks to society and citizens. They do so from the inside so to speak, basing themselves on extensive knowledge and studies of quantities of empirical material. It is not a matter of quick, opinion-based contributions to the debate but solid journalistic revelations that are based on scientific methods. Therefore in the long run nobody could successfully argue that they were wrong. These writers embodied what we today call whistle-blowers (Nader is said to have popularised the term) but in this early period, the practice was not just about revelations from within individual businesses: what they tried to tackle were whole sectors of society and established cultural patterns. They did not offer just the *exposé*, but also their own comprehensive analysis. This applies particularly to Jacobs and Friedan – but it is Jacobs alone, who, on the basis of her investigations and analysis, formulated her own carefully prepared alternative proposals for how to tackle the problems arising.

That sort of bigger picture approach at the start of the 1960s also existed in the field of town planning, which we should not forget: Jacobs was not alone when she began to formulate her critique. The first clear breaks with the basic assumptions of modernism, in the form of ambitious, consensus-busting studies came precisely in those years and Jacobs' book from 1961 is only one of the contributions (although it was the most advanced). Kevin Lynch with *The Image of the City* (1960) and Gordon Cullen in *Townscape* (1961) were among the most important and effective contributors and share with Jacobs the critical perspective in which the writers bring the observer down from modernism's lofty heights to a human level. Just a few years later, in part as a fruit of that discussion, came the ground-breaking texts of Christopher Alexander (*A City is Not a Tree*, 1965) and Robert Venturi (*Complexity and Contradiction in Architecture*, 1966), with the mathematician and design researcher, Alexander, displaying a closer theoretical connection to Jacobs.

But the compass and universal perspective that Jacobs brings to a social problem nonetheless has more in common, in approach, with an author such as Rachel Carson. We can also see the connection with a wider cultural critique, that came to be increasingly important in Jacobs' writing, and which in the early 1960s is reflected in books such as Marshall McLuhan's *The Gutenberg Galaxy* (1962), which even today is still a reference point for a new way of understanding people's environment and reality as experienced through the media, Herbert Marcuse's *One Dimensional Man* (1964) about the new oppression of the critical citizen in the consumer society, and Jürgen Habermas' *Strukturwandel der Öffentlichkeit* (1962, English title: *The Structural Transformation of the Public Sphere*), which was ground-breaking in the debate about the political sphere of urban society which has continued relevance

The writer and marine biologist Rachel Carson, 1952.

today. To complete the picture we should also mention another new departure in terms of ideas, the effects of which have increased in significance in our day, namely the work on political economics by James Buchanan and Gordon Tullock. When their book, *The Calculus of Consent* came out in 1962, it was the starting point for an economics trend that laid an important foundation for the new conservatism and marketisation of the public sphere in the 1970s and 1980s. As part of that change were two related ideological manifestos, from the ultraconservative southern Republican Barry Goldwater and the market philosopher Friedrich Hayek respectively (both 1960). In contrast to their works, but just as much of a breakaway idea with a long-term effect, was James Baldwin's *The Fire Next Time* (1963) which helped to initiate the Kennedy administration's recognition of the black population's struggle as a political issue.

Jacobs' breakthrough in a male-dominated arena – like Rachel Carson and Betty Friedan – begs the question of how she should be viewed from a feminist perspective. Several of the collaborators in this book touch on this subject. But it is not an obvious or simple thing, if our idea is to follow her own writing and thinking; in that case we should start with the issues she herself tackled – Jacobs' *own* programme – and that is the premise we have chosen for this book. On the one hand it may be difficult to draw the line when it comes to the risk of committing her, so to speak, when she did not include herself in any such discussion, even though her authorship extended right through to 2004. On the other hand, the feminist perspective is an obvious one to consider if we were to focus on her cultural and political context and the reception accorded to her books – particularly the breakthrough. How did contemporary criticism describe her? Was the judgment influenced? There is no doubt that she met with opposition as a woman, for example in the depiction of her as a housewife who wrote – an image she may have contributed to when first introducing herself to the wider reading public without making any clear reference to her earlier career (more on that in Peter Laurence's first chapter). We do not know much about the role this may have played, but it certainly warrants further investigation. The feminist perspective might thus be central to a so-called 'reception study', where the enquiry steps outside Jacobs' texts and looks at what others have written about her and her contribution. There is certainly plenty of material to work with, far more than the reference most cited hitherto: Lewis Mumford's patriarchal and sexist demolition of her breakthrough book in *The New Yorker*.[5] Starting points which scarcely need to be questioned in terms of reception and judgment are that she revealed herself to be one of the most important American social commentators just as great problems were forming at the beginning of the 1960s, and she is also probably the writer who has had the greatest influence on town planning issues since the modernist generation.

What also puts Jacobs together with writers and debaters such as Carson and Friedan – if we go back to them – is her extraordinary capacity for observation: the reader is treated to a study in the full sense of the word. When she discusses programmes and solutions, she has studied the players who put them forward. That approach goes for everything else that finds itself under her microscope: real life activities of all kinds, with their patterns, movements, processes, side effects. She tries to see where strengths and weaknesses lie, and tries to draw well-founded conclusions as to what is sustainable and what approaches and patterns have resilience or otherwise. It is from the starting point of her journalistic work that she digs deeper and deeper, gathering knowledge about an issue or a complex of issues, rather than allowing herself to be shaped by an academic 'thought-collective' and its rules. It must be a good thing for posterity that she did not succeed in academia, even though she was briefly in contact with it, as Laurence tells us in his first chapter – if she had gone down that route she would have been polished beyond recognition and may have produced much less to occupy us.

In the area of city planning, Jacobs' relevance is undisputed, even though the subject has hardly been exhausted. However, it is through her other spheres of interest, as she sought to address the difficult issues of the future, that we may seek new insights into her thinking. One such field is the economic life of society – understanding what it is and how it should be described. The economy is the most comprehensive theme in Jacobs' work, bigger than town planning and hence the clearest example of a misinterpretation of her. Jacobs herself thought that *Death and Life* was to a large extent a book about economics. Several of the headlines are sketched out in the article "Downtown is for people", published in the business journal *Fortune* in 1958, and there

are traces even in her early journalistic work.[6] The theme of economics is fully developed in three of her books – *The Economy of Cities* (1969), *Cities and the Wealth of Nations* (1984) and *The Nature of Economies* (2000) – and continues down to the last volume that she never managed to finish before dying in 2006, which was intended as a fully edited synthesis of her economic thinking.

Today there is little doubt that the current hegemony of economic theory is losing ground. This does not of course mean that mainstream economists on all sides in society will suddenly become powerless: the market as the prescribed solution to everything is still politically successful, and large parts of society are now built on those models. On the other hand, economists are already well on the way to losing their allure. Fewer and fewer people seriously believe that they serve the common good, or are in possession of a great understanding of society – as was the case as recently as the beginning of this century. Even the most sophisticated markets and business systems are quaking under the weight of quite different forces and vital issues, where the economists' problem formulations seem ineffectual, certainly in the context of questions about society's sustainability and survival. Here Jacobs may have something to offer. Her model for describing economics is linked to activity, processes and networks. It makes it possible to allow economic analysis to interact with a deeper understanding of society's vitality and survival. 'Sustainability' is a term in frequent use today, but it seems that Jacobs may give more depth to the concept: sustainable patterns of action and social norms for the way we survive, become richer on various levels and secure the development of our shared political institutions. Her economic analysis ties in with the other fields of knowledge she moves through: anthropology, systems theory, sociology and history. Jacobs' intellectual development is illustrated by Peter Laurence in his two chapters, while the other writers delve more into selected, specific aspects of her work.

The writer and feminist Betty Friedan at a press conference in New York with the National Organization of Women, 1975.

The social context she tried to place herself in is thus wider and more complex than many have been able to appreciate. Nonetheless, it should be possible to discuss straightforwardly. Can we place Jacobs' thinking and social analysis in a political context? In all her ambitious attempts to capture big social questions – on town planning, the economy, self-determination, public action – there is a political Jacobs: but which one? Left? Right? Feminist? Traditionalist? Environmentalist? Although she was gradually embraced by both libertarians and conservatives, she nonetheless was marked out as a suspected left-wing element in the 1950s McCarthy era. She played a part in the emerging alternative movement of the Sixties, and the Vietnam War and political developments in the USA caused her to choose exile in Canada for the second half of her life. Per Svensson believes that in spite of everything it is not so difficult to work out Jacobs' political home: he argues in his chapter that her central ideal has a clearly liberal character that runs like a constant line right through everything she wrote, i.e. liberal in the classical political sense. To support his conclusion Svensson cites Jacobs' claiming of *diversity* as both the means and the end, in the footsteps of John Stuart Mill. There are other things found in Jacobs that he says also show she was a liberal: the simultaneous distinction and dependency between private and universal, the individual's self-determination as something fundamental and her faith in the classic American ideal of freedom.

The political Jacobs is also the theme in Jesper Meijling's essay – if by the term 'political' we do not think primarily of elections and parties but rather the deeper meaning of coexistence in society, in our *polis*. In *Systems of Survival*, from 1992, Jacobs deals with perhaps the broadest issue in the whole of her written works, namely what guides our actions in different areas of our social life (as distinct from the individual life) and how we then determine what is right and wrong. She does not discuss private morals but what is rewarded or condemned in the different public spheres (social, political and market economy-related) in which we variously meet, and what the result might be if we thoughtlessly mix up the rules of these different spheres. Here the position Jacobs takes is far from the neo-liberal ideal that was at its zenith when the book came out, and which, in the form of the New Public Management approach to running public services among other things, was dominant for a couple of decades: seeing the individual perspective as the only valid one, the market as the only valid model for human exchange, and the existence of 'society' as an invalid illusion. Instead she tried to approach an understanding of what standards for our public coexistence make a society sustainable and which ones are destructive.

What makes society sustainable? That could be an alternative title for *Systems of Survival*, and so Jacobs discusses a question very much related to the contentions Bruno Latour put forward in his famous essay "Technology is Society Made Durable", also published in 1992. But while Latour presented technology as a joint actor with people, Jacobs makes a more complex analysis that incorporates not only the materialist perspective but also perspectives of ideas, ethics and historical development. Thus there are interesting – and apparently unstudied – parallels between Jacobs' and Latour's actor-network theory (often abbreviated to ANT): looking at reality "connection by connection", rather than jumping to big conclusions. The relational element is the subject of Ebba Högström's new interpretation of Jacobs. Rather than separate physical elements that make up reality – like sidewalks, streets, quarters and so on – Högström uncovers how Jacobs places people, things, spaces, actions and patterns of action in relation to one another. Everything that is activated in Jacobs' analysis of city life seems to hinge upon and interact with everything else, or is prevented from doing so. But at the same time there is a blind spot into which the relational in her analysis does not reach, notes Högström, namely suburban society. How was this oversight possible?

Catharina Thörn discusses another uncertainty in Jacobs, apart from, or perhaps in addition to, the close relations in the fabric of society that are Högström's theme. Thörn wonders whether Jacobs was caught in a kind of spatial determinism and therefore missed the significance of social and economic structures. Reading the classic British urban sociologist Ruth Glass in parallel raises our perspective: she is not as well-known as Jacobs, Carson and Friedan but was just as much of a decisive innovator during this period. Glass's eye for contradictions, disharmony and conflicts, and for a larger scale of economic divisions – the struggle for space and migration – enabled an analysis that led her to successfully establish the term 'gentrification' (in her book: *London: Aspects of Change*, 1964).

The relationship between the interests of individuals and wider society has become increasingly complex within one of Jacobs' topics, namely monitoring and social control – her "eyes on the street", the famous concept from *Death and Life*. Vania Ceccato is studying the transition to what she instead calls "apps on the street". Jacobs' idea of monitoring and security has its starting point in the close coexistence in urban space of residents and strangers – the relational, to use the term Högström highlights. But what happens when eyes are replaced with cameras and apps, Ceccato wonders. What does the individualised digital technology do with 'natural' monitoring of public spaces and places? Who is now the legitimate observer and monitor? This also raises new questions about environmental design in the interests of crime prevention and what environment we are actually talking about here. Are there perhaps new risks of social exclusion?

Connections and processes also characterise Jacobs' economic thinking, as Saskia Sassen shows in her text. Sassen takes up the proposition in *The Nature of Economies* from the year 2000, in which Jacobs tries to clarify the links between nature's resource and feedback flows and man-made economic processes. Jacobs establishes a perspective which seems as if it might be able to integrate the use of resources in a direct way, instead of creating a distance from it with theoretical screens like 'the market'. According to Sassen, with the help of Jacobs' approach we can clarify how different economies are linked to one another, for example in the development Sassen has studied in her now classic work: how a metropolis or *global city* is built up of diverse 'sub-economies' of professional people and services which connect the local urban with the 'super-economic' networks and are the prerequisites for the existence and rapid development of the global city. With a Jacobian process perspective, as Sassen points out, the city again becomes a lens for studying social development and economic development – like the pioneers in the Chicago school of sociology – where gentrification and the displacement of households and local businesses are not just separate phenomena but recast whole economies.

Throughout her writing, Jacobs took a special interest in concepts such as growth and innovation and what she achieved has in turn influenced eminent economists such as Robert Lucas and Paul Krugman. Lucas used her arguments in *The Economy of Cities* and *Cities and the Wealth of Nations* to revise his understanding of the significance of the social environment for economic development, and also the economic effects of an ongoing exchange of knowledge in that environment.[7] Her analysis of the growth phenomenon drew attention to the need for room for unpredictability and open paths in the companies' surroundings. She had already begun to develop the argument in *Death and Life*, and *The Economy of Cities* was entirely devoted to the mystery of growth. Jacobs' process-oriented view was completely different from Adam Smith's stylish but rigid notion of *division of labour*, which has locked in economic thinking right up to our own time.

Traces of this locked-in attitude are still current and problematic, from the modernists' rock hard construction tracks into the future to the present-day demands for predictable results from all kinds of ventures in innovation, research and social design. Unpredictability is the point that Ola Andersson highlights, based on a critique of Jacobs' starting points in *The Economy of Cities*. Andersson thinks that in her first pure economics book, Jacobs takes the focus on the phenomenon of cities quite a bit too far when she tries to make the emergence and development of cities independent of agricultural surpluses – something that we humans have always been and remain dependent on for our urban lifestyle. But in the economic analysis of the cities' inner processes on the other hand, she is almost prophetic, thinks Andersson. Many of the decisive, driving forces in the global economy today are captured by Jacobs' analysis in a way that traditionally trained economists have not been able to do: Jacobs' tools work for describing the diverse, unpredictable development and ramifications of new products and services, of the kind that have enabled Bill Gates and Steve Jobs and all the entrepreneurs who've followed in their footsteps.

Peter Elmlund also emphasises in his chapter the small and stubborn movements. The strong development of small businesses has made Jacobs' analysis increasingly relevant, thinks Elmlund, for example with a concept like *knowledge spillovers* for the exchange of knowledge surpluses between businesses in the same environment that can lead to new products and services and hence new businesses. Against this, mergers ('consolidation') and growing giants, like today's monopoly-seeking digital service companies in the retail trade for example, pose a constant threat.

Late in life, Jacobs had an ambition to summarise all of her economic thinking in a single book which had the working title *Uncovering the Economy: A New Hypothesis*.[8] She never managed to finish it, but in this volume we have enclosed an interview with Jacobs from 2002 in which

disk II
disk II
apple][

she describes, in her own words, where she stood on questions of the economy and the role of cities in future innovation.

The contributing writers' discussion of Jacobs' economic thinking could serve as a rough outline for future research: 'Jacobs and the economy' is a subject worthy of its own book, as Laurence points out. But then it might not be entirely obvious where the boundary should be drawn, since Jacobs' various fields and areas of interest overlap with one another. Basically there seems to be a unifying model, based on an interest in complex systems. Michael Mehaffy highlights how Jacobs has given the architecture researcher useable tools: analysis concepts that have their origin in a combination of clever observation and a scientific angle. She was the first to apply a new, emerging understanding of reality to the life of cities, a "web way of thinking" as Mehaffy calls it. Key terms such as organised and disorganised complexity link her to kindred thinkers like Warren Weaver, Herbert Simon, Christopher Alexander and others, and to network theories with applications within biology and data sciences as well as ANT and space syntax.

Jacobs' contested position between the domains of debate, critique and science is a prominent theme in Tigran Haas' essay, where he discusses her many shortcomings as a scientist, in the more strict sense of that word. Several authors have pointed out problems of method and transparency as well as mystifying blind spots connected to her famous observational approach, which is all the more relevant to shed light on as Jacobs' books have earned a place as a stable point of interest precisely in scholarly debate on methodology and theory among urbanists, architects and sociologists, and influenced some theory directly.

The space syntax trend – where evidence-based knowledge of spatial organisation is seen as the nucleus in city design – is today among the most active applications of a theory influenced by Jacobs. Eva Minoura argues that architecture and planning as disciplines and practice, are based on positive knowledge of the spatial organisation of the city, and that Jacobs contributes to that sort of knowledge model rather than to a prescriptive 'recipe'. Thus it is a matter of understanding and handling spatial problems – whatever the conditions – and following up, evaluating and obtaining evidence for the chosen solutions. Such an approach has great strategic potential for architects and planners when it comes to clarifying and accentuating their specific competence. In

Apple Computer co-founder Steve Jobs with an Apple II computer, 1979.

that way it can help to ensure that political notions and so-called 'dialogue planning' do not degenerate into bad solutions or even decision-making chaos that no-one can ultimately find their way out of.

The issue of 'recipes' or 'analysis and knowledge model' is one of the great divides when it comes to the view of Jacobs, perhaps the biggest. Jill Grant penetrates the dilemma of the New Urbanism movement and its use of Jacobs: how certain elements in *Death and Life of Great American Cities* inspired the movement's standardising regulations on characteristics such as density, mixed usage, walking distances, 'attractiveness' and so on, and were thus used to assert a kind of direct link to Jacobs. But Grant thinks this is to disregard too many central tenets of Jacobs' thinking – indeed, New Urbanism's representatives simply avoid reading it properly: how else could such essential themes of Jacobs as time and change be absent in their visions?

The eager embrace that came from many different directions was something that Jacobs usually accepted with tranquillity and kind interest. If there was anything that she kept her distance from, it was the academic world, which she was never a part of. As a writer and researcher she was seemingly very much driven both to understand for herself and to explain, to illustrate. (Another Jacobs can be added to the list: the teacher). The systematic nature and at the same time rich contextualising of her observations hits the deepest scientific nerve, one that is not about the number of publications but the endeavour to build new knowledge. At the same time, this seems, paradoxically enough, to have created a distance from the academic world, where the precise highlighting of a deeper understanding of problems has been in continuous decline in parallel with Jacobs' authorship – and has probably never been at a lower ebb than today. Moreover, that is one of the problems she tackles in her last book, *Dark Age Ahead*, from 2004. Regardless of other yardsticks, the questions she poses – and the answers she gives – are of great interest, not least because they take the questioning seriously: they are always about a very frank way of "wondering at society", to borrow a turn of phrase from the Swedish sociologist Johan Asplund.

Jacobs, the teacher and 'clarifier' has powerful tools to help her tackle the big questions. Something that could be worth a chapter of its own in a book about her authorship is her technique as a writer. Peter Laurence touches on the subject, highlighting her early development as a journalist and specialist writer. Her reporting technique was a significant factor in her ability to reach out, and also for the acuity of her analysis. We can also confidently assume that she gave her own thinking a good start by writing well and intelligibly – and sometimes perhaps, with that ability, she tempted herself to go a little beyond the watertight, as Ola Andersson suggests concerning her treatment of the cities' prehistoric origins. In *Death and Life* her combination of analysis, rhetoric and teaching is so refined that it might well be used as an illustrative example in the training of debaters: how she builds up some of the book's central points by cleverly turning an opponent's various arguments inside out to make them into her own.[9]

In her subsequent writing, Jacobs was even more out on her own than she was in her breakthrough book, and she often set out into uncharted territory without any waymarkers from an ongoing debate – a far harder task of course. There is definitely a strong relationship with the burning contemporary issues of the day in her later books – as in *Cities and the Wealth of Nations* from the early 1980s, about structural economic crises, or *The Question of Separatism* (1980) about the then hot topic of Quebec and other independence movements – but to a great extent she chose to go her own way there as well. Perhaps it is in her last book, *Dark Age Ahead*, published two years before her death in 2006, that she comes full circle and the relationship to the present time becomes as acute as in *Death and Life*. As with *Death and Life*, the significance of *Dark Age Ahead* seems to increase with time, and with the developments we now see around us, in contrast to the lukewarm reception the book initially received. It is only here that Jacobs seriously confronts what she is most critical of in social development at large. As the 'functionalist' that she was, she paid no attention to the dimension that deals with symbolic values and staging in the city, society and politics. This has been an intrinsic part of the analysis of other writers, from Thorstein Veblen via Robert Venturi and Denise Scott Brown down to Pierre Bourdieu and today's Joel Kotkin with his analysis of "the ephemeral city" in which the super-rich display their extravagance. In Jacobs it first came through in the last book, but now in full force: staging and image creation are not, however, in her analysis, an "interesting phenomenon" but something that with horrifying strength is now breaking down knowledge, human communication and political life.

Her criticism is directed at American society. Peter Laurence reminds us that Jacobs had actually chosen exile in 1968, but that in spite of this she continued to describe and scrutinise the USA in her writing. Her conclusion in *Dark Age Ahead* was that the USA had quite literally done away with its underlying values and instead created an internal threat to North American culture. She had no doubts that short-sightedness and contempt for knowledge were the principal factors behind this development. Jacobs adds these conclusions to a wider analysis of problems faced by the major powers and empires, and the fatal internal tensions and contradictions they build up, an analysis that now stands out as extremely pertinent. The fact that she reacted so strongly is understandable considering how far this development has taken us from the foundations of civilisation, freedom, respect and the wise creation of societies that formed her highly human, American starting point, which runs throughout her writing. That is why Jacobs' body of written work, right through from the 1930s to the early 21st century, appears to us, in the light – or should that be the shadow? – of the present day, as nothing less than the basis for a genuine political alternative.

1 See e.g. Saskia Sassen, *Territory, Authority, Rights: From Medieval to Global Assemblages* (Princeton: Princeton University Press, 2006); William J. Mitchell, *City of Bits: Space, Place, and the Infobahn* (Cambridge: MIT Press, 1995); Manuel Castells, *The Information Age: Economy, Society and Culture*, vol. I–III (Malden: Blackwell, 1996–1998).

2 Quotations from her books about cities and economics, including *The Death and Life of Great American Cities*, have increased significantly since the beginning of the 1990s, see Max Page & Timothy Mennel (ed.), *Reconsidering Jane Jacobs* (Chicago: APA Press, 2011), p. 67.

3 Sharon Zukin, *Naked City: The Death and Life of Authentic Urban Places* (Oxford: Oxford University Press, 2010). Also, together with Philip Kasinitz & Xiangmin Chen, *Global Cities, Local streets: Everyday Diversity from New York to Shanghai* (New York: Routledge, 2016).

4 Michael W. Mehaffy, *Cities Alive: Jane Jacobs, Christopher Alexander, and the Roots of the New Urban Renaissance* (Portland: Sustasis, 2017).

5 Lewis Mumford, "Mother Jacobs' Home Remedies", *The New Yorker*, 1 December 1962, p. 148 ff.

6 See Jane Jacobs, "Downtown is for People", in Samuel Zipp & Samuel Storring (ed.), *Vital Little Plans: The Short Works of Jane Jacobs* (London: Short Books, 2016), pp. 85–104. The same volume also contains a couple of Jacobs' articles from American *Vogue* 1936–1937, pp. 8–16.

7 Robert E. Lucas, "On the mechanics of economic development", *Journal of Monetary Economics*, no. 22 (1988), p. 13, pp. 37–39. See also Paul Krugman, *Development, Geography and Economic Theory* (Cambridge: MIT Press, 1995).

8 See: Samuel Zipp & Nathan Storring (ed.), *Vital Little Plans: The Short Works of Jane Jacobs* (London: Short Books, 2016), pp. 317–337.

9 For a more detailed study of this, see Jesper Meijling, *Påståenden om framtiden* (Stockholm: Axl Books, 2007), pp. 105–109.

WANTED
ATENCIÓN
HOMBRES PARA CARRERAS
EN
EL DEPARTAMENTO DE POLICIA
El Departamento de Policia de la ciudad de Nueva York
busca jovenes para carreras.
EXAMEN PARA POSICIONES DE
POLICIA Y NOVICIO
11 de mayo 1968
HAGA SU SOLICITUD ENTRE EL
3 DE ABRIL Y EL 23 DE ABRIL
Para mas informacion llame el Departamento de
Personal 566-8700 o visite su cuartel local.
YOUR

CHAPTER I

Who Was Jane Jacobs?

Peter L. Laurence

IN HIS *Pensées*, the 17th-century philosopher and scientist Blaise Pascal observed that, "A good portrait can only be made by reconciling all of our contradictory features, and it is not enough to follow through a series of mutually compatible qualities without reconciling their opposites. To understand an author's meaning, all of the contradictory passages must be reconciled."

Pascal was thinking primarily of biblical exegesis when he wrote these words, which he placed under the heading "Contradiction". However, his ideas are equally valuable for other hermeneutics – and not just literary analyses, but biographical ones as well. This, I found, was especially true when writing a biography of Jane Jacobs, as well as in analysing her canonical tome, *The Death and Life of Great American Cities.*

Jacobs, who was born Jane Butzner in Scranton, Pennsylvania in 1916, and died a Canadian citizen in Toronto, in 2006, was defined by a number of contradictions. She was a writer and an activist, with the many personal ambiguities that can entail: contemplative and militant, objective and partisan, reticent and political, private and public. She held no academic degrees but changed a number of academic fields. She was a geographer, an urbanist, an anthropologist, a sociologist, an economist, and an ecologist, but was none of these professionally. She was an insider and an outsider; a woman working in disciplines dominated (some still dominated) by men. She was as inclined to science as to literature; she was a pioneer in ideas about complexity science but wasn't a scientist. She was an expert who disdained experts and rejected a list of honorary degrees. She was modest and humble, but extraordinarily ambitious in her research and writing.

In April 1968 Jacobs made a protest against a planned expressway in New York. She was taken to the police station and released, promising to appear in court.

Before publishing *Death and Life*, she had a writing career – for industry, the federal government, and freelance – that she barely mentioned. She wrote a book on the US Constitution, published by Columbia University Press, that she never mentioned. She was a modernist who praised modern buildings as masterpieces and advocated saving old ones, albeit primarily for economic reasons. She rejected modern city planning and criticised its practitioners in the strongest terms, but helped to conceive the new field of urban design. She understood cities as ecologies and wrote about sidewalks, the death and life of cities, and the collapse of civilisations, seeing connections between phenomena of such different dimensions. Attracted to and intrigued by radicals, third-party politicians, and even communists, she was a community- and union-organising liberal who rejected Roosevelt's federalism, various liberal social programmes, libertarianism, neoliberalism, and all political labels. She loved the United States – at least the ideal of American democracy – but left it. Despite moving to New York, and later to Toronto, she never moved far from her childhood home in Pennsylvania and didn't travel beyond Canada until later in her life. Despite great interest in her life and work, writing and activism, she resisted all biographical attention.

Unsurprisingly, such contradictions, apparent and actual, led to remarkably varied interpretations of Jacobs' career, ideas, and ideology. Apart from the sexism she had to contend with (or because of it), she was as often regarded as a housewife and an amateur than as an intellectual and an expert. Despite significant attention to her ideas and life starting in the early 1960s, when *Death and Life* was published, the first three decades of her writing career were unknown – in part due to her own reticence. At the same time, her ideas were embraced by conservatives and Marxists, including such dissimilar figures as William F. Buckley and Marshall Berman, and equally embraced and rejected by many in between. In the 1960s, her attacks on post-war US public housing were accurately regarded as the slaughter of one of the liberals' 'sacred cows', and celebrated by conservatives, although she still supported subsidised housing, worked to improve a public housing project in East Harlem, and later helped to design a state-subsidised housing project in New York's West Village.

In the 1970s, as she turned her focus to *The Economy of Cities* (1969), she lost readers who were drawn to the planning, policy, and design aspects of *Death and Life*; they were often the same people who had ignored the book's economic themes. In the late 1980s, as *Death and Life* was picked up by a new generation, she was warmly embraced by New Urbanists, in part because of mistaken beliefs in her alleged hostility to modern architecture and misreadings of her ideas about old buildings, despite her clear rejections of suburbanism and architectural fetishism. In the 1990s, she was embraced by libertarians despite rejecting Reaganomics, Thatcherism, and neoliberalism in *Cities and the Wealth of Nations* (1984) and *Systems of Survival: A Dialogue on the Moral Foundations of Commerce and Politics* (1992).

With the latter book's sequel, *The Nature of Economies* (2000), her return to complexity science and economics combined with 'new' interests in such topics as biomimicry and environmental collapse to chart a path that was difficult for any siloed academic to follow. And despite her advanced years, Jacobs made keeping up with her only more difficult when she published her last book, *Dark Age Ahead* (2004), which focused on threats to what she identified as five societal pillars, including community, education, science, taxes, and public trust.

Not only was the breadth of her interests vast, when she died in 2006, Jacobs had lived a life that had spanned from the Great Depression through 9/11; she had seen the New Deal, Modernism, World War II, early post-war suburbanisation and urban redevelopment, the Cold War, McCarthyism, the social revolutions of the 1960s, the first environmental movement, neoconservatism, postmodernism, globalisation, new financial crises, new wars, the tech revolution, the urban renaissance, global terrorism, and the second environmental movement. Few of her critics or admirers had such a breadth of perspective, and, by the available evidence, few commentators had read all of her books, let alone attempted a summary of their intellectual and narrative arc.

It wasn't until 2006 that Jacobs' first biography appeared, but that book missed the unknown 'first half' of her writing career and glossed over major parts of her later work. While my own intellectual biography emphasised her writing from the 1930s up to the *Death and Life*, albeit in the context of her entire oeuvre, a reviewer fairly observed that she still found Jacobs to be an enigmatic figure after reading it.

Constitutional Chaff – REJECTED SUGGESTIONS *of the* CONSTITUTIONAL CONVENTION *of* 1787

WITH EXPLANATORY ARGUMENT

Compiled by JANE BUTZNER *from the Notes of* JAMES MADISON *of Virginia,* MAJOR WILLIAM PIERCE *of Georgia,* DR. JAMES MCHENRY *of Maryland,* RUFUS KING *of Massachusetts, and the* HONORABLE ROBERT YATES *of New York*

MCM *XLI*

COLUMBIA UNIVERSITY PRESS

NEW YORK, ON MORNINGSIDE HEIGHTS

While never intending to write a traditional biography, this would have been true even if I had delved into her personal life, which is far less relevant than other aspects of her intellectual career. Setting aside the important histories of her activism, only some of which I related, I faced the dilemma of needing another three, four, or five hundred pages to thoughtfully explain Jacobs' subsequent work on economics, ethics, and ecology, and, moreover, then facing the dilemma of not being trained in those fields.

In other words, assuming one had the room to do so, to write thoughtfully, historically, and comprehensively about Jacobs' work and ideas – which span so many fields and subjects – is to risk, as she did, valid charges of amateurism. Done well, it might require, like the story by Lewis Carroll and popularised by Jorge Luis Borges and Umberto Eco, a map "on the scale of a mile to the mile", or something close to it. To attempt to understand her is, to a great extent, an attempt to *become Jane Jacobs*, which, given her unconventional background and breadth of experience, is not an easy task.

Insofar as *Death and Life* was Jacobs' first and most impactful book, the defining mystery of her professional life was how someone without a college degree, an advanced education, a significant writing career, or any substantial expertise in the subject matter could write "one of the most remarkable books ever written about the city", a "landmark in the literature of architecture and urban design", and an "instant classic" – as reviewers quickly observed. That, at least, was how the question was framed for decades. With only one notable essay, "Downtown is for People", published in *Fortune* magazine in 1958, known to experts in architecture and city planning, it was difficult for many to accept Jacobs as a serious thinker and *Death and Life* as a paradigm-shifting masterpiece. The book appeared at a time when universities and libraries were segregated by gender, let alone race, and when the term "urban design" was still a neologism. For those she attacked (quite literally in her book), Lewis Mumford and Catherine Bauer Wurster among them, Jacobs was an "*enfant terrible*" and *Death and Life* an "emotional" but "brilliant personal diatribe", a mingling of "mature judgments and schoolgirl howlers".

While such reactions were to be expected from those Jacobs threatened professionally, even friends and supporters knew little about her

Frontispiece in classical style from Jacobs' first book, *Constitutional Chaff: Rejected Suggestions of the Constitutional Convention of 1787*, published in 1941.

career development. It wasn't until after her death in 2006, for example, that Jacobs' brief education in economic geography at Columbia University and her career as a magazine and newspaper writer, most notably for the Office of War Information (OWI), the Department of State, and *Architectural Forum*, was revealed in any detail. Missing from her first biography, it wasn't until 2007, in an obituary essay I authored, that it became public knowledge that *Constitutional Chaff: Rejected Suggestions of the Constitutional Convention of 1787* – not *Death and Life* – was Jacobs' first book.

Published under her maiden name, it was less an issue of that book being difficult to find than to have reason to look for it – because who would have imagined that Jacobs would never have mentioned it, or included any references to it in her archive at Boston College? Finding the dozens of articles and essays, many still missing, that Jacobs wrote for various commercial and government magazines, newspapers, and other publications (also absent from her archive) was more difficult and took longer. In part because many of these were ghostwritten (like the classic 1946 war memoir *The Coast Watchers*) or published without bylines, as was the practice at government publications and also for many years even at *Architectural Forum*, I was still uncovering these in the year or two before *Becoming Jane Jacobs* was published.

But the clue that initially drove my search was always in front of us: Jacobs had been hired in 1951 at *Architectural Forum* as an *associate* editor, an advanced position – meaning that she must have had a substantial writing career before then. In addition to the digitisation of historic newspapers, unavailable until recent years, it took Rockefeller Foundation documents (which documented her financial support and progress), government employment records, and Federal Bureau of Investigation files to reveal that Jacobs had risen to the level of editor-in-chief at the State Department publication, *Amerika Illustrated* – aimed for an audience of Soviet citizens – and had written and edited a list of in-depth articles about US suburbanisation, urban redevelopment, architecture, and urbanism before arriving at *Forum*. In fact, I found that, in 1951, she wrote what seems to be one of the most comprehensive articles of the time about the history of US housing and urban redevelopment published anywhere. Documents also revealed that, once at *Forum*, Jacobs had travelled, studied, and written about urban renewal far more extensively than anyone had realised—even though this was clearly evinced in the content of *Death and Life*.

So why did *The Death and Life of Great American Cities* appear to come from an amateur? At the time, Jacobs was characterised first and foremost as a woman without any relevant education or credentials. Moreover, the (auto-)biography that was initially presented to readers in the back of the original hardcover edition – later dropped from the familiar ochre paperback – was not especially convincing:

> Jane Jacobs was born in Scranton, Pennsylvania, in 1916. After high school and a year spent as a reporter on the *Scranton Tribune*, she went to New York, where she found a succession of jobs as a stenographer and wrote freelance articles about the city's many working districts, which fascinated her. In 1952, after a number of writing and editing jobs, ranging in subject matter from metallurgy to a geography of the United States for foreign readers, she became an associate editor of *Architectural Forum*. Gradually she became increasingly skeptical of conventional planning beliefs as she noticed that the city rebuilding projects that she was assigned to write about seemed neither safe, interesting, alive nor good economics for cities, once the projects were built and in operation.

While full of clues, these sentences omit her relevant work for *Amerika*, which was partly propagandist in nature, and still legitimately classified during the Cold War. Although there is a hint that Jacobs observed urban redevelopment projects before and after their construction, not mentioned, no doubt for lack of space, are the circumstances and experiences through which Jacobs became 'gradually' but "increasingly skeptical" about urban renewal. And although Jacobs' early articles about New York City's 'working districts' are, in retrospect, a decisive early moment in her study of city life and dynamics, it wouldn't have terribly impressed her readers to hear that she had written these in her late teens, and that they were published in *Vogue*. While two of them took years to find, and required poring through year after year of microfilm, the then decades-old articles would have been equally inaccessible to researchers who

ısformation: photo shows street as it ; now; sketch shows same street as of pedestrian island. Garage at right center of downtown's east side (dia- ı opp.). View is looking west. Bridge in foreground links garage to existing hotel. Four-story garages would finally park 10,000 cars each, but would begin as surface parking, grow with the city. This would be first area changed (see p. 154).

didn't know her family name. Meanwhile, writing about metallurgy and the geography of the US (for foreign readers) didn't seem particularly relevant.

Indeed, while Jacobs had few credentials, her most important and relevant credential – being an associate editor of *Architectural Forum* – was an ambivalent one when it came to promoting *Death and Life*. As discussed in *Becoming Jane Jacobs*, while her career and book project had been strongly supported by *Forum* editor Douglas Haskell, her critical opinions of the multi-billion-dollar public-private real estate business that was urban renewal were not fully embraced by Time Incorporated, *Forum*'s parent company. Well before her book was even finished, Jacobs was warned about presenting her personal opinions as those of her employer, and, planning to return to her respectable job as an editor at a widely-circulated magazine, she didn't want to lose a job that she liked and needed. While *Forum* was very much a collaborative environment, when it came to *Death and Life*, Jacobs was very much on her own. She needed the ideas in her 400-plus-page book to stand on their own.

This is not to say that Jacobs' ideas, as she readily admitted, were always right or original. In *Becoming Jane Jacobs*, I analyse the evolution of her writing and thinking in detail and show that in her early writing Jacobs held views sometimes the opposite of those she described in *Death and Life* – which was no doubt a powerful reason for her reticence about her earlier work. I also detail the important life experiences and people who influenced her thinking about cities, both positively and negatively. When a portrait of Jacobs is painted where we see her actively studying the evolution of American urban redevelopment over the course of many years, interacting with some of the most notable and respected figures in architecture and urbanism, and working through ideas, a picture emerges where the contradictions between her insider/outsider status and unconventional education are reconciled with her accomplishments.

It took almost a half century to reveal the 'unknown Jane Jacobs' – to simply understand some of the defining experiences of her life and career, and how she came to write one of the most important books ever written on cities. Going forward, this will be the foundation for better interpretations of *Death and Life*, her books and ideas on economics, moral philosophy, ecology, and public life, and her way of

Reconstruction of the downtown area in Fort Worth, Texas. A full page from Jane Jacobs' unsigned report in *Architectural Forum* showing one of the main streets in its existing state and in the future as part of a continuous pedestrian area. Jacobs held up the plans for Fort Worth as a positive example of how it was possible to manage traffic, integrate the existing urban structure and respect the user perspective. *Architectural Forum*, May 1956.

thinking. Already, in the wake of the 2016 US election, Brexit, the Ferguson Unrest, MeToo, and other sociopolitical phenomena of recent years, different aspects of Jacobs' thinking have come into new focus. With new xenophobias and attacks on immigrants, her many ideas about diverse and open cities are all the more important. With the Black Lives Matter movement and new historiographies of redlining and racial geographies, what she wrote about racism, economic injustice, and white supremacy, as well as physical segregation, have come to the fore.

With each passing year, her ideas about "the attrition of automobiles or the erosion of cities" are more evident. With a looming environmental crisis, as well as municipal insolvency in the face of mounting debts to pay for sprawl, her ideas about the ecology of cities have become critical. With increasing social complexity, her ideas about activism, governance, and localism are also increasingly relevant, as are, as I write in my other essay in this volume, her thinking about empire and democracy. Meanwhile, there is heightened awareness of what she faced as a woman and female intellectual during her lifetime, and the ways that she is still not cited today by the many authors who suddenly 'discover', as if for the first time, ideas and phenomena that she wrote about five decades ago.

So there are other books on Jane Jacobs that need to be written. There needs to be a book written about Jacobs' economic thinking – and probably by someone with deep knowledge of economics. There needs to be a book about the moral and political philosophy that she discussed in *Systems of Survival* – and by someone with deep literacy in philosophy and political science. And after those two books have been written, there needs to be another overarching analysis of her thinking, which synthesises those subjects with her ideas about the ecology of cities. These are imperative tasks that need to be done with intellectual and ideological honesty – in order to reconcile the contradictory aspects of Jacobs' ideas and to paint an accurate portrait. Because of the strength of her enduring ideas, I believe that she will remain a thinker embraced by the many partisans in today's broad spectrum of political opinions, and we need those now more than ever. But thinking and writing and debating is not enough. If Jacobs' analyses in *Dark Age Ahead* were correct, we have no time to lose.

CHAPTER II

Cities of Relationships, Not Things

Ebba Högström

THERE ARE SOME songs I've listened to so many times that they have lost their capacity to say anything to me. But there are also songs that other people have talked up so much that I believe I know exactly what they sound like even though it's ages since I listened to them myself. Then, when one day I play one of them, I can sometimes hear past my preconceived opinions. Something strikes me and the music speaks to me in a different way than previously. I am thinking about that now as I re-read Jane Jacobs' *The Death and Life of Great American Cities*, the urban planning equivalent of *Born in the USA*, so regularly referred to that it has frequently made me think "not that sidewalk again".

I would suggest that there is a general idea that Jacobs' theories of city planning can be used as a kind of recipe book – clearly formulated guidelines which, if they are followed, will lead to that sought-after living urban environment. Jacobs was after all a journalist and knew how to put across her message in a way that was as effective as it was clear. Her 'greatest hits' when it comes to examples and concepts – the sidewalk, the 'eyes on the street', the short blocks, the stranger, the shops on the ground floors – are mixed in with many anecdotal examples taken from life in New York's different districts. The butcher is a recurring figure, as are the tobacconist and other tradesmen. Her sharp criticism of everything to do with rational and large-scale planning is to be found here, as are the repeated – and to some extent sweeping – formulations for districts located at greater distances from the central parts of the city. The ones that are not so small-scale, full of shops, are seen therefore as not so 'living'.

Aerial view of the Brooklyn-Queens Expressway under construction, 1951.

Now when I read the book again, something else emerges that

extends beyond the individual urban design elements and the city's various different actors, beyond the sidewalk and the butcher. They are there too of course, and not unimportant, but the main message of the book, as I see it now, concerns diversity (and how to generate it). Jacobs compares the city to a fabric, a multi-threaded warp in which elements of different colours and qualities form a changing pattern as the fabric develops. Here I am thinking of the variations, the processes, the networks and the interactions, those elements in the warp that, in Jacobs' city planning language, are called scale, time, visual expression and function. The last-named sounds far drier than Jacobs intends, the function being the diversity itself, manifested in the everyday and varied doings of the many people. Some of Jacobs' contemporaries called it chaos. Jacobs herself called it "organised complexity".

> It is a complex order. Its essence is intricacy of sidewalk use, bringing with it a constant succession of eyes. This order is all composed of movement and change... an intricate ballet in which the individual dancers and ensembles all have distinctive parts which miraculously reinforce each other and compose an orderly whole. The ballet of the good city sidewalk never repeats itself from place to place, and in any one place is always replete with new improvisations.[1]

It is not often that Jacobs' view of cities and urban development is cited as dynamic and relational – as she makes clear for instance in the above quotation. Many of her interpreters use her ideas far more statically than she actually seems to have intended herself. Jacobs' way of analysing city life by taking it apart is then often pinned down as a set of typologies, like separate components in a recipe for successful urban planning. What the city *is,* in the form of built structures, has come to be at the forefront, instead of what the whole environment (people, built structures, objects etc.) *does.*

Death and Life is one long creed for the living urban environment, which both facilitates the diversity and is a prerequisite for it. Jacobs takes issue with the other city, the one planned from the top down, the boring, homogeneous city, even the dead city. But then what distinguishes a living urban environment? Time is one component that recurs; life takes time, people come and go, as do businesses and buildings. They are demolished, built, extended, repainted. Jacobs does not explicitly talk about relationships, instead she suggests that everything must link into everything else. Meetings, exchanges, bodies, scale, interactions, where relationships between people (the passer-by or *flâneur*, the stranger and the local), what they do (their glances) and what individual urban design elements (such as the sidewalk) have to offer, and what the connection between all of these implies (the block) – these are what drive urban development. City life, the street ballet, emerges as an outcome of this dynamic.

When a phenomenon or an activity has an effect, you can talk about its performativity. The focus is on what is done or performed, not what it means or is. When Jacobs describes how different activities on a sidewalk form part of an interplay that develops and changes, it is precisely that kind of performativity she is talking about. The city is living as long as all those involved *make* that city live. From that point of view it is not enough to have a sidewalk or shops on the ground floors. There needs to be more action, in the form, for instance, of people, goods, transport and intentions. This "ballet" that involves more actors than just the sidewalk, reminds us of the French academic Bruno Latour's description of how nothing is in itself, everything must be carried out, *made*, in order to become something. Latour has a famous example that involves the dance ceasing and disappearing when the dancers stop dancing.[2] The individual parts are not important in themselves, they have to work together and interact in order for the dance to come to life. This is precisely what relational urban planning theory formulates. It is the commitment (interaction) that arises between the different parts of the urban fabric that becomes what we experience as a living urban environment: involving the people walking on the sidewalk and the sidewalk itself, the stranger and the local resident, the tradesman and the cultural performer (but here, even so, I wonder whether Jacobs does not somewhat favour the tradesman). Connections happen in different ways, but you have to look carefully in order to see and understand them. It is in all the different doings of the daily round that urban life is called forth, through what people typically do every day: go to work, come home, go shopping, work,

Next pages: A snapshot from a pavement in Greenwich Village, New York City, 25 April 1961.

TRIPLE-S
BLUE STAMPS

TELEPHONE
EXPR
ORI

walk, collect the children, go to the gym or choir practice. All these actions conjure up the dynamic and the flow of activities that characterise the complex order of the city – in other words what Jacobs calls city life.

The American architect and theorist Stan Allen is one of the people who emphasises the relational and dynamic aspects of Jacobs' work. He picks up on her idea of organised complexity and draws on Bruno Latour among others when he discusses the difference between complex and complicated social combinations. Here it is not the dance that is used as the comparison but the machine. It is *complicated* in that it consists of a lot of parts, fairly simple in themselves but forming a complicated whole when they are put together. Perhaps Jacobs' theories could be viewed as a collection of recipes – a kind of ready tool – based on a view of the city as just such a complicated machine, with individual parts put together, each vulnerable in itself. No dynamic occurs in any way unless the parts are assembled precisely right, but if some parts break, the machine stops working.

A *complex* system on the other hand, like a city or an ecological system, is robust in a completely different way. Such a system has the capacity to absorb new experience and is capable of adapting as circumstances change. The effects become complex when the individual units and parts work together, in other words the answer to the question of what 'one plus one' makes is probably 'more than two' or perhaps even something completely different, as Allen notes in the chapter "Urbanisms in the Plural: The Information Thread" in *Fast-Forward Urbanism: Rethinking Architecture's Engagement with the City*, published in 2011.

Allen thinks that Jacobs had a strong intuition for this intrinsic complexity of the city. She sees it as unique because of its ability to maintain a balance between change and stability and by being able to combine local variations and overarching structures in a relationship characterised by what we can call a dynamic stability. Understanding the city as 'field conditions' rather than an arrangement of buildings and streets is the foundation of Allen's own understanding of city life.[3] That understanding can be seen in Jacobs' work, he asserts, and also in her fascination with the very local scale.

The complex order that characterises city life constitutes its problem at the same time. But this is not the kind of problem "which, if understood, explains all" as Jacobs puts it. No, it should rather be seen as a robust biological system with its capacity for interaction between variables and adaptation to changed situations. In order to understand it you need detailed (not to say microscopic) scrutiny. The small context must be perceived in order to understand the big one – how different parts affect one another and either adapt or stand up against that impact. To understand the city as a living environment and what Jacobs calls "the kind of problem a city is", she insists that you have to understand how life is lived. What people do in an urban environment on a daily basis must be made visible. This way of looking at the city and city life is in direct contrast, not to say conflict, with a more traditional understanding of the city as an outcome of urban planning and design.

Jacobs maintains that cities can never be works of art. The artists make a selection from everything that life is made up of and organise it in a way that to them seems appropriate. It is the actual selection, organisation and control that make it art, but life itself is not a controlled selection. Thus Jacobs claims that life can never become art, it is too tangled and too ongoing, and since the city is built up of life itself, city life gets destroyed if it is seen as art.

Relational urban theory emphasises precisely this kind of perspective. The city is described more as an environment characterised by the unforeseen, the potential, as a mixture rather than a system, a structure or a form. The city is a field condition rather than an object. The city can be described as a field of movements, a maelstrom of energies and forces in which different kinds of actors (people, machines, things, animals) are given the ability to act by being connected together.[4] Social and everyday practice is emphasised at the same time as, or even ahead of, aesthetic or technical aspects. The design of cities thus involves both social, political and economic issues and the planned and unplanned physical spaces that affect people's patterns of movement and their ideas.[5] The interaction between people, things and processes is at the centre – between the professional actors in the city's development (planners, architects, engineers, politicians) and between us all in the execution of our daily activities. We are all involved in shaping the cities. In this view of city life and urban development there are clear points of contact with

Jacobs' view of the local scale, diversity and mix as the route to a living and resilient urban environment.

> So many of the conflicts would never occur if planners and other supposed experts understood in the least how cities work and respected those workings.[6]

Local knowledge is the key, according to Jacobs. Many problems could be avoided if the planners had bothered to find out during the planning process what the various different quarters and districts consisted of and what their inhabitants valued, what their local experience was. But tackling these questions is difficult, even out of control. There are ramifications, there is no demarcation, so they cannot be stuffed into handy files in the office and be resolved one at a time. The idea that things can be put into different compartments so that we can get them under control is what we call vertical thinking. But conflicts arise between the verticals. However Jacobs puts her faith in the citizens who, according to her description, wait patiently at consultation meetings and then "they tell with wisdom and often eloquence about things they know first-hand from life". Grasping the complexity is the difficult part. Or perhaps, if we follow Jacobs' line of argument, the difficult part is grasping the fact that society and the city are an organised complexity.

If we only see disorder, it is understandable that we want to create order. Put things in files and get control. The comprehensive view, in some sense both humane and good, can be a manifestation of precisely this ordering principle. But modernist urban planning – rational and function-based – that was fashionable in Jacobs' time had, according to her, "lost the power to comprehend, to handle and to value an infinity of vital, unique, intricate and interlocked details". When, instead, Jacobs wants to find new methods for dealing with organised complexity, according to her it is a matter of avoiding dismantling and decay – the "the fate of a society which cannot maintain the complexity on which it is built and on which it depends".

Jacobs suggests that urban planning for a living city should aim instead to "stimulate and catalyse the greatest possible range and quantity of diversity among uses and among people throughout each district of a big city", which is the basis for "the city's economic stability, social vitality and power of attraction". To achieve this, Jacobs writes, urban planners must work out exactly what certain places are lacking, for such diversity to be able to develop, and then try to remedy the deficiencies in the best possible way. According to Jacobs, urban planning should therefore support the networks in individual quarters. The users and informal owners, in other words the social connections and the feeling of belonging, are important in order to feel secure in a place, for strangers to be seen as an asset instead of a threat, and for more than just the parents to supervise the children. Urban planning for living cities must also work to combat destructive barriers, the ones that do not help the dynamics and vitality that Jacobs is pursuing. The districts that inhabitants identify with must be big enough to cope with both internal and external contacts. The stranger, 'the other', must be able to find room beside those who are already at home there. To achieve that, Jacobs believes that slum quarters need to be refurbished so that people will want to stay there and live side by side with new arrivals; a good economic environment for other people's plans needs to be fostered, and a visual order also needs to be created for the city. All these guidelines are connected. We cannot just focus on some individual targets and ignore others. It's not enough for planners and civil servants to understand methods and tools – they "must understand, and understand thoroughly, specific places".

On the issue of the right to the city – in other words who the city is *for* – one might wonder how Jacobs' ideas stack up against more recent radical planning theory, for example the ideas that urban planner and academic Leonie Sandercock developed in her major works, *Towards Cosmopolis: Planning for Mulicultural Cities*, and its sequel *Cosmopolis 2: Mongrel Cities of the 21st Century*. What points of contact are there with Jacobs' vision? Both emphasise the importance of citizens being involved in their local environment and thereby acquiring an insight into how to influence planners and politicians. What separates them can be perceived in the goals they work towards or the objectives that are at the centre of their work. Sandercock has a marked emancipatory theme that is expressed in her desire to develop democracy and her view that everyone has the right to speak and influence things. Reporting as a planning method is particularly important – here it is the planners' job to make sure that different groups of people meet. By listening to each other's reports, conflicts and fears can be made visible and overcome. Sandercock maintains that it is fear of "those who have" rather than of those "who do not have" that drives urban policy. These groups are not treated equally by the authorities and, according to Sandercock, radical planning policy offers a way to change that.

Jacobs' quest for *empowerment* is not equally explicit, but where she does think along those lines, it is rather the life of the city, or simply the city itself, that should be given independent power. Putting people first, particularly as groups, may perhaps have been too radical for Jacobs, something that has maybe contributed to the fact that her ideas have been taken up by far less radical urban theories, such as for instance New Urbanism. But what is city life if not a mass of people doing things in a certain place in interaction with the built environment, with machines, with other living beings and with their own ideas? Even if Jacobs writes that it is not the physical elements in themselves that are the most important components, a sub-text emerges that defines the city and city life as ends in themselves, which take precedence over the people. This sub-text can also be read as relating to the economy, to cities as the driving force in all economic development and to entrepreneurial creativity that should not be inhibited by unnecessary boundaries.[7] Planning should not be an obstructive rule book but rather an invisible hand that ensures that the various currents in a city can flow on without major obstacles.

The American academic Richard Sennett, who describes Jacobs as a maverick with anarchic tendencies and little faith in policy-making and planning projects on a massive scale, disputes that her emphasis on the informal (street life) and the unregulated (city development processes) might be an expression of "liquid modernity".[8] The type of modernity that can fit in well, for instance, with a neoliberal agenda. But Jacobs' idea of the complex and unregulated can more readily be seen as a way of relating to time – and to informal relationships that develop over time, which have been allowed to take time to develop. According to Sennett, this also affects Jacobs' view of the political economy, since she advocates gradual and modest economic development aimed at equally modest everyday goals: building a playground, investing in street furniture and trees, or lending money to a local tradesman who needs to refurbish. Jacobs applauds the irregular, non-linear and non-time-limited (urban) development paths. This is the "slow time" that demands a smaller urban scale: slowness comes through the small scale, as Sennett suggests in his work of 2018, *Building and dwelling: Ethics for the city*.

The shortcomings of the planning that Jacobs criticises lie in its relationship to time, in the idea that it should be possible to create diversity in one fell swoop. But more time is required for variation and diversity to flourish. Allowing time to play a bigger role in the basic ethos of urban planning would revolutionise it, counteracting the principles of a quick return on money invested.

> Planners like to think they deal in grand terms with the city as a whole, and that their value is great because they 'grasp the whole picture'.[9]

Does planning have any role in Jacobs' vision of society? Yes of course it does, she acknowledges, but it must be radically changed. And this requires altering perceptions of inhabited space, expert opinion, and the right to the city. Jacobs calls the object of rational planning "the statistical city". Statistics and probability calculations are used to find out more about people's lives and constitute the knowledge base for the problems that planning is expected to solve. Problems of the nature of organised complexity are converted into simple and soluble issues by the use of rhetorical tricks. All problems (traffic, industry, parks, cultural activities and so on) can be converted so that they are accommodated in the rational order. However that is dependent on the size of the territories. The further removed from the "small" life we are (the details, the meetings, all the small everyday variables and changes), the easier it is to handle the problems rationally. When problems are viewed from an 'Olympian perspective', from above, they become more like one another and easier to handle, and the chart becomes almost more real than the reality itself.

Next pages: Housing estates laid in circular patterns in Sun City, Phoenix, Arizona, 1986.

So striving for a holistic view can lead us astray. The holistic perspective is perhaps needed for planning infrastructure projects and when it is a question of motivating and allocating funds to investments – but otherwise the planners' work has nothing to do with the

city as a whole. All urban planning is about relatively small and specific measures, in districts, residential areas or quarters. It is more important to know the specific places than to rely on statistical generalisations. As Jacobs noted in *Death and Life*: “No other expertise can substitute for locality knowledge in planning, whether the planning is creative, coordinating or predictive.”

Her criticism of rational and comprehensive planning is criticism of a Euclidian understanding of space, one which says that spatial conditions are simply those that can be measured and captured on a conventional map, and that with probability calculations one can work out which components the good city should be made up of. Jacobs emphasises that there are not many people who live in the ‘map’ world, not many who care how the city is administratively divided up and represented. Instead it is the (physical) interactions with and within their own district that create identity and belonging. “Most of us identify with a place in the city because we use it, and get to know it reasonably intimately. We take our two feet and move around in it and come to count on it”, she wrote.

Jacobs’ criticism of planning is also a criticism of the expert who prefers to coordinate vertically rather than horizontally. Horizontal integration is the hardest, maintains Jacobs, yet at the same time the most important. Here her criticism comes back to the administrative predilection for centralising and controlling from above, with a view to making things more efficient and getting control. Coordinated planning is criticised by Jacobs for taking care of bigger territories in order to facilitate the work. The challenging problems with organised complexity are thus converted into easily managed units that can be studied and understood from above: put into files, everything in its place. This, Jacobs observes, is the expression of a deep deficiency among planners – they can quite simply not understand the nature of the city or the complexity of the problems they are trying to solve.

What Jacobs does, with a view to being able to analyse what city life consists of – and here her way of arguing has perhaps invited the trivialisation of her view of city life – is to release one element at a time in her thinking. As Jesper Meijling has shown, she turns the planners’ arguments on their heads and dismantles their claims about what planning is supposed to achieve.[10] She shows how it fails precisely to do that, but also what is needed for it to actually achieve it. With this rhetorical point however she herself emerges as an enlightened strategist. By raising her everyday observations to a comprehensive, strategic level, dealing not just with individual elements of city architecture (the sidewalk, the quarter and so on) but with the planning process, the forms of city management and the citizens' possibilities for involvement, she stands out as the good strategist whilst her contemporary planners emerge as unsuccessful, ephemeral tacticians with tunnel vision.

★

However, we all have our blind spots. Jacobs, who is certain of how planning should be coordinated, how the dynamic is supported with slow and moderate interaction between many different parts, certainly has her own hinterland. It lies in what she mainly wants to see as the outcome of misdirected planning, which sees complexity as chaos.

The suburb, the residential district, the scrapyard, the large-scale. The "grey belts" that Jacobs identified. In the face of these districts and businesses in the city, Jacobs displays an attitude that is as one-sided as the one she accuses the rational planners of. It is as if Jacobs' process-based, relational attitude ends where the city ends. She cannot see how the city or life's network carries on beyond the closely packed city, nor that the closely-packed city environment is dependent on the grey belts, whether these consist of scrapyards, refuse tips, sewage works, agriculture, suburbs or smaller communities in the country, for its dynamic existence.

The suburb, and particularly the residential district, constitute a particular blind spot for Jacobs. It is not presented in any positive light at all and does not consist of dynamic people with the capacity to influence their situation (like the people who together create the sidewalk ballet that she describes so well when it comes to the closely packed city). I am not writing this in order to sing the praises of the suburb, but because I find it striking that so many people (not just Jacobs) can generalise about urban development that has been going on for almost a hundred years and in many cases has grown up as an environment full of annual growth rings in terms of memories, activities, buildings and businesses. Not all suburbs are the same, nor are those who live there. Here Jacobs falls into the same trap as she dug for the urban planners who condemned the North End district of Boston as a slum – the same slum that she saw as a dynamic, cared for place, full of activity, life and variety. Jacobs sees the residential district as just a category, a form that has sprung from an expert's (planner's) mind or from a reckless developer's pursuit of quick profits. She sees the house-owners themselves as narrow-minded people who are only interested in manicured lawns and order. She judges the residential district from above – there is nothing of what she advocated so strongly with regard to the different areas of the city. The fellowship that develops when a lot of people feel that they belong to a place is missing, as is the city life that develops when a variety of functions get together. There may be some justification for such criticism, but what is interesting, and this applies to all Swedish discussions about suburbs in principle (whether it be the housing schemes or the acres of uniform residential developments), is how an environment is judged again and again on the principles of another environment. The absence of small businesses in the residential area makes it reprehensible, according to Jacobs, who has so often sung the praises of the small movements.

But if she had picked over the stones of the residential area in the same way as she picks up every stone in Greenwich Village in Manhattan, she would have found greater diversity than one might believe – but perhaps a different diversity from the one we know from the dense urban environment? Clubs, school communities, wildlife experiences, outdoor pursuits, flora and fauna, silence, freedom from commerce.

It is clear that for Jacobs, the city is the ideal: the city is dynamic and innovative, it is made up of people and fosters tolerance of differences in people. This passion for the big city, with the suburb as its negative, dark shadow, is also apparent in Elizabeth Wilson's *The Sphinx in the City*, which came out 30 years after Jacobs' book. In contrast with Jacobs, Wilson holds great faith in the city as liberating for women. The similarity between Jacobs and Wilson is found in their view of authority, and in their view of the residential district. Jacobs for her part criticises the city's bureaucratic structures in the form of planners, civil servants and politicians who strive for physical order through separate functions and areas for traffic, homes and workplaces.[11] For

Wilson it is the patriarchal structures (and this distinction includes planners, civil servants and politicians) who on the one hand have arranged the residential suburbs in such a way that they lock women into a certain sort of life and on the other have promoted a view of the city as a symbol of terrifying and challenging femininity, that is to be trained into compliance and acceptance of their role in the ordered structures of airiness, greenness and the separation of the individual families into their own "little boxes".[12]

Sennett complicates this, just 30 years after *Death and Life,* with his description of how Greenwich Village was developing into a significantly tougher district than the one Jacobs described, a district where drug addicts and homeless people hang out in increasing numbers and where the police are conspicuous by their absence.[13] Such a development challenges the idea that diversity automatically leads to a city where different groups live and work harmoniously side by side. According to Sennett, the difficulty of putting up with 'the other' at a purely physical level means that groups which define themselves as alike tend to draw together. Each in their own place, each homogeneous neighbourhood existing separately – Washington Square, with its widespread drugs trade, being a distinct neighbourhood from the urban terraced houses of the bohemian upper middle class.

Sennett advocates the conflict as the starting point for both urban planning and city life – continuous batting back and forth. But that sort of attitude requires people to put up with those who are not like themselves. Otherwise, enclaves form that foster a kind of collective individualism of like-minded people instead of fellow-feeling and tolerance. There are no longer any "eyes on the street" in Sennett's description of Greenwich Village in the 1990s. Everyone scurries home to their own place.

★

This chapter set out from a questioning re-reading of *Death and Life* and constitutes an attempt to understand Jacobs as a relational urban theorist. That is not a position that she is usually accorded – the individual urban design elements that she used as explanations usually get in the way. What I have noted in her work instead, is the view that everything is connected, that it is not possible to isolate individual elements and parts without one appearing more important than another. It is the variation, the dynamics, the interactions, the flow, the scale and the diversity of functions that give city life its vibrancy.

This focus on, and care for place – what in modern parlance could be called "a designed living environment", as it is termed in the Swedish government report SOU 2015:88 – in all its interactions, rhythms, layers of experience in buildings, infrastructure and people's activities, is perhaps Jacobs' great contribution to urban theory and urban design theory. City life may take many forms but what they all have in common is that they arise from different people living and working in different ways in a certain place for a certain time.

One also has to ask how relational urban planning can be created. Is it a contradiction in terms to think up guidelines for something that, by its nature, is liquid and changeable? If decisive plans on how land is to be used have played their part, how should we then plan? Perhaps it is more a question of how planning should work in order to achieve the goals that have been formulated? Of whether the execution itself – in the form of codes, rules, strategies – is the means to a way forward, rather than the finality of land use plans?

Even if many of Jacobs' arguments deal with the tension between the lived and the built environment, being both in conflict with one another and complementary, perhaps a contemporary version, a Jane Jacobs 2.0 if you like, would invest more energy in the institutional arena, in planning as regulations and (a democratic) process. A representative democratic planning system should be able to work and balance different interests, and address the major societal challenges relating to short-term commercialised urban development and local needs. The city's built structures should not be subject to a vertical thinking that destroys complexity and so pulls the rug out from under what gives the city its vibrant life. Without institutional frameworks, Jacobs' freedom-seeking, small-scale approach and commitment to the local environment can clear the way for the darker sides of urban transformation: speculation, gentrification, relocation and social inequality.

The challenge for all urban development lies in balancing the planning demands of major infrastructure, in order to be able to implement radical changes, against the need to protect the existing flows of everyday practice, place memory, layer upon layer of experiences that have grown stronger over time and built up a community (but which can also become inward-looking and repressive).

A new kind of urban planning, with new narratives and new tools, would require serious engagement with the major social challenges of our time, paying attention to the true complexity of contemporary cities as described in Allen's *Fast-Forward Urbanism*. It would engender a more subtle approach that can accommodate the lived, the built and the institutional at one and the same time. Such a revised version of Jacobs' ideas could pick up on the same effective focuses as the original version: five points for institutional control, five points for participatory processes.

1 Jane Jacobs, *The Death and Life of Great American Cities* (New York: Vintage Books, 1961), p. 50.

2 Bruno Latour, *Reassembling the social: an introduction to actor-network-theory* (Oxford: Oxford University Press, 2005).

3 Allen uses the term field conditions, which may also be called field configurations. I prefer the first since, to my mind, it has clearer associations with dynamic, interplay and changeability.

4 Cf. e.g. Ash Amin & Nigel Thrift, *Cities – Reimagining the Urban* (Malden: Polity, 2002).

5 Fran Tonkiss, *Cities By Design: The Social Life of Urban Form* (Cambridge: Polity, 2013).

6 Jacobs (1961), p. 406.

7 Cf. e.g. Oli Mould, "Jane Jacobs", in Regan Koch & Alan Latham (ed.), *Key thinkers on cities* (Los Angeles: SAGE, 2017), pp. 129–134. Cf. also Jesper Meijling, *Påståenden om framtiden* (Stockholm: Axl Books, 2008).

8 Richard Sennett, *Building and dwelling: Ethics for the city* (London: Penguin, 2008), pp. 79 f.

9 Jacobs (1961), p. 418.

10 Meijling (2008), pp. 107–109.

11 Elizabeth Wilson, *The Sphinx in the City: Urban Life, the Control of Disorder, and Women* (Berkeley: University of California Press, 1992).

12 This refers to Malvina Reynolds' song, "*Little Boxes*", from 1962, a satire of the residential district and the restricted lives and opinions associated with them.

13 Richard Sennett, *Flesh and Stone: The Body and the City in Western Civilization* (London: Faber, 1994).

CHAPTER III

Diversity, Market Value and Gentrification

Catharina Thörn

The scenes that illustrate this book are all about us. For illustrations, please look closely at real cities. While you are looking, you might as well also listen, linger and think about what you see.
JANE JACOBS

Yes – London is now being 'renewed' at a rapid rate – but not on the model about which we are so often warned... The real risk for inner London is that it might well be gentrified with a vengeance, and be almost exclusively reserved for selected higher-class strata.
RUTH GLASS

DURING A VISIT to Boston, Jane Jacobs went to North End, which at that time was officially regarded as Boston's slum and a blot on its landscape. The residential area that had grown up close to the harbour's industrial zone consisted mainly of a high concentration of cheap rented apartments. Jacobs was surprised by what she saw. The streets were lively, with children playing and adults going about their business or just standing and chatting. Jacobs rang a friend and town planner in Boston. "Why in the world are you down in the North End?" was his horrified response.

When Jacobs insisted that she did not consider it a slum, the planner admitted that he himself thought it was quite a nice district – not least in summer. Moreover it turned out that infant mortality and crime in the area were among the lowest in the city.[1]

The window of a store at a market in Boston's North End, 1967.

This anecdote, which forms the introduction to *The Death and Life of Great American Cities,* says a lot about Jacobs' style and strength – through simple means she shows that the everyday experience of city life brings with it significant knowledge. For Jacobs, an understanding of the city was never an abstraction – it could only be acquired through a painstaking study of how cities actually work. Her book, published in 1961, was chiefly intended as an attack on modern city planning. The mistake of modern city planners was, according to Jacobs, that they tried to adapt the city on the basis of the abstraction that is a well-drawn map. Jacobs thought, on the contrary, that an understanding of cities must be obtained by moving about in them and using all one's senses to understand what works and what doesn't. Her four theses on the requirements for creating diversity in a city have become the mantra for city planners the world over, and sometimes it is enough just to mention her name to confirm the legitimacy of a city plan. But at the same time, as Jacobs has become an authority constantly referred to in city planning, the districts and the city life that she cherished have changed so much as to become unrecognisable. Her own quarters in the West Village have been heavily gentrified – they are inhabited almost exclusively by the white upper middle class. A few years ago, Jacobs' relatively modest house on Hudson Street was sold for over three million dollars. It seems as if modern planning and urban renewal have picked out and cultivated only certain parts of Jacobs' heritage – those parts that are about the physical environment's diversity. Today's planners seem absolutely incapable of analysing the economic conditions (for example in the form of low rents) that are required to create socially mixed cities. And of course there are aspects of *Death and Life* that can be cultivated in this way – even when the book was published, the sociologist Herbert Gans wrote that Jacobs had succumbed to the delusions of physical determinism and thus ignored the importance of social and economic structures for urban life. According to him, that rendered her blind to the fact that the real threat to the social life of the city was the developers with big resources of capital in an alliance with the politicians. For Jacobs, it was the city planners and their inability to see the street perspective that was the biggest threat to the sort of city she wanted to see flourish. Her personal commitment and activism were characterised by active resistance to large-scale planning in which older residential areas were torn down to make way for new and more efficient infrastructure.

Jane Jacobs was a child of her time. *Death and Life* captured the spirit of the age and put into words the experience and the lure of urban life that she shared with many others. The book became part of the 1960s urban wave, in which young people took flight from the countryside and the dullness of residential suburbs to the city pulse of New York. Jacobs had become engrossed in city issues when she worked as an editor on the *Architectural Forum* journal, but her attitude to the city diverged radically from that of contemporary architectural writers. According to the architectural critic Paul Goldberger, Jacobs' book should be compared with Rachel Carson's *Silent Spring* and Betty Friedan's *The Feminine Mystique*.[2] These were books written at the beginning of the 1960s, by women who challenged the establishment and consequently were also derided by that same establishment. But this changed over time and today these three books have the status of classics that have changed perspectives in their respective fields. But Jacobs was not just a writer, she was an activist and, as such, unafraid of authority. Her battle with Robert Moses, a civil servant, has gradually taken on an almost mythical character in which Jacobs takes the role of the people's champion against the power of the state and Moses' bulldozers.

Moses was also a child of his time. Thirty years older than Jacobs, he was the advocate for modernism's city planning – with its vision of new, lofty, well-planned cities. One of his first big projects was to create Jones Beach Park on Long Island in the 1920s. It is still a public beach today, which means that it is free of private housing and clubs, and almost six million people visit the beach every year.

But it is above all for his later career that Moses became famous. With a mission to modernise New York, which after the depression of the 1930s had become increasingly poor and crowded, he laid out roads, joined different districts together with the help of bridges, designed new parks, created public swimming pools and over 600 new playgrounds and also replaced older, dilapidated buildings with new-build structures. The city of New York was to be reborn and Moses saw himself as the man to realise the dream of the new modern city.

Naturally he was not the only one to have these plans. Behind Moses there was a train of civil servants, politicians and developers. But it is only Moses who has gone down in history – largely because of his position of power but also because of his charisma and tough style. From the 1930s through to the 1960s, older buildings were demolished to make way for the new city and thousands of people were forcibly moved. Moses was unmoved by the criticism from residents who complained about their houses being razed to the ground, and in spite of his anti-communist beliefs he was not afraid to use a quote which is usually attributed to Stalin: "You can't make an omelette without breaking eggs."[3] For several decades Moses was unchallenged in his power and it was from that position that he planned to build a road through Washington Square Park. But Washington Square Park was not just any park. Throughout the history of the city it had been an important public arena and from the 1950s onwards it was used by both rich and poor. From that time it also became a meeting point for the beat generation, hippies and folk musicians. It was here among other places that the photographer Diane Arbus came to take photographs. Many of New York's artists and writers also gathered there. And it was here that the story of Jacobs versus Moses began.

Jacobs lived near the park and, together with women who used the park with their children, she organised massive protests. Jacobs used the whole of her network and got well-known New York personalities such as Eleanor Roosevelt and Susan Sontag to take part in the battle for the park. Moses in turn tried to diminish the power of the protests by calling the demonstrators mothers with no experience or understanding of city planning. That was a mistake. The organised women in Washington Square Park did not belong just to a white middle class – they were also part of a cultural elite. And it was here that Moses suffered his first defeat.

Shortly after the battle of Washington Square Park, it was announced that the West Village, which Jacobs had lauded in her book, was to undergo a wide-ranging refurbishment. That became the start of a long battle between residents and city planners, and here too, in the end, Moses was defeated. Several of Jacobs' contemporaries testify to her instinct for political strategy and symbolic actions.[4] In the battle for Washington Square Park, she arranged for a ribbon-cutting ceremony in front of the assembled press, in which, in contrast to a traditional inauguration, the ribbon was tied and not cut. And it was her own children who tied the ribbon – not important men in suits. At the same time the protests that Jacobs was a part of were linked with other movements that criticised and questioned the power of the state and other authorities. In May 1968, Jacobs was arrested and accused of inciting riots in conjunction with a protest campaign. At the same time her son risked being called up to the Vietnam War, which induced the family to move to Toronto in Canada shortly thereafter, and they would stay there for the rest of their lives. Five years later came the oil crisis. The time for the kind of modernism that Moses represented, with large-scale planning and expensive projects, was over.

Even though the story of Moses and Jacobs often portrays them as protagonists in a symbolic battle between authoritarian modernism and local, small-scale activities, there were several similarities between them. Both were chiefly interested in making the city better for the middle class – albeit in different ways. Moses' modernism was based on an idea of the city as a modern public entity, clearly interconnected by bridges and roads, and with public spaces (parks and playgrounds) and public buildings. It was directed at a rising middle class and an orderly, white working class. Jacobs' vision instead focused on the street dynamic and what was required for smaller businesses to flourish and the street to be populated. Her idea of the urban, which was chiefly based on the dynamic in her own residential area, was largely a middle-class urbanity.

Both Jacobs and Moses focused on the built environment and saw physical reconstruction and design as the solution to the city's problems. And the perspectives of both were marked to the highest degree by the post-war economic boom, during which there was confidence in the ability of economic growth to solve social problems.

★

On the other side of the Atlantic, the sociologist Ruth Glass was working in London. A contemporary of Jacobs, Glass was born in Berlin, where she began studying sociology in the 1930s. Her Jewish background meant that she was obliged to flee, first to Geneva and Prague before settling in London where she resumed her studies. In 1951 she founded the Centre for Urban Studies at University College London,

Next pages: Hanover Street Market, Boston's North End, 11 August 1967.

IANNE

where she would remain until she retired. Compared to Jacobs, Glass is relatively little known as a person. No biographies or anthologies have been written about her. Yet she has gone down in history as the person who coined the term "gentrification", which opened up a whole field of research in several disciplines and generated countless books and studies. In the last 30 years, the term has gained a foothold beyond academia and is used by urban movements in resisting property speculation and rent rises.

It is a pity that Glass's legacy has been reduced to her having coined this one important term. As with Jacobs, her writings have an impact that is still relevant. And there is justification for putting these two women side by side – both were careful observers of urban life, skilled writers and far-sighted. But Glass's view is quite different from that of Jacobs. In her writing the city is presented as more contradictory and unharmonious. Conflicts in the urban space are an integral part of the hardships of daily life. According to Glass it is not possible to understand a city only from how it seems to work in the street – it requires an understanding of the city's social stratification, economy, migration patterns, culture etc. As she noted acidly in her book *Clichés of Urban Doom and Other Essays*, a dislike of statistics is usually due to the fact that the person reading them does not have a clue about the social circumstances that the statistics are about, or lacks the imagination to put themselves in other people's situations. Even though she had faith in science's ability to demonstrate social structures and change, she was also aware that a city's vibrant landscape can never be completely captured. She introduced her classic text, *London: Aspects of Change* (1964), with the words: "London can never be taken for granted. The city is too vast, too complex, too contrary and too moody to become entirely familiar. And there are moments when well-known features of her townscape stand out surprisingly, as they might to a foreign tourist, or to the expatriate who at last comes home."

Glass likens London to a woman whose shape constantly changes. The author takes her reader on a tour around London one early morning in June, as the espresso bars open their doors and the air is clear. The walk takes her through Hyde Park, Grosvenor Square, Euston Road and Tottenham Court Road – places that can call to mind protests, expectations, fear and monotony. At whatever time of the day,

Glass notes, London is, in 1963, a city that accommodates the old and the new at the same time, in an exciting dynamic. It is a place of both change and stagnation at one and the same time, a constellation of alien worlds that sometimes meet and sometimes live side by side. The city lives in constant movement – of people, goods and cars. In the 1960s, London was marked by the growth of new occupations in the service sector, advertising and design, at the same time as patterns of consumption were changing. The middle class both grew and re-grouped, which left its mark on the urban landscape in the form of ever more restaurants and bars located beside shops whose goods were being sold with a whole new sheen. Yesterday's luxury goods, writes Glass, have become today's necessities. The incipient change that Glass traces in London in the 1960s brings its own potentially destructive dynamic – the battle for space. And it is here that Glass formulates her classic definition of gentrification, in her most read paragraph: "One by one, many of London's working class quarters have been invaded by the middle class – upper and lower. Shabby, modest mews and cottages – two up, two down – have been taken over, when their leases have expired, and have become elegant, expensive residences. Larger Victorian houses, downgraded in an earlier or recent period – which were used as lodging houses or were otherwise in multiple occupation – have been upgraded once again... Once this process of 'gentrification' starts in a district, it goes on rapidly until all or most of the original working class occupiers are displaced, and the whole social character of the district is changed."[5]

Invasion, crowding out, changing. Glass's language is designed to capture the fact that gentrification is ultimately about power and resources – who is given space in the city and on what terms. Gentrification, as Glass sees it, is neither natural nor unavoidable but is facilitated by the political governing of land use and capital flows. Glass traces a change in the view of city planning and land use with the Town and Country Planning Act of 1959, when land use was deregulated and ever more scope was left to the market. Previously, she pointed out, there was a national plan of action that governed market speculation and property prices. When that was abolished, a wave of speculation and competition for properties and space was started, and Glass considered that such competition would lead to a spiralling of land values that would be out of control if it was not prevented or regulated.

Even in the 1960s, Glass suspected that this would become a stumbling block for London in the future. The displacement, she writes, had already begun. Those who cannot cope in the competition – the small businesses and the low earners – are displaced and very little has been done to counteract this development. Her vision of the future is as gloomy as it is far-sighted: unless the battle for land is contained, "any district in or near London, however dingy and unfashionable before, is likely to become expensive". London, Glass suspects, risks becoming an illustration of the principle of the survival of the fittest – in an economic sense. In her abrasive way she writes: "Thus London, always a 'unique city', may acquire a rare complaint... [It] may soon be faced with an *embarras de richesse* in her central area – and this will prove to be a problem, too."

In contrast to Jacobs, Glass was an acute observer of class differences. She noted that the changing nature of a city could never be completely separated from the movements of capital. And in her view it is precisely this capital dynamic, which demands the constant improvement of land for the best economic yield, that will kill off urban life.

Jane Jacobs left New York at a time when the future of the city was being intensely debated. The flight from the big American cities to the residential suburbs had led to poverty becoming concentrated in the hearts of the cities. Improving the living conditions, not least for the poor black population, was high on the agenda for both the Black Power movement and the civil rights movement. At the beginning of the 1970s, the world, not least the USA, was hit by an enormous economic crisis. Institutions like the New York State Urban Development Corporation, created in order to offer housing at reasonable costs, went bankrupt. At that point New York had a big public budget that was used, among other things, for works in the public sector and to support marginalised groups. The waves in the debate rose high in Congress as to who should bear the costs of the crisis – and whether the investment banks should be obliged to pay their allotted share.[6]

New York City Mayor Ed Koch walks in the Village along 5th Avenue, 1977.

The decision to allow the city's residents to bear the costs by severely

5 AVE
ONE WAY
WALK
LIBERTY
TRAVEL
LIBERTY TRAVEL

slashing the budget had major consequences for New York as a city. At the beginning of the 1970s, a large proportion of the population was young, black and unemployed. At the same time many young and creative people were moving to New York, attracted by the low rents. In SoHo a new lifestyle grew up, where the former industrial buildings were converted into dwellings, galleries and night clubs. The urban lifestyle and culture attracted the younger generation that wanted to get away from their confined existence in the residential suburbs.

The New York of the late 1960s and 1970s has become mythologised as much as Jacobs' descriptions of life in the West Village. It has been described as an intense and vibrant place where performers and artists like Andy Warhol, Barbara Kruger, Diane Arbus, Patti Smith, Lou Reed, Basquiat, Robert Mapplethorpe and others found a place for their creativity and made their names. But New York also came to be a symbol, after the Seventies, for a new kind of urban policy. After President Gerald Ford refused the city federal support in 1975, a spatial restructuring began that, with the help of increased policing and private influence on the city's development, among other things, would turn the crisis around. The solution was to attract the home-owning middle classes back to the city.

During the 1970s New York was still dominated by rented apartments, but a number of property-owner's associations ran campaigns to turn them into privately-owned apartments. The work was slow, the majority of the tenants did not just have no real interest in buying their homes, they also resisted the plans.[7] But when Ed Koch became mayor in 1978, public support for continuing changes to New York's housing market was reinforced. In his first speech as mayor, Koch promised not just better services to the middle class but also put out a general call to attract affluent people to move into the city and contribute to revitalising New York. Later, in the 1980s, when the prices of privately-owned homes in certain parts of Manhattan rose sharply, Koch declared: "We are not catering for the poor any more ... there are four other boroughs they can live in. They don't have to live in Manhattan."[8]

At the same time, in response to the crisis of 1975 when the public budget was severely cut, homelessness and unemployment increased among the city's poorer inhabitants. But it was only when Mayor Rudy Giuliani took office, in 1994, that Koch's vision of Manhattan as a place for the rich became the subject of a more focused strategy. Giuliani took office shortly after the property crisis at the beginning of the 1990s, and he set his sights on taking back the city centre which was still considered dilapidated and marked by poverty, criminality and graffiti. His strategy was in line with the campaign that had been actively working since the previous decade to brand New York out of the crisis. Now branding was to be incorporated into city planning in order to profile districts in line with ideas about what the middle class wanted. According to the geographer David Harvey, New York's handling of the crisis can be seen as a kind of dress rehearsal for neoliberal urban policy that was underway, not least because to a large extent it ignored welfare issues to focus on investment in property, exclusive consumption and a favourable climate for the big companies.

The consequence of this policy has come at a high price for the groups that were left out. Property prices have risen rapidly, with the resulting increased displacement of low-income groups. This has had major consequences, not least for the black and Latin American people of New York, whose districts are rapidly being gentrified. Furthermore, homelessness in New York today is higher than it was during the economic crisis of the 1930s. In the last ten years alone, the homeless number has increased by 80 per cent.[9]

Many cities across the world have followed in New York's footsteps and invested in strengthening their brands by building new and exclusive residential areas, hotels and shopping malls. Former working-class areas have been gentrified, and more and more cities are seeing a polarisation between rich and poor areas. Ironically enough, it is Jacobs who is the eternal reference in the new urban renaissance. But Jacobs' book was an attack on the city planning that, according to her, was obliterating the cities' history and levelling out diversity. In the 1960s it was modernism that dominated and was the focus for her criticism. But her driving force lay in finding an answer to what makes cities dynamic – what causes diversity in the city to flourish. The development we see today is the opposite of what she strove for.

Next pages: Battersea Power Station, a classic landmark of London and listed art deco building, is at the centre of a huge urban development.

In a far too rarely quoted section of *The Death and Life of Great American Cities*, where she discusses the risk of what she calls diversity's self-destructiveness, she foresaw the dangers when developers begin to build only for those who can afford the most. She wrote: "Accommo-

dations for this narrow, profitable segment of the population multiply, at the expense of all other tissue and all other population. Families are crowded out, variety of scene is crowded out, enterprises unable to support their share of the new construction costs are crowded out." The worst kind of players involved in this destruction of diversity were, according to Jacobs, banks, insurance companies and the offices of prestigious financial services.

Jacobs and Glass were contemporaries, and their most influential texts were published at the beginning of the 1960s. Both of them, albeit in different ways, were of enormous significance to our understanding of the dynamic of cities. Both were fascinated by urban life – precisely because it was not boring or monotonous. Instead they found a dynamic and unpredictability for which they both expressed appreciation. But while Jacobs' descriptions of the city were inclined to be black and white (either dismal or lively streets), Glass stuck to an image of the city as contradictory and changeable.

Jacobs had a great belief in small-scale city life and the communities that grow out of it, and she was generally suspicious of state intervention. Glass's focus lay instead on the social dynamic, migration, capital movement and class differences. While Jacobs is revered and widely loved, Glass's ideas and thinking have been largely forgotten or ignored. It is impossible to overlook the fact that both were women writing at a time when women's thinking still tended to be marginalised or trivialised. Jacobs was often dismissed as a housewife with no education. When the famous urban sociologist Lewis Mumford reviewed her book, he ridiculed it under the heading "Mother Jacobs' home remedies".

Glass was a new thinker and an original researcher. As head of the interdisciplinary Centre for Urban Studies at University College London, she initiated and was responsible for research about London – with a focus on social structures, economies and migration. Although she is so little remembered, her influence is enormous – she not only gave impetus to a whole new direction within urban research but also influenced urban movements the world over, which, without having heard of Glass, use the term "gentrification" in their fight against rent rises and compulsory removals. Few people with such great influence have been so little read. And that is a pity because the reader who picks up Glass's texts will soon notice their remarkable relevance when it comes to understanding urban development in our time.

Perhaps it is the case that neither of these women received the kind of readership they deserved. Even though Jacobs is read and admired, her legacy seems largely to consist of simple forms of city development, falling far short of giving her wider thinking the attention it deserves. And although she was an activist, it is chiefly among the city planners she criticised that she has achieved high status. She herself wrote: "I hope any reader of this book will constantly and sceptically test what I say against his own knowledge of cities and their behaviour."

But few of those who now take her word as true seem to be taking up her invitation. Instead, her careful observations of a specific urban place, in a specific historical context, are generalised to the extent that her thoughts have become pointless. The strength of Jacobs' most famous book is her indispensable ability to observe and appreciate city life. And that is not something that can be formalised but something that has to be practised with our own observations. To understand the dynamic of cities, just reading Jacobs is not enough. For a deeper understanding of developments in today's cities we also need Glass and a clear analysis of both class differences and the land speculation of financial capital. Otherwise, Jacobs is at risk of becoming yet another building block in what will ultimately be the death of diversity, in all cities.

1 Jane Jacobs, *The Death and Life of Great American Cities* (New York: Vintage Books Edition, 1961/1992), pp. 9–10.

2 Paul Goldberger, “Uncommon Sense”, in *The American* Scholar (1 September, 2006).

3 Marshall Berman, *All that is solid melts into air. The experience of Modernity* (New York: Simon & Schuster, 1982), p. 294.

4 This is described in the documentary *Citizen Jane: Battle for the City* from 2016.

5 Ruth Glass, *Clichés of of Urban Doom and Other Essays* (London: Blackwell, 1989), p. 138.

6 David Harvey, “Economic crisis and rebel cities” in Thörn & Holgersson (ed.) *Gentrification* (Lund: Studentlitteratur, 2014), p. 257.

7 Benjamin Holtzman, “I Am Not Co-op: the struggle over middle-class housing in 1970s New York”, *Journal of Urban History*, vol. 43, issue 6 (2017), p. 865.

8 “The revival of Cities: How to bring cities back from the brink”, in *The Economist* (4 May, 2017).

9 Information from Coalition for the homeless homepage. According to them almost 130,000 people spent a night in one of New York’s hostels in 2017, and of these over 45,000 were children.

Conscience
the
Ultimate
Weapon!

CHAPTER IV

The Political Jacobs

Per Svensson

Jane Jacobs attends a boycott at a public school, New York City, 1964.

Next pages: Jane Jacobs grew up in Scranton, Pennsylvania, the centre of a seething industrial district with ironworks, steelworks and coal mines.

JANE JACOBS GREW up in Scranton, Pennsylvania. Her father was a doctor, her mother a teacher and a nurse. The family lived in a house with a veranda, which Jacobs would talk about for many years with warmth and affection.

Scranton was an industrial town that lived on its coal mines. When Jacobs was born, in 1916, it had a population of over 100,000. The big expansion had taken place in the second half of the 19th century when a large number of immigrants went to the town to work in the mines: Italians, Poles, Irish. In the child's eyes, Scranton was an exciting, teeming place. In an interview for the Canadian literary magazine *Brick,* in the early 21st century, Jacobs claimed that she had enjoyed going to the dentist as a child because it meant that she got to go "downtown".

You can never get away from your childhood. For Jacobs it was perhaps natural in later life that she saw the big city as an idyll, and that, when she moved to the global metropolis of New York, she literally took the veranda with her.

Is she nostalgic or a visionary, a reactionary or a radical, a romantic or a clear-sighted analyst, left wing or right wing? It has sometimes been claimed that Jacobs is difficult to place in political terms. On one level that is a strange assertion. You do not need to read much of her work or her story to recognise her as a bona fide liberal – that is, in the classical sense: not a conservative, not a socialist.

For her it is the diversity, the differences it contains that make the city the beating heart of history. Here she shares her views with classical liberals. Diversity is both the means and the end in the liberal tradition. John Stuart Mill's most famous work, *On Liberty*, from 1859, has a

BREAKER

motto taken from the liberal and university founder Wilhelm von Humboldt's essay "The Limits of State Action". The quotation points out precisely the decisive importance of diversity: "The grand, leading principle, towards which every argument hitherto unfolded in these pages directly converges, is the absolute and essential importance of human development in its richest diversity."

Jacobs applies this principle specifically to the actual physical social structures: town planning, architecture, traffic systems. It leads her to applaud the traditional city street with its many players and functions. It also leads her to distance herself from a monolithic modernism that spoke the language of power even when its advocates believed they were speaking for the powerless.

So far, no problem. But there is also, in liberalism's DNA, a great capacity for moralism. Historically the connection between liberal ideas, the middle class and Protestantism places great weight on individual morality. Liberal diversity tends in practice therefore to have certain limits: certain environments, people, behaviours and attitudes are seen, quite simply, as 'not nice'. Perhaps even then the best is the childhood village but with lots of fun shops and snug bars? And perhaps best a society in which it is precisely just we, who recognise each other as level-headed and liberal, who set the tone and the agenda.

One of Jacobs' admirers and successors was the philosopher Marshall Berman, best known for his volume of essays on modernity and urbanism, which was clearly influenced by Marx and his own childhood in the Bronx, *All That Is Solid Melts Into Air* (1982). On page after page he praises Jacobs and her observations and the ideas contained in her great work, *The Death and Life of Great American Cities.* It is obvious that Jacobs is one of Berman's main sources of inspiration, not least because they have a common enemy: Robert Moses, in his time the all-powerful 'master builder' of New York. It was Moses who drove the Cross Bronx Expressway straight through Berman's beloved childhood quarter. And it was Moses who was Jacobs' opponent when she emerged in the early 1960s as an activist in the fight against a planned motorway, the Lower Manhattan Expressway, through the quarter she had made her own.

Berman highlights Jacobs' affirmation of diversity, movement, and differences, writing:

> Any careful reader of *The Death and Life of Great American Cities* will realize that Jacobs is celebrating the family and the block in distinctively modernist terms: her ideal street is full of strangers passing through, of people of many different classes, ethnic groups, ages, beliefs and life-styles [. . .] Jacobs' street and family are microcosms of all the diversity and fullness of the modern world as a whole.

But in spite of this, Berman notes later, her ideal picture has appealed to groups and individuals who stand for quite opposite values: traditionalists, reactionaries, bigoted guardians of public morals, people who want to avoid having anything to do with minorities. Even 'the new right' can evidently be attracted by such ideas of the urban idyll. "Is this connection entirely fraudulent? Or is there something in Jacobs that leaves her open to this misuse?" asks Berman, and he provides the answer himself: Yes, there is. Diversity has its limits, there are no "blacks" in her quarter. He continues:

> This is what makes her neighborhood vision seem pastoral: it is the city before the blacks got there. Her world ranges from solid working-class whites at the bottom to professional middle-class whites at the top. There is nothing and no one above; what matters more here, however, is that there is nothing and no one below – there are no stepchildren in Jacobs' family of eyes.

One is reminded, through this, that Von Humboldt was a Prussian official, and that John Stuart Mill was a civil servant in the British East India Company. His freedom was not a freedom available to all. Berman's conclusion is that, in Jacobs' modernist-tinted affirmation of diversity, there is also at the same time "an anti-modernist subtext, a sort of undertow of nostalgia for a family and a neighbourhood in which the self could be securely embedded, *ein' feste Burg*, a solid refuge against all the dangerous currents of freedom and ambiguity in which all modern men and women are caught up".

This duality is a characteristic not just of Jacobs and the liberals, but of western modernity as a whole. More recently it has been brought up to date in the political arena with *The Road to Somewhere*, the British journalist David Goodhart's acclaimed book about two 'tribes' in contemporary society: the *Anywheres*, the mobile meritocrats with acquired identities, and the *Somewheres*, the security-seeking traditionalists who defend their given identities. This is a description that can be used to explain the forces and structures behind phenomena such as Trump's election victory, Brexit and the success of populist and authoritarian political trends and parties all over Europe.

But a model is only a model. In real life the two attitudes always overlap one another, even within each individual. Liberalism acknowledges the duality. That is why the demarcation between private and public is so important in the liberal tradition. It is in their private lives, in their circles of friends and in family life that people expect their need to belong and their need for unconditional solidarity to be met. In public the culture is different; in that sphere, life is not composed of organic ties and personal bonds but of impersonal transactions, agreements and rules. That is also why the traditional city is the obvious symbol for the liberal lifestyle, and not just because it requires and creates diversity. The wall of façades marks a boundary between the two spheres of life, street life and home life.

But this too is in many ways a theoretical model. There are no truly sharp dividing lines in a person's life. The threats against our own existence that we feel, for more or less good reason, are something that we take with us from one sphere to the other. So it can be tempting to dream of a home which is always safe and a society that is always like a home. That is the dream that populists and other anti-liberals exploit. And that is also the temptation that liberals can give in to, openly and uninhibitedly or covertly, more or less consciously (they kind of secretly imbibe forbidden fantasies about the "lotus land") or by establishing such narrow and strict boundaries around their own open and diversity-affirming society that in practice it can appear to be a (globalised) middle-class village where curious doctors and teachers open the morning paper eagerly every day to see what their favourite columnist has written today – just as Jane Jacobs used to do.

One of the most central commandments of liberalism is that nobody should be locked into a given identity beforehand. Everyone should have the right to become something else and someone else. That is why the school and the city play such prominent parts in liberal rhetoric.

Both are engines for change. But the older one gets the clearer it usually becomes just how difficult it is to get away from one's life story. Childhood impressions can have a completely irrational influence long into our adult years. In that interview for *Brick*, Jacobs told how she had avoided pink lemonade all her life because her mother had told her that the colour came from wrung out red ties.

Her mother also affected her in other ways. Like her husband, Jane Jacobs' mother was socially aware and involved. Jacobs also went on to become actively involved in politics and social issues herself, throughout her life. Was she left or right wing? She was a registered supporter of the American Labor Party in the 1940s, a member of the civil service union, and was suspected of being a communist sympathiser during the McCarthy period. An activist in the Sixties, she was accused of rioting and instigating rebellion after protesting loudly at a meeting against the planned motorway in Manhattan, and she was a signatory to an appeal on behalf of activists who stood accused of inciting a riot in conjunction with the Democratic Party Convention in Chicago in 1968. Her emigration to Canada was seen as being in part to save her sons from being drafted into military service in Vietnam. It is clearly a CV with a left-leaning profile.

And yet Jacobs was one of the most eloquent advocates of the ideal market economy, a position adopted typically on the right of the conventional political spectrum. How does that hang together? The simple answer is that the contradiction is actually illusory. In spite of everything, classic liberalism was a 'left-wing' movement fighting for both economic and political freedom. And there is nothing to suggest that Jacobs professed anything other than values in the liberal tradition throughout her life. The difference in her political profile was possibly due to the fact that she articulated and displayed her beliefs more consistently and radically than most. If 'diversity' was her overriding ideal, homogenisation was the danger, regardless of whether it was created by megalomaniac modernist city developers, tyrannical regimes or monopolist mega-businesses.

In a discerning essay in *The Atlantic* magazine issue of November 2016, the author Nathaniel Rich noted: "Urban life was Jacobs' great subject. But her great theme was the fragility of democracy – how difficult it is to maintain, how easily it can crumble." The city was, dare I say it, the good antithesis of the state in the world as Jacobs saw it. According to the 17th century philosopher Thomas Hobbes, the state develops when, in fear of one another, people swap freedom for security by subordinating themselves to an almighty ruler, as represented by his idea of the Leviathan.

According to Jacobs, the city develops through free people exchanging goods with one another. In books like *The Economy of Cities* (1969), *Cities and the Wealth of Nations* (1985) and *The Nature of Economies* (2000), Jacobs proclaims her thesis: cities are not the result of economic and political development. It is in the cities that everything begins. Cities are the starting point for political and economic development. And according to Jacobs, since the city as a phenomenon originally developed as a market – a place where hunters and gatherers met to barter for meat or edible seeds – the market economy was fundamental to her conception of the world.

What is the source of Jacobs' conviction that diversity is a necessary prerequisite for a decent human existence? Rich highlights an experience from Jacobs' youth. She never went to college. Instead, she took an unpaid voluntary job as a teenager with a local paper in Scranton. After that she spent a year with a relative who worked as a missionary in a godforsaken village, Higgins, in the Appalachian Mountains. It was a poverty-stricken dump in Jacobs' words, where a broken pitchfork or a rusty plough were tantamount to "a serious financial crisis". But Higgins had once flourished, when the village's inhabitants had possessed a range of different tools and pursued a variety of occupations. But by the time of Jacobs' visit, its development had gone backwards, to a miserable, abject monoculture. The villagers made their living from a single trade – the manufacture of molasses.

Jacobs claimed that such setbacks can happen to whole societies. Developments in Venezuela, once one of South America's richest countries, are a contemporary example of the justification of those fears. Owing to dictatorial misrule and its one-sided dependency on oil, Venezuela has become a poorhouse of a nation.

The year in Higgins undoubtedly played its part for Jacobs in establishing and reinforcing her conviction of the importance of safeguarding the prerequisites for diversity and freedom, democracy and economic development. But she also took from it a whole series of other experiences, at least equally profound, that helped mould her writing and activism. The urban studies theorist Richard Florida, also one of Jacobs' disciples, summed them up concisely in a short article on the *CityLab* website (December 2016), in which he wrote:

> In Scranton, she saw first-hand the devastating toll of the Great Depression on industries and workers. As a young woman, she saw the rise of fascism and totalitarianism in Europe. During the 1950s, she witnessed the chilling effect of McCarthyism. Robert Moses-style urban renewal reflected the same unbridled top-down power.

Jacobs' answer to this was wholehearted opposition. After her first two years in New York, when she worked as a freelance journalist, she began working for the armed forces information service in 1943. From there she moved to the Department of State and the editorial office of the PR magazine *Amerika*. Since falling under suspicion during the years of state alarmism over communism, she was obliged on several occasions to account for her political activities and sympathies. In March 1952, she wrote a long, thorough and brilliant response to a questionnaire that had been sent to her by the chairman of the State Office's "Loyalty Security Board".

In point after point she rejected all the insinuations and suspicions that she might not be loyal to the USA and the American ideal, presenting herself as "a citizen with a deep commitment to the preservation of traditional American freedoms" and emphatically denying having any sympathies with the Soviet Union:

Next pages: A protest march in New York against the Vietnam draft, December 1967. Jane Jacobs in the middle of the picture, flanked by the poet Allen Ginsberg and the writer Susan Sontag.

> I abhor the Soviet system of government, for I fear and despise the whole concept of a government which takes as its mission the molding of people into a specific 'kind of man', i.e. 'Soviet Man', that practises and extols a conception of the state as 'control from above and support from below' (I believe in control from below and support from above); that controls the work of artists, musicians, architects and scientists; that controls what people read and attempts to control what people think.[1]

NEWS
Bread

An exemplary liberal profession of faith and, interestingly enough, initially an ideological contextualisation of Jacobs' and many other people's aversion to the modernist, monolithic town planning, whose generally power-crazed representatives sometimes thought they could create not just a new and better society but even, in the longer term, a better human being. Jacobs did not believe in a society or a city that was created on the drawing board of power. Perhaps, in spite of everything, this is all that is needed to define her position.

But if she was so critical of collectivist and centralised systems and ideologies, how could she then explain her commitment to the American Labor Party, a socialist-inclined party that she gradually came to see had ideas and sympathies that she could not share? Her answer, which is apparent in her letter to the Department, is interesting. Firstly, Jacobs felt it important for American democracy that there should be alternatives to the two dominant parties, "dissident third parties", as she called them. Diversity was obviously also a priority for her in the political arena.

Secondly, she noted: "The reason I continued to register with the American Labor Party in 1947, 1948 and 1949 was that I wanted to combat the idea that I might be afraid to register with the American Labor Party." She hereby appreciates the intrinsic value of the refractory, the importance of claiming the right to go against the flow, break with the norm, deviate from what is conventionally seen as desirable.

At an earlier point in her response to the Department, Jacobs establishes that there are two major threats to the American tradition. One is constituted by the Soviet Union and its satellite states. The other is "the current fear of radical ideas and of people who propound them". That is her central argument. Jacobs repeats and develops it further on in the text: "Ideas and ideologies become an internal threat if we fall into the trap posed by believing that each and every one of us should think like all the others." Yet again: Diversity. Freedom.

Her reply is interesting not least because Jacobs traces her ideas of freedom, independence, courage and diversity to her own growing up in Scranton and the morality she was taught in her parents' home. As a child she had learned that there was nothing virtuous in meekly agreeing with public opinion. Instead it had been impressed upon her that conformism leads to social stagnation.

She also highlighted her maternal grandfather, who had belonged to alternative parties in the agricultural populist tradition all his life and stood, in 1872, in the congressional elections for the so-called Greenback Labor Party. "The fact that he could do that and still be a successful and respected lawyer makes me proud of my country", Jacobs maintained. And perhaps her grandfather was implicated in a deeper way in her writing and thinking.

The characteristic of 19th-century American populism was its battle against 'the monopoly', predicated on a not entirely unfounded conviction that a few robber barons were swindling the workers, small businesses and poor farmers, with the help of the state. The late 19th-century was the era of the railway magnates and the quick making of enormous fortunes. And, as the *Atlantic* reporter Jack Beatty observed in his book *Age of Betrayal: The Triumph of Money in America 1865–1900*, a railway king like Jay Gould never needed to worry about standing in any election. He and the other robber barons controlled the country anyway, through their representatives in politics: "Of the seventy-three men who held cabinet posts between 1868 and 1896, forty-eight either served railroad clients, lobbied for railroads, sat on railroad boards, or had railroad-connected relatives." The state and the capital sharing the same compartment.

It is against the same background that one should also understand Jacobs' distinctly American aversion to all forms of monopolised power. Democracy demands diversity. Jacobs' last book was published in 2004, two years before her death. Its title clearly and simply expresses what a liberal often feels when confronting the world two decades into the 21st century: *Dark Age Ahead*.

Diversity does not seem to be so much of a priority in our time. Instead we have Chinese and Russian state capitalists, Californian digital monopolies and political populists of a different sort, I would guess, from Jacobs' grandfather. The world is racing towards uniformity.

1 Peter L. Laurence, *Becoming Jane Jacobs* (Philadelphia: University of Pennsylvania Press, 2016), p. 87.

CHAPTER V

New Urbanism, Jacobs and the Concept of Change

Jill L. Grant

AS ONE OF the key urban thinkers of the 20th century, Jane Jacobs has had a major impact on the theory and practice of community design, especially in North America. In this chapter I briefly consider some of the ways that Jacobs influenced New Urbanism – through a community design approach that advocates dense, walkable, mixed, and attractive urban settings. Linked to ideas of smart growth and sustainability, New Urbanism appears frequently in contemporary approaches to planning new residential areas.[1]

With its critique of modernist planning, New Urbanism reiterated many of Jacobs' principles of good community design, including the importance of diversity, mix, compactness, visibility, and connectedness.

To what extent did Jacobs explicitly inspire the new urbanists in their theory and practice? Several key thinkers in the New Urbanism movement seem to echo her judgments. Some follow her rhetorical strategy of journalistic bombast and bold assertion without specific evidence. Yet New Urbanism includes divergent voices and approaches. Its practice and discourse is continually morphing in response to challenges and opportunities, which makes generalising about it difficult. Consequently, I will narrow my gaze as I explore some of the links between Jacobs and New Urbanism, focusing primarily on the writings of Andres Duany as a key New Urbanism practitioner and Emily Talen as the principal theorist working to integrate Jacobs' insights into New Urbanism. I consider how the theories and practices of New Urbanism do and do not reveal lingering influences of Jacobs' ideas about physical planning. While Jacobs certainly said many things that the new urbanists find inspiring, key writers conspicuously set aside

Dilapidated empty classical townhouses in a once well-to-do area of Detroit, Michigan, 2014.

some of her views about the requirements for good community design and governance. In particular, they overlooked some of Jacobs' ideas about the significance of time, scale, and control in generating vital urban environments.

The Right Behaviour Through Design

While Jacobs often suggested in *The Death and Life of Great American Cities* that urban vitality emerges from unplanned juxtapositions and time-dependent processes, she also affirmed that good design makes a difference in outcomes. Jacobs argued for creating physical diversity within the urban environment to provide a basis for mixing uses; the mix of uses generates a mix of users and thus produces social diversity.[2] Jacobs identified the multiple diversities that characterised the areas that she loved, and postulated causality from the physical to the social. The underlying environmental or spatial determinism of this theory troubled social planners and sociologists like Herbert Gans who emphasised the significance of social networks and individual choices; Gans saw the vitality of ethnic neighbourhoods and new suburban communities as deriving from the cultural values and commonality of experiences and class conditions the residents encountered, not from the physical form of the spaces they inhabited.[3] By contrast, the notion that form could shape behaviour resonated with physical planners and designers who believed in the efficacy of good design, and Jacobs afforded them a theoretical foundation to legitimate their work. The prominence Jacobs gave to the influence of the spatial earned her continuing respect within movements like New Urbanism but it remains her Achilles' heel for many critics.

Generalising from conditions in Greenwich Village in the 1950s to the prerequisites for good urban design, as Jacobs did, warrants careful dissection. Jacobs witnessed a particular moment in American culture: the end of one era and transition to another. In the 1950s any responsible adult could reprimand an errant child and assume responsibility for disciplining rowdies on the street. In those days America appreciated its power and sense of cultural superiority; European immigrants celebrated their cultural heritage as they immersed themselves in the melting pot. Jacobs described days when TV was such a novelty that owners brought sets out onto the street on summer evenings to share with their neighbours. The New York of the 1950s represented a time before air conditioning drove people inside behind closed windows and before widespread ownership of cars gave working-class people the means to commute to homes in the suburbs. The vitality, social control, and intense interaction of Jacobs' home district of Hudson Street reflected the social, economic, and cultural conditions of that particular era. While conceding that physical form likely played a role in the urban qualities Jacobs saw in the 1950s, I'm not convinced that form merited the supremacy Jacobs gave it. The short blocks and dense mix of uses of Greenwich Village accommodated the intense street theatre that Jacobs described, but it did not produce that interplay. The social and economic conditions of the 1950s, and the complex history of the people and businesses thriving in New York at that time, certainly took advantage of that form; however, as Gans argued, similar working-class dynamics also generated lively suburban communities in that era. Social and economic conditions are as much – if not more – a product of time and human history as they are an artefact of spatial configurations.

Throughout their writings the new urbanists indicate that they covet a similar social moment as the one Jacobs described. They seek to build the kind of social vitality that flourished on Hudson Street or that generations of novelists imagined on the front porches of small-town America. As Jacobs did, they conflate urban form with a particular type of cultural behaviour. If only homes are dense enough, close to the street, on small blocks, and with a mix of uses, people should behave in the way someone (usually the designer or planner) thinks is respectable: fit for upstanding, civic-minded, and responsible citizens. Keeping windows lit, managing graffiti, ensuring an attractive urban realm, and mixing affordable housing in small proportions into development projects thus serves as part of a civilising process.

Next pages: Residents of the New Urbanism-style settlement of Seaside, Florida, 1988.

Jacobs said relatively little about housing types but Duany and his colleagues settled on the small-town American houses of the early 20th century, with elevated front steps and porches for New Urbanism's designs. The porch would function as a transition space between the private and public realm and permit occupants to interact with passers-by, analogous to the front stoops that Jacobs described a generation

SEASIDE
TOWN LIMIT
POP. 203
ELEV. 28
GROVE ALLEY
COUNTY ROAD 30A

earlier; however, in the age of air conditioning, TV, internet, and long work commutes, residents may not use the porches in the same ways their grandparents did.

Launching her critique just as modernism and garden city ideas reached their zenith in North America, Jacobs received mixed reviews within the planning community.[4] By the 1970s, she had moved to Canada where she joined protests about highway extensions and urban renewal projects.[5] Before long her ideas about density and mixed use were influencing urban planning policy and redevelopment projects in Toronto and Vancouver.[6] Her analysis of the failures of modernist projects in major American cities proved increasingly persuasive as suburban growth proliferated and old urban cores were hollowed out. Planners looking for new strategies began to accept the merit of her ideas.

In the early 1980s, architect-planners like Andres Duany and Peter Calthorpe designed suburban and exurban developments that articulated design principles similar to those Jacobs espoused. The proponents of this new way of building often implemented elements of her prescriptions for physical form without explicitly acknowledging Jacobs' influence.[7]

Duany and his wife, Plater-Zyberk, initiated neo-traditional town planning with Seaside, a small resort town they designed for developer Robert Davis in 1982.[8] With its compact form, mix of uses and housing types, traditional-style homes with front porches, distinct edge and civic centre and attractive public realm, Seaside captured attention as an alternative to conventional development patterns. Seaside exemplified Duany's commitment to employing the design principles that characterised small-town America.[9] Through his writings and lectures Duany discussed several thinkers who influenced his work, including Camillo Sitte, Raymond Unwin, and Lewis Mumford.

Duany's most important intellectual mentor, however, is clearly Léon Krier, the European architect who advocated building according to traditional principles proven in the past.[10] Although his work occasionally includes cryptic quotes or citations from Jacobs, Duany has more commonly drawn on fellow architects for inspiration and supportive arguments. In 1993, Duany, Plater-Zyberk, Peter Calthorpe, and several colleagues formed the Congress for the New Urbanism (CNU) to coordinate the planning and design principles they were developing, and to initiate a systematic campaign to influence urban planning.[11] Over the next decades the New Urbanism movement grew into a potent force in North American planning while scholars like Emily Talen and Reid Ewing worked to give it intellectual coherence and methodological rigour.[12]

Which Elements of Jacobs' Argument Did New Urbanism Accept?

A close reading of Duany's work finds relatively few explicit connections to Jacobs; however, new urbanists use some of her clever quips to illustrate important points. For instance, the following quote from *Death and Life* appeared in several New Urbanism books: "The pseudoscience of planning seems almost neurotic in its determination to imitate empiric failure and ignore empiric success."[13]

Despite the paucity of direct citations, many of Jacobs' ideas seem implicit in new urbanist thinking and prescriptions. Like Jacobs, Duany accepted that developing a mix of uses, short blocks, and continuous networks can foster lively streets; that integrating parks, squares, and public buildings with the street fabric enhances the public realm; that emphasising the identity of districts helps to connect people to place. Perhaps Duany employs the same style of architectural critique as Jacobs – dispensing with academic citations that might have shown his reading of Jacobs. Or perhaps Jacobs' insights have become conventional wisdom that no longer merit explicit acknowledgement.

Jacobs stipulated four requirements to generate what she called exuberant diversity in the city.[14] Duany and other new urbanists have commonly promoted three of these requirements: districts must serve multiple functions; most blocks should be short; and density is required. Jacobs' fourth requirement – that buildings should vary in age and condition at close grain – received less attention, especially in the early years of New Urbanism.

While Duany focused on designing New Urbanism projects and refining tools to implement the vision, academics involved in the movement began to develop its theory. One of the most prolific of these scholars is Talen, a planning professor at Arizona State University. Talen's writings have often discussed the pragmatic and theoretical implications of diversity within New Urbanism, trying to make explicit connections between physical form and social outcomes while side-stepping and down-playing the physical determinism that can crop up in the writings of practitioners.[15] In an effort to enhance the academic credibility and authority of the movement, Talen worked within New Urbanism organisations to encourage practitioners to tone down the overt spatial determinism that the movement's critics[16] found problematic, and to embrace a wider understanding of what diversity can and should mean in practice. She wrote: "New Urbanism without social complexity is dreary. In the coming decades this simple truth will compel new urbanists to do more than create a physical shell of hoped-for diversity; it will force them to master the art of creating social mix in the same way that they have mastered the art of civic design."[17]

With criticisms of New Urbanism mounting within the academy[18], Talen sought to establish solid theoretical foundations for New Urbanism's principles and practices. In this task Talen drew extensively and explicitly on Jacobs' work.[19] Talen accepted Jacobs' arguments about the importance of social diversity and the potential that physical diversity has for producing social diversity, saying "there *are* design principles that can help sustain diverse neighborhoods".[20] She elaborated on "place diversity" that she argued constituted an element of the conditions required for social and economic mixing.[21] Talen did not abandon the idea that place plays a role, but she acknowledged its limitations.

Although practitioners cite Jacobs selectively, and theorists have worked assiduously to link Jacobs' insights with New Urbanism's design principles, close reading suggests that some of Jacobs' teachings failed to gain traction within new urbanist thinking. I turn now to a few of these points.

Which Elements of Jacobs' Argument Did New Urbanism Set Aside?

While Jacobs suggested that form had an essential effect on social and economic outcomes in the city, *Death and Life* pointed to other significant factors that New Urbanism has tended to set aside in formulating its principles and practices. For instance, in Jacobs' thinking, time, scale and control affect urban outcomes in significant ways.

Jacobs argued that buildings of varying age and condition provide opportunities for different kinds of uses and classes of people to co-exist in a district:[22] "Cities need old buildings so badly it is probably impossible for vigorous streets and districts to grow without them."[23] Spaces become meaningful, differentiated and organised by temporal processes. Jacobs saw time as a pre-requisite for developing social networks and building commitment to place.[24] Social capital and connections emerge as a consequence of the passage of months and years: they cannot be rushed or pre-planned. For instance, Jacobs critiqued the planners' notion that zoning for corner stores can increase diversity as a patronising gimmick that failed to understand social and economic conditions.[25]

New Urbanism involves building communities over a relatively short period of time with a planned mix of housing types and uses, including corner stores.[26] While some older structures may be retained in redevelopment, most of the structures are built (or renovated) within a few years. Given designers' concerns about the quality of the public realm, little variability in building age or condition results. New urbanists recognise this problem as intrinsic to their practice. "True towns take time; a designer can only provide the ingredients and conditions most likely to lead to a mixed-use future."[27] Differentiated spaces provide a veneer of history but little temporal depth.

Time matters to the new urbanists more as a design reference point than as an unfolding process. CNU founding executive director Peter Katz noted that the years 1900 to 1920 serve as the architectural and urban model for New Urbanism and provide benchmarks for urban design.[28] Alex Krieger suggested that New Urbanism seeks to short-cut the temporal process that transforms the fringe into a centre.[29] While Jacobs valued the variation in form that time affords cities as they age and transform, Duany argued that compatibility of design and conformity in relation to the street can create appropriate and perhaps even timeless form.[30] For the new urbanists, time constitutes a potential enemy, threatening the longevity of the vision: hence covenants and design codes limit the potential for design changes, seeking to freeze form in a unique moment in time. The libertarian streak within Jacobs would rebel at New Urbanism's unwillingness to let time exert its traditional influence on the city.

Jacobs clearly liked large cities and deplored planners' efforts to create small self-contained neighbourhoods.[31] Jacobs thought that planners insisted on working at inappropriate scales (like the neighbourhood unit). She saw meaningful social units at the street level, where neighbours formed "webs of public surveillance" that created "trust and social control",[32] but also at the functional district level (or political ward) where significant numbers of residents exert political influence within the city.[33] Jacobs argued that cities have natural advantages over towns and suburbs because size gives them the diversity that generates vitality.[34]

New Urbanism works primarily at the neighbourhood scale that Jacobs criticised.[35] In its early years New Urbanism was promoted as a better way to design subdivisions.[36] Instead of ugly and dysfunctional suburbs, Duany designed small towns and urban villages with apartments over the shops and civic uses around a town green or square. New urbanist communities were intended to permit a five-minute walk to important destinations and include a mix of living, working, and shopping uses within "true neighbourhoods".[37] The principles of New Urbanism have increasingly been applied to the kind of infill redevelopment projects that Jacobs favoured,[38] but green-field "complete" communities remain part of the practice.

Jacobs revelled in small-scale neighbourhoods operating at the street level, like Hudson Street. She saw these small districts as important for organising political action: small-scale social networks could mobilise to fight unwanted developments.[39] While Jacobs embraced citizen engagement for urban change, Duany and his colleagues described such intervention as Nimbyism, and decried the tendency of people to resist growth.[40] Jacobs conceived of scale as creating a matrix for social, political, and economic action, while New Urbanism accepted scale as a spatial constraint fixed by development economics and planning conditions. In her later work, Jacobs elaborated on her ideas about urban and economic scale, identifying the critical importance of cities in producing wealth and innovation;[41] these later writings get little attention from new urbanist practitioners or writers.

The new urbanists have followed Jacobs' legacy in voicing strong criticisms of conventional planning practice, but their strategies for resolving the problem differed. The libertarian streak running through Jacobs' writings led her to conclude that planning induces conformity, homogeneity, and sterility in the urban environment. She

Sankt Erik neighbourhood in Stockholm, built in the 1990s according to New Urbanist ideas, has been criticised with reference to Jane Jacobs for not being part of the surrounding city.

hoped to see cities break with the control that planning imposes so that social and market forces might operate more freely. Jacobs argued that monopoly planning cannot generate diversity.[42] Building areas all at once cannot create vitality. She wrote that "neighbourhoods built up all at once change little physically over the years as a rule"[43] – because they cannot update or repair themselves, they are dead from birth.

In drawing on Jacobs' insights, Talen recognised the inherent problem that New Urbanism faces: comprehensive planning by a master planner is intended to foster diversity.[44] New Urbanism applies a unifying vision yet seeks to produce diversity and vitality. Talen argued that planning for place diversity will encourage social and economic mixing, but Jacobs doubted that monopoly control could generate the requisite variety or distributed power.

Duany suggested that because infill alone cannot accommodate the urban growth required, planned developments must continue: New Urbanism, he noted, must accept the power that master planning endows and wield it responsibly.[45] In its efforts to promote "authentic urbanism",[46] New Urbanism has used the powerful control of the master planner to deploy covenants and codes to safeguard the quality of the public realm. Setting up homeowners' associations to monitor covenant compliance provides the necessary governance mechanisms to protect the designer's vision.[47] Duany and Talen collaborated to develop a theoretical framework (informed by ecological theory) for explaining and justifying the widespread application of "smart codes" to replace municipal land use regulations.[48] For the new urbanists, replacing what they saw as anti-urban planning regulations with urbanistic codes that govern form represented a positive step forward, but both versions reflect the kind of monopolistic control that Jacobs resisted. If Jacobs was correct that places need to have the ability to transform as conditions change, then New Urbanism codes and covenants may limit the potential for adaptive responses. Should the traditional forms that New Urbanism designers favour go out of fashion in the decades to come, then the districts that feature them may struggle to maintain market relevance.

While New Urbanism borrowed extensively from Jacobs' concepts in framing its approach to planning and design, it defied Jacobs' teachings in critical ways. New Urbanism projects emblemise the monopolistic control of the master planner who designs projects scaled not for appropriate social or political action but because of serendipitous land assembly factors, built not to accommodate time but to freeze it in place with codes and covenants. Jacobs' vision of the city as adaptive space within which citizens constructed their identities and shaped their own prospects in a sometimes messy urban context got lost in the picture-perfect images of New Urbanism.

Jacobs' Legacy

New Urbanism theory and practice reflects Jacobs' vision of lively urbanity: a diverse range of people densely interacting within a finely-grained mixed-use context. Like Jacobs, the new urbanists rejected modernism and garden city ideals, and blamed planning for the problems of the North American city. Yet New Urbanism did not merely parrot Jacobs' message. Indeed, some of New Urbanism's methods violated Jacobs' libertarian notions and reproduced the monopolistic processes that initiated her attacks on planning.

While Jacobs celebrated individual voice and community initiative in the city, New Urbanism has left relatively little space for democratic action or organic transformation of urban form over time. The centralising power of modernists like Robert Moses has transferred in New Urbanism to a new generation of architect-planners and developers who apply their expert judgment through increasingly universalised codes, design guidelines, and preferred forms.

Jacobs understood that her 1961 book transformed planners' theories about the good community, but she expressed reservations about how contemporary practice was implementing her observations and insights. For instance, in 2000 she told the social critic and author, Jim Kunstler that standardised approaches were not helpful, and she reminded him that places differ and have to be able to adapt in their own ways.[49] She found the codes imposed on new projects "very constricted".[50]

Despite Kunstler's best efforts to entice Jacobs to praise New Urbanism, she retained an aura of scepticism, telling him:

> I do not think that we are to be saved by new developments done to new urbanist principles. That's all of the good and I am very glad that new urbanists are educating America. I think that when

> this takes hold and when enough of the old regulations can be gotten out of the way – which is what is holding things up – that there is going to be some great period of infilling. And a lot of that will be makeshift and messy and it won't measure up to new urbanist ideas of design – but it will measure up to a lot of their other philosophy. And in fact if there isn't a lot of this popular and makeshift infilling, the suburbs will never get corrected. It's only going to happen that way. And I think that it will happen that way.[51]

The history of planning reveals the systematic simplification of powerful visions in practice. Thus Ebenezer Howard's garden city, committed to urban containment and social reform, now stands accused of complicity in producing suburban sprawl. Great theorists run the eternal risk of being only partly understood. To the extent that Jane Jacobs' ideas have permeated North American planning theory and practice, they tend to be linked to New Urbanism principles and methods embedded within smart-growth strategies and wedded to ideals of sustainability. Certainly it has become challenging to find a plan in Canada that does not espouse these ideas and recommend new urbanist methods.[52] Jacobs' belief that design influences urban vitality and economic growth has been so widely accepted that cities with the means to do so generally hire staff urban designers or commission urban design guidelines or form-based codes that reflect New Urbanism principles. Thus it seems that Jacobs became a guru of contemporary planning even as her admonishments about the undesirability of comprehensive planning fell on deaf ears.

This text is an abridged version of an article previously published in Max Page & Timothy Mennel (eds.), Reconsidering Jane Jacobs *(Chicago: APA Press, 2011) and reprinted with permission of the author, Jill L. Grant.*

Older buildings facing new constructions in Gelsenkirchen, Germany, 2017.

1 Jill L. Grant, *Planning the Good Community: New Urbanism in Theory and Practice* (London: Routledge, 2006).

2 Jane Jacobs, *The Death and Life of Great American Cities* (New York: Vintage Books, 1961), p.96.

3 Herbert J. Gans, *The Levittowners: Ways of Life and Politics in a New Suburban Community* (New York: Vintage Books, 1967); Herbert J. Gans, *The Urban Villagers: Group and Class in the Life of Italian-Americans* (New York: Free Press of Glencoe, 1962); Herbert J. Gans, *People and Plans: Essays on Urban Problems and Solutions* (New York: Penguin Books, 1968).

4 For instance, while planners in Toronto found Jacobs compelling and began to apply her principles in the 1970s, as late as the 1980s planners in smaller cities like Halifax, Nova Scotia, were openly critical of Jacobs' naivety. See John Sewell, *The Shape of the City: Toronto Struggles with Modern Planning* (Toronto: University of Toronto Press, 1993); Jill Grant, *The Drama of Democracy: Contention and Dispute in Community Planning* (Toronto: University of Toronto Press, 1994) pp. 129–130.

5 Sewell (1993).

6 Jill Grant (2006), pp. 153–156; Jacqueline Vischer, "Community and Privacy: Planners' Intentions and Residents' Reactions", *Plan Canada*, vol. 23, issue 4, pp. 112–122.

7 For instance, early writings by Peter Calthorpe and discussions of Duany's early projects do not cite Jacobs as a source. See P. Calthorpe, *The Next American Metropolis* (New York: Princeton Architectural Press, 1993); Alex Krieger, Andres Duany and Elizabeth Plater-Zyberk, *Towns and Town-Making Principles* (Cambridge: Harvard University Graduate School of Design, 1991).

8 David Mohney and Kelly Easterling, *Seaside: Making a Town in America* (New York: Princeton Architectural Press, 1991).

9 Andres Duany and Elizabeth Plater-Zyberk, "The Second Coming of the American Small Town", *Wilson Quarterly*, vol. 16, issue 1, 1992, pp. 19–48; Krieger (1991)

10 Salingaros calls Krier the "intellectual godfather of the New Urbanism movement": N. Salingaros, "The Future of Cities: The Absurdity of Modernism", online at *Planetizen*, www.planetizen.com/oped/item.php?id=35, (accessed 8 January 2004). Scully points to Krier's influence on Duany and Plater-Zyberk: Vincent J. Scully, "Seaside and New Haven", in Krieger (1991), pp. 17–20. Salingaros includes a quote from Duany indicating that Krier inspired him to create traditional communities: Nikos A. Salingaros, "Léon Krier: Architect and Urban Planner", online at applied.math.utsa.edu/krier/ (accessed 8 January 2004).

11 Michael Leccese and Kathleen McCormick, *Charter of the New Urbanism*

(New York: McGraw-Hill, 2000). See also Nico Calavita, "The New Urbanism", *Journal of the American Planning Association*, vol. 60, issue 4 (1994), p. 534; Peter Katz, *The New Urbanism: Toward an Architecture of Community* (New York: McGraw-Hill, 1994).

12 See, for example: Reid Ewing, *Best Development Practices: Doing the Right Thing and Making Money at the Same Time* (Chicago: APA Planners Press, 1996); Emily Talen, *New Urbanism and American Planning: The Conflict of Cultures* (New York: Routledge, 2005).

13 Jacobs (1961), p. 183; Krieger (1991), p. 70; Andres Duany, Elizabeth Plater-Zyberk, Jeff Speck, *Suburban Nation: The Rise of Sprawl and the Decline of the American Dream* (New York: North Point Press, 2000), p. 88.

14 Jacobs (1961), pp. 150–151.

15 Emily Talen, "Design that Enables Diversity: The Complications of a Planning Ideal", in *Journal of Planning Literature*, vol. 20, issue 3 (2006), pp. 233–249; Emily Talen, *Design for Diversity: Exploring Socially Mixed Neighborhoods* (Oxford: Architectural Press, 2008).

16 For instance, see Alex Marshall: *How Cities Work: Suburbs, Sprawl, and the Road Not Taken* (Austin: University of Texas Press, 2000).

17 Emily Talen, "The Unbearable Lightness of New Urbanism", *New Urbanism and Beyond: Designing Cities for the Future*, Tigran Haas, (ed.) (New York: Rizzoli, 2008), p. 77.

18 Evaluations of New Urbanism practices identified challenges with meeting its social agenda as early as 1994. See Ivonne Audirac and Anne H. Shermyen, "An Evaluation of Neotraditional Design's Social Prescription: Postmodern Placebo or Remedy for Suburban Malaise?", *Journal of Planning Education and Research*, vol. 13, issue 3 (1994), pp. 161–173.

19 The index of Talen's book on New Urbanism and American planning listed 61 page references where she highlighted Jacobs' work and influence. See Emily Talen (2005), p. 313.

20 Talen (2008), p. 7.

21 Talen (2006), p. 234.

22 Jacobs (1961), p. 150.

23 Jacobs (1961), p.187.

24 Jacobs (1961), pp. 138–139.

25 Jacobs (1961), pp. 190–191.

26 Codes in New Urbanism projects set out the requirements for corner stores: see Kurt Andersen, "Oldfangled New Towns", *Time,* vol. 137 (20 May, 1991), pp. 52–55. See also *Newsweek* , "15 Ways to Fix the Suburbs", Newsweek, vol. 125, issue 20 (15 May, 1995), pp. 46–53.

27 Duany et al. (2000), p 190.

28 Katz (1994).

29 Krieger (1991), p. 15.
30 Duany and Plater-Zyberk (1992).
31 Jacobs (1961), p. 114.
32 Jacobs (1961), p. 119.
33 Jacobs saw 30,000 residents as sufficient to constitute a functional district in cities like Boston, but suggested they might need to include 80,000 or more in larger cities like New York. Jacobs (1961), pp. 130–131.
34 Jacobs (1961), pp. 145–146.
35 While the Charter of the New Urbanism advocates planning at all scales from the region down to the neighborhood, in practice most development projects occur at a smaller scale. See http://www.cnu.org/charter .
36 Jerry Adler, "The New Burb is a Village", *Newsweek*, vol. 124, issue 26 (26 December 1994–2 January 1995); Krieger (1991).
37 Duany et al. (2000), pp. 148, 191–192.
38 Kunstler (2001). McInnes includes a similar comment from Jacobs: "Instead of aiming at big projects, it's much better to aim at the small ones, like infill projects." Craig McInnes, "Toronto Planners Praised by Jacobs", *Globe and Mail* (Metro Edition, 7 September 1991), p. A4.
39 Jacobs (1961), pp. 122–129.
40 Duany et al. (2000), pp. 42, 194.
41 Jane Jacobs, *Cities and the Wealth of Nations: Principles of Economic Life* (New York: Vintage Books, 1984).
42 Jacobs (1961), p. 192.
43 Jacobs (1961), p. 198.
44 Talen (2006), p. 234.
45 Andres Duany, "Our Urbanism", *Architecture*, vol. 87, issue 12 (December 1998), pp. 37–40.
46 Andres Duany, "A Common Language of Urban Design", Places, vol. 11, issue 3 (1998), pp. 76–78.
47 Duany et al. (2000), p. 149.
48 Andres Duany and Emily Talen, "Making the Good Easy: The Smart Code Alternative", *Fordham Urban Law Journal*, vol. 29, issue 4 (2002), pp. 1445–1468.
49 Kunstler (2001).
50 Bill Steigerwald, "Urban Studies Legend Jane Jacobs on Gentrification, the New Urbanism, and Her Legacy", *Reason.com* (June 2001), online at http://reason.com/archives/2001/06/01/city-views (accessed 20 August 2010)
51 Kunstler (2001).
52 Jill L. Grant, "Theory and Practise in Planning the Suburbs: Challenges in Implementing New Urbanism and Smart Growth Principles", *Planning Theory and Practice*, vol. 10, issue 1 (2009), pp. 11–33.

CHAPTER VI

The Economies of Nature and Man

Saskia Sassen

JANE JACOBS' WORK and long life stretched across multiple epochs, each with its distinctive markers. I want to start with a lesser known part of her work, and the book *The Nature of Economies*, which, written towards the end of her life, was published in 2000. One of the key struggles in this book is the attempt to reconnect to nature while maintaining the specificity of the man-made world. Here Jacobs takes on economics as a discipline as opposed to economies as complex systems subject to laws and dynamics not fully captured in standard economic models. She does this not by providing the 'treatise' treatment of the subject. Rather, she makes us part of the life of a few friends who spend time talking, and talking is what this book is about. She used this format frequently in her later work, as a way, she hoped, to include the non-expert.

Working out ideas and contesting each other's thoughts and beliefs, these friends take us through an enormously broad range of subjects and erudite illustrations. The book is modelled on the Platonic dialogues, yet after some initial resistance that many a contemporary reader might have, one is captured by its dynamics. There is a clear organising passion that drives the talking and that keeps this account moving. It is the effort to situate economies within a broader set of possibilities and limits, laws and contingencies, and to show the many ways in which the discipline of economics has become stuck within a very narrow range of issues and has failed to work with a broader range of possibilities and limits.

Cutters at work at Dege & Skinner on Savile Row – the exclusive gentlemen's tailoring street in the financial district of London.

This was a bold experiment by an intellectual who had long shown herself to be daring. It moves far away from her two classics, *The Death and Life of Great American Cities* and *Cities and the Wealth of Nations*. And yet, as was also the case with these two classics, Jacobs takes on economics as a discipline and *economies* as complex systems subject to laws and dynamics not fully captured in standard economic models.

In what follows I navigate these two sides of Jacobs, one belonging to her earlier period and the other to her late period.

★

The conditions that make and constitute a metropolis – the enormous diversity of workers, their living and work spaces, the multiple sub-economies involved – are seen as irrelevant to today's global city, or as belonging to another era. But a close look, as encouraged by Jacobs, shows us this is wrong. She would ask us to look at the consequences of these sub-economies – for the city, for its people, its neighbourhoods, and the visual orders involved. Today she would ask us to consider all the other economies and spaces impacted by the massive gentrifications of the modern city – not least, the resultant displacement of modest households and profit-making small neighbourhood firms.

How do we see those aspects that are typically rendered invisible by modern narratives of development and urban competitiveness? In the early 1900s, the city was a lens for understanding larger processes – but half a century later, it had lost that role. It was Jane Jacobs who taught us to look again at the city in a deeper, more complex way. She helped us re-emphasise dimensions that were usually excluded – indeed expelled – from general analyses of the urban economy. I can imagine she would have affirmed that, no matter how electronic and global the city might one day become, it still has to be "made" – and therein lies the importance of place.

The city has long been a strategic site for the exploration of major subjects confronting society. In the first half of the 20th century, the study of cities was at the heart of sociology – evident in the work of Georg Simmel, Max Weber, Walter Benjamin, Henri Lefebvre and the Chicago School of Urbanism. These sociologists confronted massive processes: industrialisation, urbanisation, alienation, and a new cultural formation they called "urbanity". Studying the city meant studying the major social processes of an era.

And yet, by the 1950s, the study of the city had gradually lost this privileged role as a producer of key analytic categories. The social sciences, we might say, lost their capacity to 'see' the city and all that it made visible. But not for Jacobs. For her, the barricades – both figurative and literal – played a role not merely as part of the battle to preserve one of the oldest parts of Manhattan, but in her entire analysis of the urban economy. Jacobs' passionate fight to protect 'the Village' in Lower Manhattan was about much more than preserving an old urban landscape – although this in itself was enough to warrant a fight in a city like New York where the developers ruled, and basically did not care about legacy or visual orders or urbanity.

Social theory pioneer Richard Sennett, who was often on the 'picket lines' with Jacobs, talks of her calm ferocity. She was relentless and stood up to anyone, regardless of her age. But it also became clear that community battles were, for her, simply part of a wider inquiry than just a 'neighbourhood fight' as she sought to better understand, and develop concepts for, the role of cities in the wider economy.

Why is it so important to recover the sense of place, and production, in our analyses of the global economy, particularly as these are constituted in major cities? Because they allow us to see the multiplicity of economies and working cultures in which regional, national and global economies are embedded. But Jacobs went much further than this. What she showed us, crucially, is that urban space is the key building block of these economies. She understood it as the weaving of multiple strands that make the city so much more than the sum of its residents, or its grand buildings, or its corporate economy.

In *The Economy of Cities* Jacobs mentioned how she had already understood the central role played by the economy in cities when writing *Death and Life*. She saw the need to make it clear that without an economy there is no city. This became the key argument in *The Economy of Cities*, in which she wrote: "It doesn't matter what else cities have, what grand temples they have, what beautiful scenery, wonderful people, or anything else – if their economy doesn't work."

Most big cities in the 1960s and 1970s were rather poor, as I noted in my work *The Global City*, published in 1991. New York went bankrupt, and other major cities abroad, from Paris and London to Tokyo, were broke. The key economic sectors were basically not urban: mass manufacturing, the building of suburbs, and the development of infrastructures. Especially in the United States, people were drawn to suburbs, and the highway construction was embodied there by Jacobs' most well-known antagonist, Robert Moses.

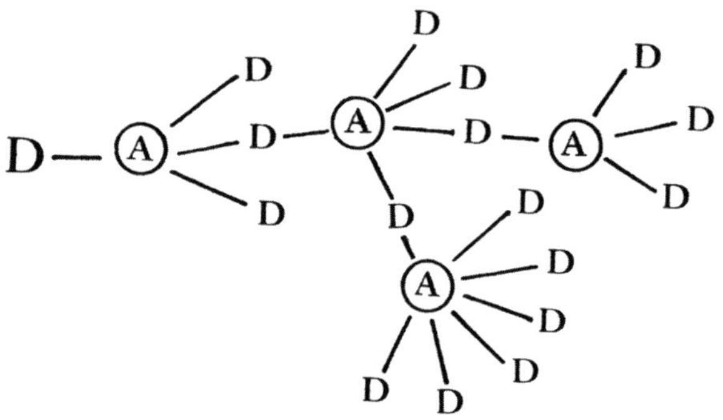

When the global economy got going in the 1980s, cities once again become rich and strategic. They became the places for the production of the diverse instruments needed to handle the global operations of companies. In my analysis, the global city function is an intermediation function: when firms go global they need access to a broad range of highly specialised inputs, often quite diverse across the world.[1] This type of production cannot be done in-house. It requires a highly networked concentration of diverse specialised services for corporations and the financial sector, and it is in the metropolitan areas that these services are developed.

★

As an activist, Jacobs made a knowledgeable case about whatever the issue of concern was, and she succeeded in mobilising others. As a writer, she exposed the inner workings of cities. Yet it is the economy of cities that unites Jacobs' work and connects her most famous trio of urban studies – *The Death and Life of Great American Cities* (1961), *The Economy of Cities* (1969) and *Cities and the Wealth of Nations* (1984). Even though Jacobs did not engage directly with the global economy, she demonstrated through her work that she had good insights into how it worked.

Diagram illustrating Jacobs' theory of growth. Work multiplies by branching out, from a speciality or product (division of labour, D), which generates and branches off a new activity (A) which in turn leads to new specialities or products – and so on. *From The Economy of Cities*, 1969.

Jacobs' later books were more daring still, both in terms of her ideas and the means through which she shared them. *The Nature of Economies* is not among her best known works but it is here that Jacobs takes on economics as a discipline and economies as complex systems subject to laws and dynamics not fully captured in standard economic models (particularly environmental destruction). The intellectual struggle in her book is the attempt to reconnect to nature while maintaining the specificity of the "man-made world".

She does this, as I mentioned at the outset, not through learned interpretations, but rather by making us party to fictional conversations, modelled on Platonic dialogues, between a group of friends as they challenge each others' ways of thinking about certain interrelated issues. A theme in the conversations is, for example, the need to stop focusing on *things* and instead shift attention to the *processes* that generate the things, which, in turn, should blur the difference between nature and economy. Thus airplanes are made by engineers; yet engineers use the laws of nature to make planes. As do winemakers and bakers in their own production processes: the profits made is just a feedback information mechanism. Jacobs is at pains to situate economies in a broader set of possibilities and limits, laws and contingencies, and to show the many ways in which economics had become stuck in a very narrow range of ideas – namely the production of goods – and failed to consider the extent to which such product growth rested on the destruction of often non-replaceable natural resources.

Towards the end of her life, Jacobs began work on a new book, to be called *Uncovering the Economy*, but death interrupted her. The opening section of this uncompleted work was included in *Vital Little Plans: The Short Works of Jane Jacobs*, which, its editors tell us, "reveals her final understanding of how economic growth unfolds".[2] Jacobs argues that healthy cities are where "new work"[3] springs up, where the "dense fabric of interdependencies incubates economic expansion and innovations at large". "Cultivating vibrant urban centres with small, diverse commercial and industrial enterprises", she writes, "is the linchpin of any meaningful strategy to combat decline." This has become a widely accepted notion today. But that wasn't the case when Jacobs invoked it in her battles to save downtown Manhattan.

Engagement with nature is not typically associated with Jacobs' work. But she does indeed seek to engage with it, on her own terms. The friends' conversation in *The Nature of Economies* contains a journey of insightfulness and breadth that finally convinces even those who are at first sceptical of the somewhat unusual narrative form. The theme of not seeing nature as distinct from the world we humans have built is most eloquently developed by a kind of alter ego to Jacobs, the character Hiram, who stresses the need to focus not on "things" but on processes that generate those things. The friend Armbruster, who is sceptical of the nature perspective, asks how money, the ultimate man-made item, gets handled in this type of logic. And even this, Hiram tells us, is an information mechanism, a kind of feedback system similar to others in nature.

The book contains multiple disquisitions such as these and builds up the level of complexity of the argument as it proceeds. This produces interesting logic. While ecology is the "economy of nature", Hiram is studying the nature of economy. "Nature affords foundations for human life and sets its possibilities and limits. Economists seem not to have grasped this reality yet", she writes, and yet, she points out, "economic life is ruled by processes and principles we didn't invent and can't transcend."

More understanding of these processes and principles would lead to better economies. Working with the limits is part of this. Thus alchemists did better once they gave up trying to turn base metals into gold, and instead studied chemistry. Limits also lead to producing substitutes for that which becomes subject to diminishing returns: domesticated animals raised for food replacing a scarcity of wild game, plastics instead of tortoise shell; and so on.

The wreck of the Titanic illustrates some of these possibilities and limits. At the time the ship was built and launched, metallurgy had not advanced as much as engineering. Engineers were able to design the largest man-made movable object, but the steel available could not withstand the stress of the ship's size, so it cracked under low impact with the iceberg. Yet it was the best steel of its time.

The question of economic development raises another question: where do new things come from? Jacobs allows the discussion to build arguments that it does not follow a straight line or sequence, but is about a network of mutually dependent events. It's not the same as

Jane Jacobs and the architect Philip Johnson (on the right) taking part in demonstrations against the demolition of the monumental Penn Station in 1963.

AGBANY IS HERE
SAVE PENN STATION

cooperation, Jacobs thinks, because a lot of it is random and also may entail competition. Development is not driven by any invisible force that strives for greater complexity, away from simpler stages. Although we do not know why development occurs, we can say more about how it happens.

However, Jacobs' notion that growth depends on a system's capacities to continue transforming energy is not entirely correct, because the more the system in question can do before releasing that energy, the greater the growth. This is clearly a formula for maximising sustainable sources of energy and for recycling. The reasoning is also applicable to successful cities with diversified economies that are not dependent on a single sector, however high-yielding it is. I have also pointed out that cities can become too dependent on, for example, the financial world. If a country reduces its dependence on unilateral exports and invests more in internal diversification, it is also the equivalent of delaying the release of that energy.

Herein lies a severe critique of the discipline of economics that somehow became stuck on supply and demand and an associated emphasis on specialisation rather than diversification as the best way for economies to develop. This economic logic is a failure to understand the 'nature' of economies, and it brings to mind the observation of the economist John Maynard Keynes on how the continuation of business cycles in England, in spite of government interventions, might signal the existence of deeper structural flaws in the economy that could not be remedied through monetary, budgetary or tax manipulations.

As the book proceeds, the various characters at times almost have the function that a Greek choir could have in a play: images that have been constructed through conversation on a particular subject become recurrent expressions in an increasingly broad range of subjects and settings. If I have one critique of this text, it is that it carries a risk of becoming mechanical in the effort to trace back to nature what we experience or represent as 'artificial' in the sense of being human-made. But the remarkable little book is like a living seminar, and should be made for teaching.

Jacobs' analysis is built largely from the bottom up, via a process of detecting the dynamics embedded in urban space itself. This also ensured she would keep discovering newly emergent conditions, that would then feed into an expansion of the domains she would address in her writing, notably her later focus on the environmental question. Her many short stories capture the evolution and accumulation of her knowledge about cities and how their economies feed larger economic systems, but also how they fit into the ecological challenge. She was a champion in the genre itself, and knew how to extrapolate a larger history or dynamic from micro-conditions.

1 Saskia Sassen,"The Global City: Enabling Economic Intermediation and Bearing Its Costs", *City & Community*, vol. 15, issue 2, June 2016.

2 Samuel Zipp & Nathan Storring (ed.), *Vital Little Plans: The Short Works of Jane Jacobs* (New York: Random House, 2016).

3 Cf. Jacobs' special concept of economic growth, *new work*, in Jane Jacobs, *The Economy of Cities* (New York: Random House, 1969), pp. 49–84.

CHAPTER VII

Unpredictability and the Wealth of Cities

Ola Andersson

IN THE SPRING of 1968, Jane Jacobs had had enough of New York. She was 52 years old and had been arrested twice in a year, firstly during a protest against the Vietnam War, along with Allen Ginsberg and Susan Sontag, among others. The protest ended for Jacobs in a discussion with Sontag about the dynamic of the dissenting view, beneath the harsh, fluorescent lighting of the local jail.

The second time she was accused of having disrupted a public consultation arranged by New York's transport department which was designed to drive through the Lower Manhattan Parkway, a motorway which would have meant devastating demolitions in the Manhattan area of SoHo. Jacobs risked being prosecuted for inciting a riot, criminal damage and obstructing the exercise of authority. She had reasons to leave not just New York, but also the USA, since her sons James and Ned, aged 18 and 20, were at risk of being called up for military service in Vietnam.

When her husband, Robert, was commissioned to design a hospital in Toronto they left the house at 555 Hudson Street where she had written *The Death and Life of Great American Cities*. They packed their belongings in a Volkswagen van and moved to a red-brick house in the Canadian city, where they would remain for the rest of their lives. Another important purpose of the move was that Jacobs should have the opportunity to finish writing the follow-up to her successful book. "I get upset when I think how much time I had to spend on those things", she said. "The new book was begun two years later than planned because of that motorway and the fight against demolitions in West Village. It is a terrible abuse of power when a city threatens its inhabitants so that they can't carry on with their work."

In her book *The Economy of Cities*, Jacobs imagined that the agricultural revolution began in towns. Two farmers in East Anglia sharpening up their scythes, September 1946.

PLAZA
RESTAURANT
PARK
HOSTEL
OFFICE
INDUSTRY
DRY GROCERY
DRY GROCERY
BUTTER & CHEESE
CHEESE
POULTRY & EGGS
FRUITS & VEGETABLES
HOUSING
BROAD STREET
ALLIED
CITY
MEATS
FISH
INCINERATOR
PATTISON AVENUE
GARAGE
FRUITS & VEGETABLES
LEAGUE ISLAND PARK
ALLIED INDUSTRY
DRY GROCERY
GROCERY
FROZEN FOOD
DRY GROCERY
MEATS
MOTEL
DRY
ALLIED INDUSTRY

The book she tried to write but was unable to complete before she had left New York was *The Economy of Cities*, which came out in 1969, the year after she came to Canada. There is no doubt that Jacobs considered it to be an important book. However, other people around her did not share that view to any great extent, which is not so surprising. The book begins with a theory that lacks both evidence and logic, namely that the agricultural revolution began in towns. She imagines an invented town that she calls New Obsidian; the fact that the town shares the first part of its name with New York is scarcely a coincidence. According to Jacobs that town is a "pre-agricultural metropolis". Concerning her imaginary city she says: "I shall not allow New Obsidian to be controlled by any other economic processes than the ones I have found in cities in our own and historic times." Quite an extraordinary way to describe the agricultural revolution about ten thousand years ago, you might think. Rather than a theory though, it is, at best, a wild guess. Quite a poor one too.

Her thesis is that agriculture and animal husbandry arose in cities because, she asserts, all development always takes place in cities. According to this logic, the origins of cities must therefore have preceded the emergence of agriculture. The fact that this was in conflict with contemporary archaeological knowledge may not have seemed such a great problem to her. Her previous book, *Death and Life*, was based on a rejection of all accepted theories of town planning, and time proved her right. The accepted truths about town planning turned out to be wrong, not to say absurd.

The problem with her theory about agriculture is that, from start to finish, it makes no sense. Ten thousand years ago there were two to four million people in the world who were dependent on hunting, fishing and wild plants for their survival. They were obliged to roam over wide areas in order to catch and gather enough food. But the emergence of agriculture enabled humans to be raised within a much smaller area. When we learned to harvest crops and domesticate and breed animals we could then settle in one place to a great extent. Resources, above all in the form of grain, could be gathered and stored to be consumed all year round, not just at harvest time. This also meant that it became possible to produce a surplus. That surplus could be exchanged for goods and services, and could be seized by those who obtained the power to do so.

Plans for a new food distribution centre in Philadelphia, Pennsylvania. From an unsigned report by Jacobs, "Philadelphia's Redevelopment – A Progress Report", *Architectural Forum*, July 1955.

This in turn made job-sharing possible on a whole new scale. Smiths, carpenters, potters, basket-makers and others could make a living by swapping their services for food. States could develop by taxing the people who farmed the land in return for administrative services and military protection. When agriculture reached the level of development at which it could produce a surplus, the city was able to develop.

Jacobs does not seem particularly interested in what the people living in her imaginary city might have eaten – "food is imported from hunters and gatherers", she states nonchalantly. The underlying weakness in Jacobs' view of the city can scarcely be demonstrated more clearly.

It has always been possible to conquer cities by siege. However much a city has in terms of high walls and fortresses, sooner or later it will be vanquished by hunger if its exchange with the surrounding world's production of food dries up. The city is and remains dependent on agricultural surplus. We still live on the bread made from grain from the fields, fish from the sea and lakes and meat from cattle. Thus it was not the cities that invented agriculture. It was agriculture that gave rise to the cities, because agriculture needed them in order to be able to exchange its surplus for goods and services. In order for that to be done efficiently the exchange needs to be concentrated in certain places, in cities.

Even today there is no way of reducing the geographical radius of the content of our meals so drastically that a concentration of people can be self-sufficient.

Jacobs' ideas of the superiority of the city should perhaps be seen rather more as a battle cry, an index finger directed at the forces that could not see any points at all in favour of city life or the crowded city and wanted to abolish them. There are also other reasons why *The Economy of Cities*, 50 years after it came out, is chiefly of historical interest. When the book was written it was taken as a matter of course that the capital that caused cities to grow came from the local production of goods. Today it is equally a matter of course that welfare in the western world's cities is based on quite different production. Jacobs' view of the city's economy was wholly characterised by the conditions for the production of goods. For her the export and import of goods formed the foundation on which the economies of cities had always rested. The growth or stagnation of cities was therefore dependent on their ability to export goods and to be able to substitute imports with their own production.

When the book was written it was scarcely controversial. The greatest part of global industrial production took place in the industrial cities of the Western world. Industrial products manufactured in Japan and Hong Kong were exceptions and were seen in the West as inferior, cheap copies. China was in the middle of the convulsions of the Cultural Revolution.

But at the same time as Jacobs was battling to finish her book, the world was changing, even though few people understood the consequences. It was only during the 1970s that the contours of the new division of labour that we take for granted today became clear. The production of goods moved from the Western world to other parts where labour costs were lower. The industry that survived in the West was rationalised and automated in order to become less labour-intensive. The number of jobs in industry was thus drastically reduced. The once great industrial cities of the West began to stagnate.

Ten years after Jacobs' book was published, the unthinkable had happened: Japanese car manufacturers had taken over the American car market. Detroit, *the* motor city, the symbol of the USA's superior technology that led people all over the world to dream of big American cars, was becoming depopulated. The roads and car parks in the USA were increasingly dominated by small Japanese cars.

In order to be able to move the surplus from production in countries with low labour costs to owners and financiers in rich countries, the global mobility of capital became a necessity. The global flow of capital that constitutes the foundation for welfare in the growing cities of the Western world has entailed a drastic transformation in their economies. The provision of services and private consumption are the dominant features there today, not the production of goods. Cities like Detroit, that have been unable to convert the production of goods to the provision of services, have stagnated and for many of them the stagnation looks like being permanent.

Jacobs' refusal to understand the cities' eternal dependency on agriculture was clearly indefensible, even when *The Economy of Cities* was written. On the other hand she can scarcely be blamed for not foreseeing the release of industrial production from the working classes of the Western world. Few people foresaw that development, which only became evident ten years later.

In other words, Jacobs was not an eminent historian. That was not where her strength lay. It was her keen observations, her ability to see what was happening in front of her eyes, things that others took no notice of that made the *Death and Life* ground-breaking.

But even if, like most others, she was unable to see the new economic division of labour that was emerging as she wrote *The Economy of Cities,* she does display an almost prophetic capacity, based on what she observed in her own time, to pinpoint exactly what it is that distinguishes the stagnating cities from the growing ones in our own time. The fact is that in the chapter "The Valuable Inefficiencies and Impracticalities of Cities" she points out what was to become the dividing line between the cities that were able to adapt to that development and those that were not.

Jacobs' writes that manufacturing will no longer be what economic activity is organised around. Instead it will be services – and it will be this that also sets off other activities, including manufacturing. She points to the example of office machines, which in their earlier form were just machines (typewriters, calculators, dictaphones etc.). But we buy a modern office machine first and foremost as a service: the service that analyses and programmes the work in an office, where the machines are just a part of the whole.

However, it is not rationality that leads this development. The impractical and the inefficient, she writes, are necessary to economic development and that is precisely what makes the cities particularly valuable to economic life. She explains that they are not valuable *in spite of* that, but *because* they are inefficient and impractical. Her point is that the rational city that streamlines its economy to satisfy the demands of a certain type of production will find it difficult to develop what she calls "new work" – new products and services that arise out of the existing ones. Efficiency in work and production is something that follows on from all the more messy development work: a time and energy-consuming business of trial, error and failure. Trial and error are the certainties, not success. And even when the result is ultimately a successful one, it is often a surprise and not what people were actually aiming for.

Thus, according to Jacobs, what causes cities to develop is development work, not efficiency. On that point, the 50 years that have elapsed since she wrote the book have confirmed her thesis. The transition from an economy based on the production of goods to a service economy based on the global flow of capital was to turn the old industrial quarters of SoHo on Manhattan, where she had made a decisive effort to save them from demolition, into an exclusive district of the city. The houses she saved became lucrative investments. The fact that Detroit, which built its success on Henry Ford's efficient conveyor belt principles, was not capable of changing when it faced competition from Japanese car manufacturers proved to be its downfall. With less efficiency and more irrational development work, full of failures, Detroit might have maintained its lead. But the big car manufacturers, obsessed with efficiency, were not interested. It is a city's capacity to retain a high proportion of inefficient and irrational development work, in a wide range of different organisations, at different levels and in different fields, that keeps stagnation at bay. It is the irrationality and the impractical that make it possible for the city to continue to flourish.

Even today our understanding of this fundamental fact is imperfect, and in 1969 Jacobs' theory must have appeared extremely odd. The idea that there could be a clear line of development from hippies and gays in San Francisco's Haight-Ashbury and Castro neighbourhoods to today's Silicon Valley must have seemed preposterous. But Jacobs suspected it and the decades since have given us countless examples.

Yet there is often a lack of understanding of the fundamental unpredictability that characterises all development work. It is not just the labour-intensive, time-consuming development of new products that creates success. It is the multitude of new ideas, most of which are never realised, the wide range of people willing to risk failure, that build a flourishing city.

A city where the price of risk-taking is far too high, where failure is punished severely, is a city on the road to stagnation. The idea that a city's development potential can be measured by the number of failures is no exaggeration. For every successful development project there are at least three failed ones. The more failures there are, the more successes there will also be. The fewer that have the chance to fail, the gloomier the city's future prospects.

A Jacobs example which has only become clearer with time is that of Rochester, New York. At the end of the 19th century and the beginning of the 20th, the city was a hothouse for the development of scientific

FORECLOSURE
RECORDS
80
24 St
Brillo
Brillo

and high-tech equipment. The city was thought to be heading for a bright future. The person who stopped it in its tracks was George Eastman. The company he founded, the camera and film manufacturer Kodak, was one of many that emerged from the favourable conditions for technological development work that prevailed in Rochester. But when Kodak had achieved a sufficiently strong position, through their own and others' development work, Eastman ruthlessly opposed anyone who tried to leave Kodak to start their own businesses. When Eastman Kodak gradually came to dominate not just the economic and political life but also the cultural life of Rochester, the good development climate disappeared.

In 1950 Rochester had 330,000 inhabitants. Since then the population has shrunk in every decade. In the 1990s Kodak lost market shares to the Japanese film manufacturer Fuji, who made cheaper and better films that were easier to develop. In the new millennium the competition from digital cameras took over and, in January 2012, Kodak went bankrupt. By 2016, the city had 208,000 inhabitants, one third fewer than in 1950.

There was only one firm in Rochester that could compete with Kodak. Xerox originated in 1906, before Eastman Kodak got a grip on the city, under the name of Haloid. In 1946, Xerox reached an agreement with the inventor of a process that could print images with an electrically-charged photosensitive plate and powdered ink to develop it as a commercial product. After long and costly development work, the copying machine became an enormous success in the mid-1970s, and became synonymous with the Xerox trademark. But by then the company had moved several years previously from Rochester to Stamford, Connecticut.

Xerox was at that time also developing a computer which was never sold commercially but was used internally by the company and by the US military. It was called Xerox Alto. In 1979, a 24-year-old college drop-out, who had travelled to India and studied Zen Buddhism and experimented with marijuana and LSD, realised the potential in Xerox Alto. The 24 year-old's name was Steve Jobs. He recruited the development team from Xerox to his own company, Apple. In 1983 they had developed Xerox Alto into a product that they launched under the name Macintosh. I am now sitting here in Stockholm typing this text

A colourful mural in the Castro district, San Fransisco.

KODAK

on a modern Mac. Manufacturer Apple's even newer product, the iPhone, has fundamentally changed our society, and Apple is one of the world's most valuable companies. How many people could have anticipated that in 1969? There was certainly one – Jane Jacobs. To expect her to have foreseen that, as of today, I can't know in what city or part of the world they are actually manufactured, or by whom – that would perhaps be to expect too much.

The head offices of Eastman Kodak in Rochester, New York, with the 19-storey Kodak tower from 1914.

登龍軒
登龍軒
林鋼鉄店
シマダ

CHAPTER VIII

The Great Importance of Small Movements

Peter Elmlund

ONE ASPECT OF Jane Jacobs that is rarely, if ever, commented on is her storytelling technique. Jacobs was a journalist and knew how to write for the public in an intelligible way and at a fast pace. The style and the manner in which she narrates and describes, for example, in *The Death and Life of Great American Cities*, encourages the reader to read quickly. At the same time, and this is what gives the book its special character, though it may irritate some readers, the pages burst with observations, analyses, ideas, conclusions, reflections and anecdotes. Her ambition to explain the social and economic functions of the big city, once and for all, has resulted in a book that is as complex, tight-packed and diverse as the big city itself.

Jane Jacobs should therefore be read slowly and contemplatively, regardless of the fact that the text flows on like a river in spring. Readers often forget this and consequently miss a good deal in their understanding of her work. She frequently delivers complex analyses which are boiled down to just a couple of sentences that could easily be developed into free-standing books in their own right. Such as when, in *Death and Life*, she writes: "Great Cities are not like towns, only larger. They are not like suburbs, only denser. They differ from towns and suburbs in basic ways, and one of these is that cities are, by definition, full of strangers."

Even today we tend to consider cities of different sizes as variations on the same theme. In the Swedish debate, there has been criticism of the division of the analysis of the city into the 'classic city environment' and the 'suburb' because such a division is presumed to belittle the suburbs. The response has been that 'everything' is a city, which is a perspective that conceals valuable knowledge, for example the fact

A delivery boy on his bicycle carrying lots of noodles, Tokyo 1956.

that major cities have a significantly larger proportion of small businesses than small towns and suburbs. This has major implications for both social and economic life. Jacobs pointed this out as long ago as 1961 and it is still true.

Examples of an insufficiently close reading of Jacobs can be found even among prominent academics. Margaret Crawford, an architecture professor at Berkeley, wrote that it was remarkable that the activist Jacobs did not take up issues of race in her famous breakthrough book.[1] This might seem a rather odd comment, since Jacobs was essentially trying to explain how cities work. In my view, the aim of the remark is rather to cast suspicion on the type of classic city environment that is rapidly being gentrified today, and that many architects consider to be old-fashioned. Crawford dutifully added that Jacobs was not racist, noting that "her silence on issues of race was typical of unbiased liberals at that time, who preferred to emphasise the similarities between people rather than their differences."

One may say that but it is not correct at all. Jacobs took up the issue of race in *Death and Life* and introduced her argument thus: "Sidewalk public contact and sidewalk public safety, taken together, bear directly on our country's most serious social problem – segregation and racial discrimination." She believed that the key to tolerance in the big city was a living city life where strangers could share the urban space in a peaceful and civilised way. She also pointed out that it is difficult to solve the problem of housing segregation in areas where there is no city life and where strangers feel unwelcome.

If the book's complexity has sometimes led to misunderstandings and superficial reviews, economic development has also influenced the ways in which it is seen, at first to its detriment and later to its advantage. An important part of Jacobs' analysis of cities is her appreciation of small businesses, which are important not just because they ensure safe streets where people from different backgrounds can meet, but also because they constitute important factors for economic growth.

Her preoccupation with the merits of small businesses was probably the main reason why her book did not have the impact it should have had when it was published, nor in the following decades. The number of micro-companies, defined by her as companies with up to five employees, had dropped continuously in the Western world ever since Karl Marx proclaimed his prophecies of their demise. In the USA they also decreased dramatically in number from 1950 to 1970, which is interesting since that period coincides with a dramatic change in the city landscape.[2] One might wonder whether the habitat for micro-companies was quite simply planned away together with an urban life able to integrate people. In any event, the 1960s were dominated by large-scale corporate thinking, and many town planning experts saw Jacobs' passion for small businesses as backward-looking.

Economic development would, however, soon endorse the relevance of her analysis. The technological advancements of the 1970s began a change in the economy that Alvin Toffler addressed in 1980 in his book, *The Third Wave*, which can most simply be described as the transition from an industrial society to an information society.[3] A developmental shift began here which was to fundamentally change our cities. It is often attributed to an increased interest in our inner cities that became perceptible in the 1970s. New lifestyles, above all among the young, were becoming possible, but what propelled the development of cities forward was, as Saskia Sassen suggests, a new technology that enabled what could be called the urbanisation of economic activities.[4]

Up until the 1960s, company head offices were as a rule located in the same place as their production works, but with new telecommunications it was suddenly possible to separate them. The result was that factories remained in the countryside or in small towns – or moved abroad in pursuit of lower paid labour – while their head offices began to move to bigger cities where they could purchase advanced services from specialised companies. This progression was so manifest by the 1990s that American researchers began to write about "the new urban revival of the United States".[5] And, in turn, it led to many head offices being reduced in size or at least being reorganised. It was simply more efficient for businesses to buy qualified services from specialists in the areas of finance, economics, advertising, IT, and the law etc. than to have their own employees perform these functions. Sassen also points out that the smaller service companies have strong agglomeration advantages and therefore "tend to be concentrated in cities".

The increased urbanisation of economic services, the urban growth of the business-to-business sector, and the influx of people into bigger cities resulted in a rapid multiplication of small businesses. This development came as a shock to economists, and sociologists in the Marxist tradition, and many observers at first doubted the validity of the statistics and called them into question.[6]

There is no doubt about the matter today, and the Organisation for Economic Cooperation and Development (OECD) notes in a current report that small businesses have a key role in all OECD countries where they represent the majority of the workforce.[7] Also, the very smallest businesses, the so-called micro-businesses, make up between 70 and 95 per cent of all businesses in OECD countries.

We may have a different economic structure today than when Jacobs wrote her classic, but her economic analysis is more relevant now than it ever was. She should certainly be considered one of the most significant urbanists of the post-war period, but she herself felt that her greatest contribution had been in the field of urban economics.

Among economists, Jacobs is best known for having developed the term "knowledge spillovers", sometimes called "Jacobs spillovers". The term encompasses all the human currents in which knowledge is exchanged informally and free of charge, and which sometimes lead to new types of products and businesses. Ultimately, she claims, this is the basis of prosperity. The term is well established today among innovation researchers.[8]

But for Jacobs the term is not a pure abstraction, distinct from physical place and urban space. She points out that the spread of knowledge takes place in the physical space of the cities, on the sidewalks and in other types of urban locations. As she wrote in her major work: "Lowly, unpurposeful and random as they may appear, sidewalk contacts are the small change from which a city's wealth of public life may grow."

In her later work, specifically in *The Economy of Cities* of 1969, she expanded this "wealth of public life" to include more literal wealth, such as came from innovation and economic growth. From Jacobs' perspective, this wealth grew from the soil of small businesses. It was their independence and ability to develop new, specialised products, fitting into a wider network of relationships and synergies, which form the core of a city's economic growth and expansion.

In that book, Jacobs gives several remarkable instances of how this process works. One relates to the city of Tokyo, which at the end of the 19th century was a significant importer of bicycles. When the bicycles fell apart, small businesses began to specialise in making the various components needed to repair them. It was not long before these businesses communicated with one another, sharing knowledge, and found new ways of making the larger component parts and, eventually, entire bicycles. This 'import exchange' continued and began to expand to other sectors such as the car industry, for example, in which Japan has global dominance today.

Jacobs told a similar story about Detroit. At the end of the 19th century, many small engineering businesses had begun to share knowledge about the specialised components used in the shipbuilding industry – pulleys, belts, wheels, engines, chassis and so on. And many of them succeeded in finding new markets in the growing field of motorised transport, later to develop into the American automotive industry, which was very successful for a time.

The decline that followed is something that Jacobs links to the negative development for small businesses. In Detroit, smaller businesses were bought up and merged into larger corporations; the most famous example is General Motors, under the management of Alfred P. Sloan. As a result of the consolidations and loss of smaller businesses, the entire United States motor industry lost its creative energy and ability to develop new work by sharing knowledge. This led to the stagnation of the industry in the 1970s and 1980s and, in the end, to Detroit's slow death as a city.

Jacobs enjoys great respect among economists. Such critical voices as are heard often come from sociologists who believe that it is no longer possible to have truly mixed city districts, where residents of different ethnicities, from different social classes and of different ages and lifestyles, can share their city space with visitors. Sharon Zukin, for example, has pointed out that the districts that Jacobs admired have now been comprehensively gentrified and hence developed into exclusive neighbourhoods.[9]

Next pages: In many places cafés act as flexible offices and co-working spaces. Bean & Bean Coffee shop in Chelsea, New York, 22 March 2016.

But of course New York, San Francisco and other gentrified US cities are not the only examples in the world. In the southern hemisphere there are plenty of examples of city life as described by Jacobs.

seasonal
LATTE
pumpkin spice
gingerbread
AUTUMN
GOLD

The Habitat III meeting in Quito, Ecuador, in the autumn of 2016 attracted more than 35,000 people with an interest in cities, who were able to see with their own eyes exactly the sort of city life that Jacobs described.

Others, have claimed that small shops, restaurants and cafés are dying out. The geographer Joel Kotkin argued in 2016 on his New Geography blog that Jacobs' vision of the good city fails because the economic role of today's cities is different from the one they had at the time of her analysis. Kotkin writes: "The economic basis of her New York – small businesses, manufacturers, business service firms employing masses of middle-class workers – has declined while the city has evolved into what Jean Gottman called the 'transactional metropolis', dependent on the most elite financial services, high-end consumption, and the all too present media industry."

It is fascinating that the well-documented structural change that economic life has undergone in the West, with the urbanisation of economic activities and the increase in the number of small businesses and micro-businesses, has escaped the notice of so many analysts of the city.

Admittedly the development in commerce has been going in the opposite direction for a long time, but in most other sectors small business entrepreneurship in cities has increased. But now even commerce has been hit by structural change – downsizing is taking place because of competition from e-commerce, which will affect the city landscape of the future.

There is no doubt that we are living in a time of increasing, almost brutal segregation in some cities. Yet we can also see that mixed city districts are attractive even to well-to-do people, which is something that Jacobs pointed out as long ago as 1961. Perhaps the real problem is that so many cities seem unable to build the kind of urban environments that people actually want.

Finally, we are seeing a whole range of development lines that point towards increasing complexity in city life. The reduction in motor car travel that will arise from new transport technology may change the balance of power on our streets, which for a long time have had their function as public spaces threatened by the automobile. Commuting from the countryside never became the big trend that was predicted, and many people do now work from home one or more days a week. Another trend is that the workplace as such is no longer sacrosanct – in the IT industry above all, it is now increasingly common to work remotely from the office, and even the home, at nearby coffee shops for example.[10] A brief stroll around the cafés in many central urban districts around the world quickly testifies to this emergent reality.

1 Margaret Crawford, *Public Space: From the 'Feel Good' City to the Just City*, keynote-speech at Contesting the Streets II, (University of Southern California, October 2015).
2 Erik Olin Wright, *Class Counts: Comparative Studies in Class Analysis* (Cambridge: Cambridge University Press, 1997).
3 Alvin Toffler, *The Third Wave*, vol. 484 (New York: Bantam Books, 1980).
4 Saskia Sassen, "Cities Today: A New Frontier for Major Developments", *The Annals of the American Academy of Political and Social Science*, vol. 626, issue 1 (2009), pp. 53–71.
5 William H. Frey, "The New Urban Revival in the United States", *Urban Studies*, vol. 30, issue 4–5 (1993), pp. 741–774.
6 Peter Elmlund, *Företagande som livschans och klassresa* (Stockholm: Timbro, 1998).
7 *Small, Medium, Strong: Trends in SME Performance and Business Conditions* (OECD 2017).
8 Zvi Grilichesv, "Issues in assessing the Contribution of Research and Development Productivity Growth", *The Bell Journal of* Economics, vol. 10, issue 1 (1979), pp. 92–116. Bert Verspagen & Wilfred Schoenmakers, *The spatial dimension of knowledge spillovers in Europe: Evidence from patenting data*, (AEA Conference on Intellectual Econometrics, 19–20 April 2000).
9 Sharon Zukin, *Naked City: the Death and Life of Authentic Urban Places* (Oxford: Oxford University Press, 2011).
10 Juliana Martins, "The Extended Workplace in a Creative Cluster: Exploring Space(s) of Digital Work in Silicon Roundabout", *Journal of Urban Design*, vol. 20, issue 1 (2014), pp. 125–145.

TOBY

CHAPTER IX

Apps on the Street

Vania Ceccato

SINCE JANE JACOBS' 1961 seminal work *The Death and Life of Great American Cities*, we have heard countless times about the powerful key concept of "eyes on the street". Jacobs wrote that, in order for a street to be a safe place, "there must be eyes upon the street, eyes belonging to those we might call the natural proprietors of the street". But what happens when 'eyes' are replaced by 'apps' and mobile cameras in our phones?

A safety or emergency app falls within the technological domain of location-based services (LBS), which is a generic term for applications integrating geographic location, such as x/y coordinates, with the general notion of services. In other words, these services combine information with location so as to provide new added value to the user. In the era of smartphones, 'eyes' are complemented by 'apps', giving expression to new ways of depicting what happens in the streets and perhaps redefining how we capture what happens in public places – the very act of surveillance in the public realm. This chapter explores the nature of natural surveillance as captured by new smartphone-based tools (safety apps) that are developed to assist citizens in reporting incidents ('events') in public spaces. We revisit the concept of natural surveillance that was linked to the original work by Jacobs in the 1960s by comparing it with new types of exercises of social control performed when we use safety apps in mobile phones. We conclude this chapter by reflecting upon the role of these new technologies in safety planning. We look in particular at the potentialities and the challenges they may impose to the democratic values that legitimise the exercise of social control in public spaces.

Police using early CCTV to combat crime: OPS Cameras positioned around Croydon in south London, January 1968.

Jacobs' eyes on the streets, surveillance and public safety

Consideration of surveillance in urban spaces emerged in different fields, for example architecture, sociology, and environmental psychology, in the 1960s and 1970s. And by surveillance we take the definition of surveillance studies pioneer David Lyon who described it as "the monitoring of behaviour and activities for the purpose of influencing and directing them".[1] Such monitoring can take place in real time, through, for instance, a CCTV camera.

One of the best known ways of thinking about this surveilling of public spaces was suggested in Jane Jacobs' seminal work *Death and Life* – and her phrase, "eyes on the street". With this notion, Jacobs highlights the suitability of certain types of environment to enable the opportunity for visual and auditory surveillance. Jacobs wrote that in order for a street to be a safe place, "there must be eyes upon the street, eyes belonging to those we might call the natural proprietors of the street".

Jacobs was worried about the shape and design of housing developments in the USA at that time. She was a fierce opponent of modernist developments of monotonous high-rise buildings which she argued denied residents the very basic conditions that would allow observation of what happened on the streets to take place – something which she maintained was fundamental for a neighbourhood's safety. She used examples from New York's districts where she suggested that "natural surveillance was functional and part of everyday life – portrayed by a 'sidewalk ballet', where people of different races and income levels mixed without conflict". Jacobs also emphasised that people may not engage in watching a street because of a sense of it being their duty, rather that there must be something in the environment that allows for natural encounters. She wrote:

> You can't make people watch streets they do not want to watch. Safety on the streets by surveillance and mutual policing of one another sounds grim, but in real life it is not grim. The safety of the street works best, most casually, and with least frequent taint of hostility or suspicion precisely where people are using and most enjoying the streets voluntarily and are least conscious, normally, that they are policing.

Already, in the early 1960s, practical principles were developed that highlighted the importance of the design and structure of public places and their relationship to the whole neighbourhood's capacity to promote natural surveillance. An urban planner in Chicago, Elizabeth Wood had put forward guidelines for improving such natural surveillance long before Jacobs' refinements. Wood's project was never implemented as initially conceived but it did inspire what would emerge afterwards. An advocate of low-rise projects scattered throughout the city, Wood worked closely with the Parks Department to assure tenants had adequate recreation space, and she advocated the construction of community and cultural facilities alongside the housing provision.

This notion of natural surveillance was taken up not only in architecture by Jacobs and the architect Oscar Newman (in his book *Defensible Space*, published in 1972), but also by the criminologist C. Ray Jeffery with the publication in 1971 of his work, *Crime Prevention Through Environmental Design*.[2] In criminology, the notion of surveillance overlaps to some extent with the concepts of 'guardianship' and social control; in both cases the intention of observing what happens on the streets is to prevent a criminal act from taking place, which is similar to Jacobs' initial conception. This notion was further developed by the American academics Marcus Felson and Lawrence E. Cohen in a 1979 piece for the *American Sociological Review*, in which they suggested that guardianship was a "spatio-temporally specific supervision of people or property by other people which may prevent criminal violations from occurring".[3] In 2011, Danielle Reynald offered a detailed description of the process of guardianship, suggesting that a guardian needed first of all to be available and present at a particular place to be able to monitor and supervise, which can then lead to the prevention of a crime.[4]

However, we know that not everybody who witnesses or notices an incident, a call for help or an emergency, reacts or takes preventative measures. It was actually an incident that happened in the 1960s in New York that led scholars to investigate the role of bystanders in emergency situations and the reasons behind what came to symbolise urban apathy in the United States.[5] The iconic case was the murder of Catherine Genovese, a young woman who was stabbed just outside her apartment block in New York. What was curious about this case was

MOWBRAY DR
BOOKS

the fact that more than 30 people had heard the attack and some people had seen parts of it, yet none of them made an attempt to intervene.[6] This occurrence triggered a vivid discussion about the types of people living in cities, but more importantly led to research on intervention and responsibility in such events.

Although most people would want to discourage crime from happening, not everybody wants to be 'responsible' for intervening (or not) in a particular situation. In *Situational Crime Prevention: successful case studies* (1992), the volume's editor Ronald V. Clarke indicated the varying degrees of responsibility for discouraging crime depending on the place and time, postulating the notion of "intervention by duty". In a chapter for *Crime and Place* (1995) – "Those Who Discourage Crime" – Felson, of Rutgers University, adapted these responsibilities by listing four steps of crime discouragement: *personal discouragement* exerted by family and friends; *assigned discouragement* exerted by those employed in a particular place; *diffuse discouragement* exerted by those employed but not assigned to that specific task; and *general discouragement* exerted by unpaid persons lacking a personal tie or occupational responsibility. Felson wrote: "The level of responsibility affects not only the likelihood that crime will be discouraged but also that such discouragement will occur directly and quickly." From the point of view of the criminal, it has been noted, guardianship activities must be visible to be an effective deterrent.[7]

Beyond 'intervention by duty', recent research shows that there are several factors affecting people's decision to intervene or not. Increased social interaction in neighbourhoods has long been associated with a willingness to intervene, as has been the relative stability of a community and the neighbourhood's collective efficacy.[8] Reynald showed the importance of neighbourhood conditions in facilitating surveillance and individual intervention to prevent crime. Individuals in low-crime neighbourhoods, for instance, were found to be considerably more willing to intervene and to stop a crime than elsewhere in the city. Also, individuals in low-income neighbourhoods are the least willing to supervise their surroundings, while individuals in high-income neighbourhoods are the most willing. The findings also indicated that the highest number of individuals who were unwilling to supervise their surroundings or to intervene came from neighbourhoods with a

The place in Kew Gardens, Queens, New York, where Catherine "Kitty" Genovese was stabbed to death in 1964.

high percentage of ethnic minorities. Yet, even if individuals do not intervene, their presence might make a difference.[9] Recent research confirms the importance of the presence of a potential guardian for reducing the risk of crime or at least for disrupting and reducing its severity.[10]

The challenge here is to plan environments that make surveillance a natural part of everyday life, especially when we spend a number of our waking hours working in other parts of town, away from our own neighbourhoods. Yet the challenge remains to promote the creation of public places in which the involvement in crime prevention activities, police-community partnerships, and neighbourhood exchange make people feel safe, in an inclusive way. Which is of course easier said than done. We have far too often the seen the "eyes on the streets" argument being used to legitimise social exclusion; in other words, actions that earmark public spaces for those who are the so-called "legitimate users" only. Research and practice have long illustrated that it is not always easy for residents and visitors to identify who are "the proprietors" and "the non-proprietors of the streets". This challenge does not disappear, when 'eyes' are replaced by 'Apps' on the streets; in fact, the challenge escalates to another level in times when cultural and ethnic diversity are an important and desirable quality of neighbourhoods.

The nature of surveillance in the safety app era

Are smartphones and apps capable of redefining the exercise of natural surveillance and crime control and therefore improve safety conditions in a place? Here we discuss what it means to use this new set of technologies as well as some of the potentialities and challenges it may impose. Safety apps have become part of crime prevention packages designed to improve safety interventions in areas with problems of crime and disorder around the world. As I noted in my article "Eyes and Apps on the Streets" in a 2019 edition of *Criminal Justice Review*, compared with the old "eyes on the street", the new exercise of social control invites the involvement of a number of other senses, such as touch and sound. An incident that happens on the street is still local (attached to a physical place and a set of coordinates), but it can now be seen by far-away eyes, literally by the whole country. Jacobs' sense of "natural proprietors of the street" acquires an entirely different meaning – since those taking notice of a location may not be resident there but can be temporary visitors or transients, perhaps with no attachment to the area.

Safety apps on mobile phones and other location-based services have changed the way that individuals interact with the city. Note that the way we conceptualise natural surveillance has so far been in line with what has been expected elsewhere (e.g. Felson and Reynald) but its nature is challenged with the emergence and wide diffusion of apps on mobile phones and other devices. These applications vary from emergency/safety services to navigation systems, tourist tour planning or other information delivery services. And the technology has imposed new challenges, both technically and conceptually, that are exemplified below.

Firstly, the original ideas of surveillance and guardianship are based on the one-to-one effect of action; for example, a bystander, just by virtue of his or her presence, could prevent a crime. However, with networks of smartphone app users, the process might look more like one of *sousveillance* (as in the French for "to watch from below') instead of surveillance ("to watch from above"). The term *sousveillance*, coined by the Canadian researcher and inventor Steve Mann, refers "both to hierarchical *sousveillance*, e.g. citizens photographing police, shoppers photographing shopkeepers, as well as personal *sousveillance*, bringing cameras from the lamp-posts and ceilings, down to eye-level, for human-centred recording of personal experience", as Mann puts it in his groundbreaking article of 2004, "Existential Technology."[11] In other words, *sousveillance* describes the present state of modern technological societies where anybody may take photos or videos of any person or event, and then diffuse the information freely all over the world, as noted by the French academic Jean-Gabriel Ganascia.[12]

Secondly, it is also suggested here that traditional principles of guardianship become problematic when surveillance is linked to non-physical (remote) intervention and responsibilities that are attached to information attained remotely via smartphones. As with any other technological innovation, its diffusion and use depends on the purchase of the technology, which cannot, at least in the initial stages, be attained by all segments of society.

Next pages: Pedestrians absorbed in their mobiles on a crossing in Bologna, Italy, 2013.

In the context of planning, these challenges are not limited to crowdsourcing data; participatory schemes in the past using other

WIND
TIM
vodafone
LEGNO lab
IKEA
300 POSTI

technologies have faced similar problems. Critics of crowdsourcing data are eager to suggest that the technology creates a potential bias of information and preparedness between those who have access (to these apps and the information that is shared) and those who do not (data samples may be completely self-selected). Research on crowd-sourcing data has pointed to the problem of 'participation inequality' and inaccurate information.[13] Despite these risks, other researchers claim that properly designed apps can be a tool to build community life while preserving privacy. Moreover, the problem of inaccurate information is said to be self-regulated and self-managed by the community themselves because, as the University of Manchester academic Reka Solymosi suggests, those who add information to the system "tend to strive to ensure the accuracy of the information they provide", since they are also the consumers of that information.[14] But this issue is far from being a problem simply of the information's reliability, it is also about the content of the information. The process of information sharing and who manages first to "tell the story".

Table 1 – Re-conceptualisation of surveillance: From 'eyes on the streets' to 'apps on the streets'[15]

	Eyes on the streets	*Apps* on the streets
Basic requirements for action	Presence and availability lead to potential action	No need to be present. App and smartphone in hand
Type of activity	Surveillance	Sousveillance
Level of responsibility	Personal/assigned	Diffuse/general
Senses	Visual real time, auditory, all senses	Visual remotely, touch the screen
Status of action (engagement/ neglect)	Immediate and known by the group	Not known by the group
Scale	Uniscale (Local to local)	Multiscale (Local, global, global to local). Information is added and spread remotely
Common environment	'Context dependent', micro environments, e.g. windows, façade	Meso-macro context, street, neighbourhood but also 'context irrelevant'
Cohesion	More dependent on local social ties	Less dependent on local social ties
Access to 'the event'	Time-specific	Priori and posteriori
Participation	Imposed by presence, location	Voluntary, at individual and group level

The danger of putting forward a particular discourse on what is observed in public spaces is not inherent to this new technology, but it is surely facilitated by its speed. Why is this problematic? Because not everybody takes part in this digital arena in the same way. A research paper compiled by Uyi Stewart, David Lubensky and Juan M. Herta placed individuals into three groups of participants – the super contributor, the contributor, and the outlier (who rarely participates) – and they noted that those who are very active participants are highly motivated in their participation. Solymosi characterised the super contributors in the context of crime prevention as "super guardians", those who may play a key role in reducing criminal opportunities in public places. It is important to note that there is a risk that these super guardians may also create a bias in the planning process and in the outcomes of interventions. The advantage with apps on the streets is that information can be shared on social media and other virtual channels, which open up to a wider audience (a group of stakeholders and the population in general), in a way that was not possible in more traditional public participation schemes. Yet this does not mean that these new groups, possibly activated by social media, will engage in the process. Table 1 summarises the potential differences between the two processes, pointing out both the potentialities and the challenges.

Eyes or apps on the streets: drawing conclusions

In this chapter, we have looked at Jacobs' concept of "eyes on the street" from a new perspective. What can we learn from transplanting the traditional ideas of natural surveillance via those "eyes on the street" to the new ways of exercising social control in public space using ICT technology such as safety apps?

Following the traditional meaning of Jacobs' 'eyes on the streets', we argue that the original idea of natural surveillance is based on the one-to-one effect of an action; for example, through a bystander who, simply by his or her presence, would improve safety and/or ensure that nothing bad happens in a given street. Nowadays, with networks of smartphone app users, the process might look more like a process of *sousveillance*, instead of natural surveillance, presaged by Jacobs and other researchers from the 1960s and 1970s. This new way of capturing what happens in public space is bound to affect not only the way public space is produced but also ourselves, as observers. In this new role of 'proprietors of the streets', we are given new agency by these safety apps. Urban planners, for instance, might have now a better basis from which to work on safety issues, by shifting the focus from large contiguous areas as neighbourhoods to patterns of individual interactions collected in real time, revealing multiple perspectives on public spaces.

These new practices of public space surveillance have become problematic. One of the problems is that it is not easy or even possible to detect who the 'proprietors of the streets' actually are just by observing them. Nowadays most of us are mobile, spending more time elsewhere than we do in our own neighbourhoods. We cannot take for granted that temporary visitors and passer-by individuals would act openly in favour of the common good. Would they be willing to intervene if something happened?

The other problem is that by being an active safety app user, our role is supposedly to help ward off potential threats from our streets in order to make them safer. As previously discussed, this exercise of social control unravels a complexity that goes beyond issues of surveillance and technology, and it leads us to reflect more widely upon issues of urban diversity, social inclusion practices and principles that we all share in a democratic society. It is not always clear who are the 'legitimate' and who the 'illegitimate users' of those public spaces surveilled by the apps. Can safety apps lead to surveillance practices that generate safer and more inclusive public spaces? That is the challenge!

1 David Lyon, *Surveillance Studies. An Overview* (Cambridge: Polity Press, 2007).

2 C. Ray Jeffery, *Crime Prevention through Environmental Design*, 2nd edition (Beverly Hills: SAGE, 1977).

3 Laurence E. Cohen & Marcus Felson, "Social change and crime rate trends: A routine activity approach", *American Sociological Review*, 44 (1979), pp. 588–608.

4 Danielle M. Reynald, *Guarding against crime. Measuring guardianship with routine activity theory* (Farnham: Ashgate, 2011).

5 John M. Darley & Bibs Latane, "Bystander intervention in emergencies: Diffusion of responsibility", *Journal of Personality and Social Psychology*, vol. 8, issue 4 (1968), pp. 377–383.

6 A. M. Rosenthal, *Thirty-Eight Witnesses. The Kitty Genovese Case* (New York: Open Road Media, 1964/2015).

7 Meghan E. Hollis-Peel, Danielle M. Reynald, Maud van Bavel, Henk Elffers & Brandon C. Welsh, "Guardianship for crime prevention. A critical review of the literature", *Crime, Law and Social Change*, vol. 56, issue 1 (2011), pp. 53–70.

8 Robert J. Sampson, Stephen W. Raudenbush & Felton Earls, "Neighborhoods and Violent Crime: A Multilevel Study of Collective Efficacy", Science, vol. 277, issue 5328 (1997), pp. 918–924.

9 Alana Cook & Danielle M. Reynald, "Guardianship Against Sexual Offences. Exploring the Role of Gender in Intervention", *International Criminal Justice Review*, vol. 26, issue 2 (2016).

10 Benoit Leclerc, Stephen Smallbone & Richard Wortley, "Prevention Nearby. The Influence of the Presence of a Potential Guardian on the Severity of Child Sexual Abuse", *Sexual Abuse: A Journal of Research and Treatment*, vol. 27, issue 2 (2015), pp. 189–204.

11 Steve Mann, "Sousveillance: inverse surveillance in multimedia imaging", *Proceedings of the 12th annual ACM international conference on Multimedia* (New York: ACM, 2004).

12 Jean-Gabriel Ganascia, "The generalized sousveillance society", *Social Science Information*, vol. 49, issue 3 (2010), pp. 489–507.

13 Sonja Marjanovic, Caroline Fry & Joanna Chataway, "Crowdsourcing based business models: In search of evidence for innovation 2.0", Science and Public Policy, vol. 39, issue 3 (2012).

14 Reka Solymosi, *Exploring spatial and temporal variation in perception of crime and place using crowdsourced data*, Diss. (London: Department of Security and Crime Science, University College London, 2017).

15 Vania Ceccato, "Eyes and Apps on the Streets: From Surveillance to Sousveillance Using Smartphones", Criminal Justice Review, vol. 44, issue 1 (2019).

CHAPTER X

What was Jacobs Thinking?

Michael W. Mehaffy

While city planning has thus mired itself in deep misunderstandings about the very nature of the problem with which it is dealing, the life sciences … have been providing some of the concepts that city planning needs …
And so a growing number of people have begun, gradually, to think of cities as problems in organised complexity – organisms that are replete with unexamined, but obviously intricately interconnected, and surely understandable, relationships.

JANE JACOBS, "The Kind of Problem a City is", from *The Death and Life of Great American Cities* (1961)

AS A PERSON who regularly uses Jane Jacobs' texts in my teaching and research, I am often struck by the relevance of her observations for challenges right up to the present day – and yet some of her most important ideas were advanced well over half a century ago. That is why I find her to be such a remarkably perspicacious thinker, and also such a useful one for us today.[1]

Jacobs took an interest in the relationship between the new complexity science and nature's own complex patterns and systems. Here a chambered nautilus as a negative print, circa 1950.

For me, Jacobs offers a way out of the current darkness, so to speak – a path through the confused and short-sighted thinking that too often characterises our collective approach to growing crises within ecological, economic and social systems. Hers is, I think, an extremely useful intellectual framework for thinking about our modern predicament, and for finding actual workable solutions. In this chapter, I will explore some of the elements of that framework, and the key lessons it provides for managing our present challenges.

Of course, Jacobs is thought of first and foremost as an urbanist, and understandably so, since her first book, *The Death and Life of Great American Cities,* is also her most famous. But less well known are her later books on economics, sociology, and political philosophy, including *The Economy of Cities* and *The Nature of Economies.* Common to them all was an understanding of the central role of cities (and settlements more generally) in our economic and social life, and so it is appropriate that we start out by considering the major contribution of *Death and Life.*

On the occasion of the book's 50th anniversary we saw a remarkable series of re-assessments and, in some cases, revisionism. The US professor of urban studies and city planning, Thomas Campanella, criticised Jacobs' "evisceration" of planning, which created a vacuum into which privatising interests rushed; the Harvard economist Ed Glaeser argued that Jacobs fed gentrification with her call for preservation of some old buildings instead of all-new towers; and sociologist Sharon Zukin attacked Jacobs' alleged fantasy of the "social-less" urban block. Most recently, the author Anthony Flint suggested that Jacobs was a libertarian with a mixed legacy of NIMBYism.

What I find remarkable about these accounts – speaking again as an instructor who regularly uses her texts – is that, in almost all cases, these were things that Jacobs herself simply never said. She was clearly not against planning, but against *failed* planning; not against government, but against government badly organised; and not against new buildings, but against rushing monocultures of the new. She was reaching for a deeper tactical understanding of how the "inherent regenerative force" of "self-diversification", as she termed it, can be put to work to provide more diversity of income and opportunity, as has clearly happened in cities throughout history.

She was not, let me assert, a blind theoretician or ideologue, but a good empiricist, using theory as a helpful tool along the way. This may be part of the problem. After all, the professions of planning and architecture, to which I myself belong, do not have a particularly good history when it comes to escaping ideological or *ex cathedra* thinking. We don't seem particularly good at learning from the evidence of our mistakes – even when they are explained to us in painfully lucid detail.[2]

But I think there is a deeper explanation for the persistent misreadings of Jacobs. She was the first to apply a dawning new human understanding of the natural world to cities – an understanding that even now is slow to be grasped by built-environment professions. It's an understanding of "organised complexity", as she called it – the dynamic inter-relationships of systems, of processes, and, especially, of the important phenomenon of self-organisation. This was not a mysterious world, but a comprehensible one – it was just a different *kind* of world than we had been envisioning. A city, certainly, was a different *kind* of problem than we had thought. And therein she identified a huge obstacle to learning and progress, and one that is largely still with us.

Other fields of thinking and action have made great progress on these insights: ecology, biology and medicine, to name a few. There are astonishing things happening today in genetics, in network theory, and in mathematics and computer science. Even economics, a field that has historically been more dominated by simplistic ideology than most, is beginning to use more reliable evidence-based theories of how complex economic interactions actually work. Such models now seem essential in learning how to make cities more successful and more sustainable.

But all these fields are informed by what Jacobs called a new "web way of thinking" – employing not simple formulas or templates applied from above, but catalytic changes to a network of dynamic relationships. Doctors do this kind of thing routinely when they give medicine to boost the immune system, or prescribe changes to diet – or indeed, when they recommend that a patient adopt a healthier lifestyle or environment. They are changing the dynamic mix of variables within a complex, interactive web, going on a testable, refinable idea of how that will turn out.

So, too, Jacobs argued, a city is a diverse mix of people and processes, with its own self-organising dynamic. We can exploit this dynamic by design – but this is a different idea of design, perhaps. Top-down interventions can certainly be part of this process (Jacobs mentions, for example, the use of public projects as "chess pieces" to trigger other changes), but we understand that we have to pay attention to multiple factors and multiple relationships. We have to use different tools for different conditions – "tactical" urbanism as it has been called. We have to figure out where – and how – to change the "operating system", the rules, processes and standards that constrain and corrupt our intended outcomes. And we have to plan *with* self-organisation, in a way that exploits its inherent capacity to solve our problems.

Next pages: The larger urban area of Moscow appears at the centre of this night-time image photographed by the Expedition 30 crew aboard the International Space Station, flying at an altitude of approximately 240 miles.

This approach may not have the compelling simplicity of big-thinking, 'silver bullet' solutions, but history shows it can achieve more durable successes over time, where the big plans often lead to slow unfolding disasters. History also shows this approach can be extraordinarily hard to implement by 'siloed' professionals accustomed to specialised, linear formulas and templates. But that too is a dynamic problem, to be studied and remedied.

Of course, Jacobs was by no means the only thinker to offer us insights on these topics, or even the first to do so on the topics of "organised complexity". Indeed, in the last chapter of *Death and Life,* she cited Warren Weaver, an early visionary in what we now know as "complexity science". Since that time, there has been an explosion of knowledge in this area – in the mathematics of networks, the geometry of fractals, the understanding of algorithms and iterative evolution, the dynamics of phenomena like "strange attractors" and "cellular automata". All these phenomena have in common what Jacobs called "organized complexity" – or as we might refer to them today, "complex adaptive systems".

In the remarkable last chapter of her book, Jacobs described Weaver's account of the history of scientific thought, and its relation to the ways in which we think about and act upon cities. She noted that modern science really took off, around the time of Newton, when it mastered so-called two-variable problems, like linking how many houses one has over here to how many stores one can have over there. In physics, the laws of motion, for example, are also two-variable problems: we look at the relationship between, say, mass and acceleration. In this way, we can 'daisy-chain' these coupled variables into long linear sets of relationships, and get a very good approximation of reality. This approach has certainly been very useful – indeed it has helped us to do remarkable things, including landing on the Moon.

However, in the early 20th century, something interesting had begun to happen: through statistics and probability we learned to manage very large numbers, where we had not just pairs of variables, but myriad variables all interacting together. The interesting thing we found was that one could manage these phenomena as statistical averages, without knowing much about the actual interactions involved.

We can do very useful new things with this new kind of scientific knowledge as well. For example, without needing to know precisely who is going to get sick, we can provide health insurance for large groups at a cost that assures that everyone is treated, and, at the same time, ensures that the insurance provider will almost certainly not go bankrupt. Or we can conduct reasonably accurate polling, or manage large quantities of sampling data, or handle other complex phenomena – of the kind that Jacobs termed "disorganised complexity". That is, the individual entities could be treated as if they were only randomly related to one another. Of course that was often not true – for example, in reality people often got sick because of related factors, like flu outbreaks – but we could get a reasonably accurate working model that ignored those interrelated factors.

This statistical science translated into the phenomenal technological power of the industrial revolution of that period. Much of our industry and the prodigious output of 20th century modernity was rooted in these powerful new statistical methods. Indeed, Jacobs pointed out that the early ideas of Le Corbusier and other leading planners, leading up to the later ideas of planners – often to this day – have relied upon this notion of large statistical populations.

Just as there has been this progression in science to phenomena of "disorganised complexity", there has been a progression from, say, the rigidly formal, 'rational' plans of, say, Haussmann, or of Ebenezer Howard and his neatly segregated Garden City plans, through to the more statistically informed plans of Le Corbusier, implemented around the world by the likes of Robert Moses and others.

In either case, however, the problem of cities was seen as one of devising reductive engineering schemes, seeking to isolate smoothly-functioning mechanical parts in place of 'messy' organic conditions. This was seen as advancement and modernisation. But in the former case it was two-variable engineering, and in the latter case the problem of cities was also seen as one of statistical mechanics operating on large numbers. The newer science was added to the old.

Meanwhile, however, yet another momentous new change was occurring in the sciences. The biological sciences had to move beyond the statistical world of so-called "disorganised complexity", and had begun to understand the phenomenon called "organised complexity" – the area in the middle, between simple two-variable problems and large numbers of random or poorly interacting variables. In this area, the way the variables interacted was much more important, even critical. However, this was not a simple linear relationship, but a complex network of relationships that had interacting influences – as, for instance, in a game of "rock-paper-scissors". You couldn't know the impact of one set of variables (rock to paper, say) without simultaneously knowing (or finding out, by learning what your opponent has secretly chosen) the condition of the other sets (paper to scissors and scissors to rock). Such variables are inter-dependent and interacting, within a network of relationships.[3]

This is Jacobs' "middle zone" between what she called "simplicity" and "disorganised complexity" – where the number of variables is less important than their interdependent relationships. It is in this middle zone, said Jacobs, that the phenomenon of life occurs. The elements of a living system or an ecological system are "interrelated into an organic whole", as she put it. They cannot be reduced to a simple set of variables that are relatable in linear fashion, nor can they be treated as only randomly related. Indeed, their patterns of interrelationship are of the essence.

It turns out that the problems of the human environment are a lot like these biological problems of "organised complexity" too – as Jacobs wrote in the last chapter of *Death and Life*. While city planning had "mired itself in deep misunderstandings about the very nature of the problem" with which it was dealing. The life sciences had already provided the conceptual framework for problem-solving that city planning needed. Now we were able to think about cities "as problems in organised complexity – organisms that are replete with unexamined, but obviously intricately interconnected, and surely understandable, relationships".

She proceeded to point out how the planning and architecture professions were at that time – 1961, we must remember, over half a century ago – mired in the earlier, less relevant models of science:

> Today's plans show little if any perceptible progress in comparison with plans devised a generation ago. In transportation, either regional or local, nothing is offered which was not already offered and popularised in 1938 in the General Motors diorama at the

> New York World's Fair, and before that by Le Corbusier. In some respects, there is outright retrogression. None of today's pallid imitations of Rockefeller Center is as good as the original, which was built a quarter of a century ago.

Then she summarised what she considered the lessons of organised complexity:

> In the case of understanding cities, I think the most important habits of thought are these:
> 1. To think about processes;
> 2. To work inductively, reasoning from particulars to the general, rather than the reverse;
> 3. To seek for 'unaverage' clues involving very small quantities, which reveal the way larger and more 'average' quantities are operating.

In this respect she was counselling planners to work more like good doctors, not formulaically applying rigid measurements and prescriptions, but looking for clues, looking for particular signs of more general issues, and considering the kinds of processes that might be under way – a disease, a nutritional imbalance, or, in the case of a city, an unhealthy degeneration of a street or neighbourhood. From there we could begin to see the remedies that were needed.
She summed up the problem as follows:

> As long as [we] cling to the unexamined assumptions that [we] are dealing with a problem in the physical sciences [that is, of mechanics], city planning cannot possibly progress. Of course it stagnates. It lacks the first requisite for a body of practical and progressing thought: recognition of the kind of problem at issue. Lacking this, it has found the shortest distance to a dead end.

Today we have certainly begun to think differently about "the kind of problem a city is". Most planners have adopted the most prominent of Jacobs' ideas, including mixed use, concentration, diversity of people and buildings, and walkable street patterns. Yet there is still a long way to go in understanding the deeper implications of Jacobs' "web way of thinking," not only for models of urban planning, but for other kinds of modern challenges.

To be sure, much has been accomplished in the sciences since *Death and Life* was published, as I mentioned earlier. Network science is proving to be a remarkably fruitful topic across many domains – not only biology but also computer systems, the Internet, economics, sociology, and other fields. Bill Hillier's "space syntax" methodology is one direct application of these insights to the built environment.[4] So are the architect Christopher Alexander's "pattern languages", which allow a designer to create web-networks of design elements. Pattern languages have proven surprisingly useful in the software world, where they have spawned new "design pattern" software, and led to the development of Wiki, Agile, and Scrum methodologies.[5]

Alexander was also famous for a 1965 paper titled "A City is Not a Tree".[6] Echoing Jacobs, and moving further into a mathematical and cognitive analysis, Alexander argued that "the kind of problem a city is" is more web-like, and much less like a simple, hierarchical, "tree-like" relation of parts and wholes.

Those insights were also echoed by the great polymath and design theorist Herbert Simon. In another classic paper in *Proceedings of the American Philosophical Society*, in 1962, he described the "architecture of complexity" as having "nearly-decomposable hierarchies". The "near-decomposability" was the part that also fascinated Alexander. Simon is also famous for giving a definition of design not as an innovative composition by geniuses, but as a kind of transformation, "from existing conditions to preferred ones". That definition is wonderful, not least because it asks more questions than it answers. But they are the right questions! Who is doing the preferring? How do we know what is preferred? What systems will we use to transform the existing to the preferred, and how will we know they are working?

Simon's definition also reminds us that we are not creating a design from scratch, as a purely "top-down" process. Rather, we are working with the natural processes of "self-organisation", the phenomena of "emergence" that occur when many agents – including people – work within systems governed by "generative" rules. Our job as designers is to steer these natural processes – including the actions of people – into a more 'preferred' direction. (Sometimes we can do it by changing the 'generative' rules, and sometimes we can use other methods – like evolutionary selection, or catalytic nudging, or a range of other strategies. Jacobs hinted at all of these approaches.)

There are many other philosophers, mathematicians and thinkers in other fields with notable contributions to this process-based 'web way of thinking'. I'll only mention here the philosopher Alfred North Whitehead and his 1937 work, *Process and Reality*;[7] René Thom's 'catastrophe theory' (which describes the phenomene of 'attractors' and 'tipping points') from the 1960s;[8] sociologist Bruno Latour and his 'actor network theory' (describing a web of interactions within society),[9] as set out in *Reassembling the Social: an introduction to actor-network-theory*; and a new generation of complexity theorists, working on problems of biology, ecology, economics and urbanism – among them Brian Goodwin, Luis Bettencourt and others.

Yet for all this progress, the transformation needed in the design and planning worlds has been slow to appear. In part that is because the old ways still work reasonably well, and there is little motivation at present to make the needed transition. The trouble is, of course, that the current arrangement is unsustainable, and the need for transition is becoming urgent. We are a little like passengers in a jetliner, finding that we must overhaul the plane in mid-flight. We desperately need practical tools and strategies to accomplish this feat – not only in planning and design, but in the other fields in which it is embedded.

In her later works, Jacobs did turn to economics, cultural systems, and other broader topics – and, indeed, one of her most important contributions was in the field of economics. We must come to understand that economics is a dynamic system, she said, like any natural system (argued most powerfully in her book *The Nature of Economies*). In any such system, the feedback within that system can become disrupted, or provide false signals. Thus, our culture can experience perverse incentives and behave irrationally. What seems sane and rational can in fact be a kind of noise from the echo chambers of specialists.

In the case of economics, we can fail to value so-called "externalities" – things like natural resources, and other elements that are "external" to our valuations, our transactions and their costs – and thereby we can destroy, often unintentionally, the common structures on which our future depends (a phenomenon known as "the tragedy of the commons").

The threat of this kind of degradation also extends into our institutions and their integrity. That danger was the subject of her last cautionary book, *Dark Age Ahead*, in which she warned of an oncoming breakdown of the integrity of our cultural systems, in critical fields like politics, law, journalism and academia. Indeed, I believe that what we are seeing today is once again proving Jacobs' perspicacity, and the importance of her warnings. We must learn to account for the connected patterns of things, to put into practical application a "web way of thinking" – or we will continue to make increasingly catastrophic mistakes.

A full discussion of this issue is beyond the scope of this chapter. A more complete consideration of it can be found in my book, *Cities Alive: Jane Jacobs, Christopher Alexander, and the Root of the New Urban Renaissance*, in which I compare Jacobs' ideas with those of another remarkable polymath, the aforementioned architect Alexander. But short of that, I will do my best to close with the most relevant practical 'takeaways' for urbanism. Below, then, is a list of what I believe to be Jacobs' 'Top Ten' most important – and most misunderstood – lessons for the urban professions in particular.

1. *The city needs to maintain a continuous walkable fabric that promotes "thoroughgoing city mobility and fluidity of use"*. This is a key to promoting diversity, and unlocking the capacity of cities as engines of mobility. This alone does not guarantee diversity – but it *is* a prerequisite for it. This means, among other things, that alternatives need to be found to disruptive uses, such as freeways, large parks and the various "campuses" that might interrupt this fabric.
2. *The antithesis of this approach is to create isolated "projects" or project neighbourhoods* – large, disruptive superblocks of monocultures, featuring artfully designed, unchangeable buildings, surrounded by amorphous 'no-man's-land' areas that she dismissively termed 'project land oozings'. A particularly destructive example is the Clarence Perry 'Neighbourhood Unit' – a standardised planner model of inward-turning neighbourhoods surrounded by 'fast car sewers'. But other examples include large shopping centres surrounded by oceans

of parking; large industrial users (also surrounded by parking); large hospitals; large university campuses; and other variations of the destructive 'campus' model. Examples like Portland, Oregon show that it *is* possible to integrate these uses into a modern city.

3. *The best way to fight gentrification is not to demolish old buildings and build high-rises, but to go into other depressed areas and regenerate them.* Jacobs did not argue exclusively against the construction of new buildings, but she did emphasise the importance of retaining a mix. What about Manhattan, which is almost fully gentrified? Well, how about Brooklyn, The Bronx, Queens? There is far more that can and should be made more economically diverse – short of toxic gentrification – before we resort to colonies of massive new buildings. Because we are failing to heed the dynamics of balanced growth, that can only fuel more toxic gentrification.[10]

4. *The city must not be treated as a work of art, or a sculpture gallery.* This silver-bullet sensibility – encouraged by many architects and developers – has favoured scraping away all existing context, in exchange for new, untested, and out-of-scale 'projects'. These projects are often supposed to be 'sustainable' – but they rely on almost no evidence of what has actually been sustained anywhere. Indeed, they often explicitly reject it. As Jacobs said in her characteristically pithy tone, "the method fails".

5. *Zoning is not inherently bad, but should be liberal with regard to use, and prescriptive with regard to the way buildings address the street.* To a remarkable degree, Jacobs pre-figured form-based coding.

6. *Density is a valuable urban ingredient in context, but is not an end in itself.* Again, we must be wary of single variables and single-variable solutions, like 'skyscraper cities'. What we value is not sheer aggregations of people massed together – or separated by 'open space' – but the web of connections and ordinary encounters between people. This is what compact, walkable urbanism can give us, in a range of conditions, including big cities and smaller towns.

7. *Cities are engines of knowledge synergy that create economic prosperity.* As a mark of respect to Jacobs, economists now call this phenomenon a "Jacobs Spillover". There is a physical web of relationships that starts at the pedestrian scale. "Sidewalk contacts are the small change from which a city's wealth of public life may grow", she said.

Very hopefully, there also appears to be a corollary in the conservation of resources, that does not come only from reduced driving and from compact buildings, but in fact comes from the "metabolic efficiency" of dense networks of connection within cities.[11]

8. *Diversity does not by itself guarantee avoidance of economic stratification.* But lack of diversity does guarantee more stratification. Again, we should not be looking for single-variable solutions, but for an interplay of relationships. In human affairs, that interplay is best facilitated through strategies of diversification.

9. *"It's the economics, stupid."* We need to recognise that economic systems are feedback mechanisms for the values we seek, and we must treat economics as such – recognising that there is as much danger in "money floods" (as Jacobs called them) as in "money droughts". Our job is to select the right tool for the job, and make sure that things are working optimally. They do not do so by themselves, but only with an active citizenry and a lively culture.

10. *The capacity to solve our problems rests with the informal web of creative and regulatory relationships we have – our culture – and less so with specialised "experts".* To rely too much on experts in silos is to reinforce their siloed condition, which threatens us all. Certainly this does not mean that there is no role for experts, or for government. It does mean that this role must be more catalytic, more 'bottom-up' – more with the grain of the culture, than against it.

In the end, Jacobs' message was a hopeful one. We broke cities – we "broke" our built environment, and the other systems on which it depends – and we can fix these systems. Or perhaps "heal" is a better word in this context. We do have the power to make walkable, thriving cities and towns, and to erase the disastrous course of suburban fragmentation we set ourselves on several generations ago – not easily, but diligently, with work, cooperation, and learning. The kind of problem a city is, is one that can, in fact, be solved, or perhaps more accurately, managed – if we will only take the trouble to understand it, and learn from it.

1 This paper is derived from a talk I gave at KTH University, Stockholm, in December 2016, and from a previous essay that appeared on the *Planetizen* web journal. I am grateful to my hosts, Jesper Meijling and James Brasuell, for these previous invitations.

2 A number of other commentators have made this point at greater length, including Alexander Cuthbert and Stephen Marshall (see A. R. Cuthbert, "Urban design: requiem for an era–review and critique of the last 50 years", *Urban Design International*, vol. 12, issue 4 (2010), pp. 177–223, and S. Marshall, "Science, pseudo-science and urban design", Urban Design International, vol. 17, issue 4 (2012), pp. 257–271.

3 This interrelatedness is also the characteristic of what is sometimes termed "wholeness", as in, "the whole is greater than the sum of the parts". The additional contribution comes from the interrelated patterns of the parts, not just their discrete relationships to one another.

4 See for example Bill Hillier, *Space is the machine: a configurational theory of architecture* (London: University College London, 2007).

5 I wrote about this more extensively with my colleague Ward Cunningham, who played a key role in this development. See Ward Cunningham & Michael W. Mehaffy, "Wiki as Pattern Language", *Proceedings of the Pattern Languages of Programming 20 Conference* (Monticello IL: The Hillside Group, 2013). Available on the web at http://hillside.net/plop/2013/papers/Group6/plop13_preprint_51.pdf

6 Christopher Alexander, "A City is not a Tree" (1965), in Michael W. Mehaffy (ed.), *A City is Not a Tree*, 50th Anniversary Edition (Portland: Sustasis Press, 2015).

7 Alfred North Whitehead, *Process and Reality* (Cambridge: Harvard University Press, 1937).

8 René Thom, "Leaving mathematicians for philosophy", *Mathematical Research Today and Tomorrow* (Berlin & Heidelberg: Springer, 1992), pp. 1–12.

9 See e.g. Bruno Latour, *Reassembling the social: An introduction to actor-network-theory* (Oxford: Oxford University Press, 2005).

10 I discuss this at more length in: Michael W. Mehaffy, *Cities Alive: Jane Jacobs, Christopher Alexander and the Root of the New Urban Renaissance* (Portland: Sustasis Press, 2017), and especially in the chapter titled "Beware of 'Voodoo Urbanism'".

11 See also my paper exploring this topic: Michael W. Mehaffy, "The 'Jacobs Spillover' as a model of urban dynamics: Can we describe a similar mechanism affecting urban resource use and greenhouse gas emissions?", *On Resilient Settlement* (15 October 2011).

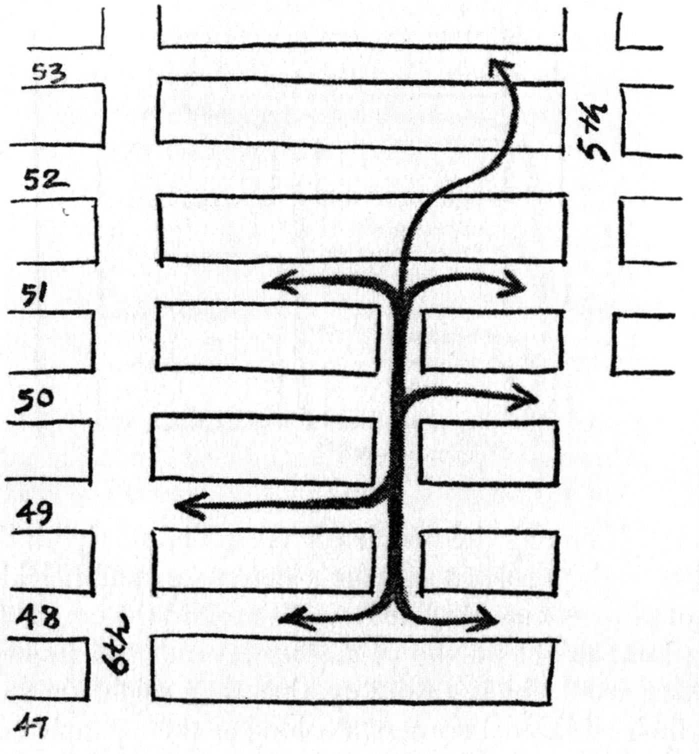
53
5th
52
51
50
49
48
6th
47

CHAPTER XI

Belief and Knowledge in City Planning

Eva Minoura

AS WE LEARN from the way she sets out her arguments, Jane Jacobs' critique of how architecture and planning are practised is not an *ideological* objection. Rather, she makes a critique of knowledge, which calls into question how it is that a practice in which massive building proposals are realised can be carried out with at times no more legitimacy than "a pseudoscience built on a foundation of nonsense". It is therefore ironic that, while being almost universally accepted, Jacobs' ideas are current because architecture is still, even today, a practice weighed down by the imprecision and insecurity she identified, as above, in her book *The Death and Life of Great American Cities*. The issue at hand here is by what justification those of us who practise architecture may claim that we know what we are doing. If knowledge is broadly understood as the theoretical or practical understanding of a subject, architecture has not just symbolic, technical and functional demands but must also perform at many scales, relate to a historic context and do all these things over time, all the while supporting environmental, economic and social sustainability. The built environment is, after all, the most visible and effective bearer of societies' norms and standards.

Figure from the chapter "The Need for Small Blocks" in which Jacobs analyses the spatial organisation of the densely packed city life. *The Death and Life of Great American Cities.*

When Jacobs articulates her objection to planning praxis in *Death and Life*, she does so with the question, "Why have people professionally concerned with cities not identified the *kind* of problem they had?" Today, half a century later, we may have finally established the nature of the problem. The interesting question today is: Are we any nearer to coming up with the right solutions?

The knowledge-critique of today is that we have tools at our disposal to assess planning proposals based on empirical evidence, but we do not always apply them as a matter of course. We simply do not ask the right questions of the design. Architectural renderings convey the desired outcome, but the methods to achieve it are not always understood or compared in the early stages of design. For instance, ample research exists to establish that neighbourhoods deemed unattractive are prone to social segregation over time,[1] and a fairly common practice within planning today is to opt for what is seen as contextually-sensitive densification – namely to reproduce not only the same typologies but also the same tenancy forms that are already present. As it is, one consequence of such supposedly contextual infill proposals is that areas with renter-occupied point-and-slab buildings are densified with more of the same, while areas with owner-occupied perimeter blocks are densified with more of the same. Although oversimplified, this is a not uncommon situation which may be described as a 'tyranny of good intentions'.

Other research supports the opposite approach – by adding owner-occupancy housing, a greater mix of socioeconomic classes occurs and the attractiveness of the neighbourhood generally improves. Additionally, to the extent that social sustainability can be promoted not just by adding new housing but also by addressing the needs of a place, an opportunity is missed to add the affordances and diversity that come with other urban forms than are already present. As can be expected, the uncritical adoption of *formalistic* rather than *performance* criteria for a design will often reproduce the same social conditions that were there to begin with. When we consider that, for example, tenure types implicitly regulate the residents' control (and hence agency) over their immediate environment, then this same agency (or lack thereof) is reproduced when form is foregrounded ahead of function. To be fair, this scenario is not entirely a fault of planning per se, but of any market-driven development that fails to deliver the diversity and equitable distribution of a city's spatial affordances justly. As such, it is a failure of policy as much as architecture.

In part, a reluctance to adopt a more critical stance on our own production through architectural design and planning is rooted in a misconception that we lack the tools to do so. In fact, we don't lack the tools, they are just not broadly taught in architecture schools or implemented 'on the job', and have therefore not become a practice. This is now changing, although some observers "are wary of the potentially 'reductionist' application of science to urbanism", or the foregrounding of scientific over other forms of knowledge.[2]

As a profession, we have readily embraced Jacobs' catch-phrase "eyes on the street", yet we struggle to apply other concepts in practice. Certainly, Jacobs is more relevant than this more superficial appropriation allows, suggesting that if there is an inability to apply Jacobs to design problems at hand, it may lie in a broader inability or unwillingness to apply evidence-based approaches to urbanism. Stephen Marshall has argued that urban design theory needs precisely this – namely a more scientific knowledge base. Marshall calls for "reform from within" the practice in order that theories and solutions be tested and evaluated in relation to others and not just uncritically incorporated at whim as trends emerge. More than many other professions, architecture can be practised without reference to theory or research.

Architectural design and urbanism practice play by their own rules. Design is often prized for innovation, a by-product of which, according to this line of thought, is an abundance of conjecture. However, ours is a field that currently lacks a framework for refutation. Design proposals that strive to reinvent, test new ideas and push boundaries are the "conjecture" but rarer is the more systematic evaluation of prior works by the architect or firm responsible in order to see how a completed project has performed over time. Only by seeing how buildings and spaces are actually used and even altered over time, can we assess which ideas had merit against which ideas were "refutable", hence worth abandoning to the scrap-heap of history. In architecture, the notion of refuting a design concept is rarely considered necessary. Rather, the success (or failure) of a design can always be brushed-off with the qualifier that 'everyone is entitled to their opinion'. But if we do not hold architecture to the standards by which, once new knowledge is accrued, old (unsuccessful) theories can be abandoned, then it can't claim to exist as part of a knowledge-tradition at all.

Next pages: The morning rush hour in New York City with commuters hurrying to catch departing trains from Penn Station, 2015.

In other creative production, there simply is no right or wrong answer – this we learn in most architecture schools. Rather, the merit of a design is gauged by the consistency of the concept or execution of an idea. But the leeway granted to artistic endeavour, well-intentioned as it may be, never forces the architecture profession to own up to its

420←458
Eighth Ave
Joe Louis Plaza
TAXI
Eighth Ave
ONE WAY
POLICE

ONE WAY
Eighth Ave
PARK

mistakes. This is very different from the practice of medicine, for instance, where bad practices generally end up being abandoned in favour of better ones. In architecture, the potential feedback loop isn't in place which might otherwise guard against repeating past mistakes. Instead of being cast aside to the trash heap, 'bad' design practices become a sort of treasure trove of inspiration to be drawn upon again and again. As urbanist William Whyte noted in *The Social Life of Small Urban Spaces*, "very tall, free-standing towers can generate tremendous drafts down their sides. This has in no way inhibited the construction of such towers, with the result, predictably, that some spaces are frequently uninhabitable." This is problematic and speaks precisely to the knowledge-critique Jacobs formulated. Even when the problematics of wind are known, the social arguments against producing such environments are perhaps not given adequate consideration. The architect Bill Hillier suggested as much and, in his book *Space is the Machine: A Configurational Theory of Architecture*, he echoed Jacobs when writing: "Relics of an outdated paradigm do not derive from an understanding of cities. On the contrary, they threaten the natural functioning and sustainability of the city."

We too rarely take the time to follow up and evaluate the social effects of the built form in a systematic way. But this is precisely what Jane Jacobs did. In every urban context she came across, she analysed and assessed in quite a methodical and empirically sound way (by way of interviews and observations) how the built form was doing what it set out to do, and what the design promised to deliver. Too often, the more organically emergent urban environments performed far better for city-dwellers, Jacobs found, which led to a deep-seated suspicion that planners either really didn't know what they were doing or simply didn't care about city-life at street-level.

Even today, research backing, for instance, spatial analysis of the built form is not embraced. This is due to a foregrounding of what Lars Marcus of the Chalmers University of Technology calls the *first form*, i.e. the built form's symbolic and aesthetic value to the *second form*, i.e. how the built form performs. Architectural performance can be assessed not only in terms of energy efficiency and ecological footprint, but also in terms of social sustainability. For instance, how a street network supports patterns of movement has great bearing on the loca-

Top: schematic plan of a suburb, 2016. Dwellings and social amenities grouped around a suburban station with approximate building shapes. From the Swedish lobby project Activity Based City (ABC) by the consultancy firm WSP, the construction company Skanska, the bus manufacturer Scania and the Chinese public transport operator MTR.

Bottom: schematic plan of a suburb, 1945. Dwellings and social amenities grouped around a suburban station with approximate development ratios. From the planning work within Stockholm city council which formed the basis for the Fifties' so-called ABC town. Sven Markelius (ed.), *Det framtida Stockholm: riktlinjer för Stockholms generalplan* [The future Stockholm: guidelines for Stockholm's general plan], 1945, p. 57.

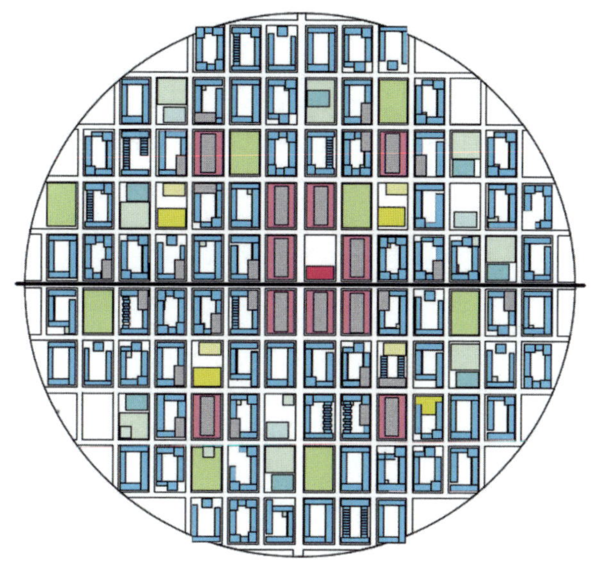

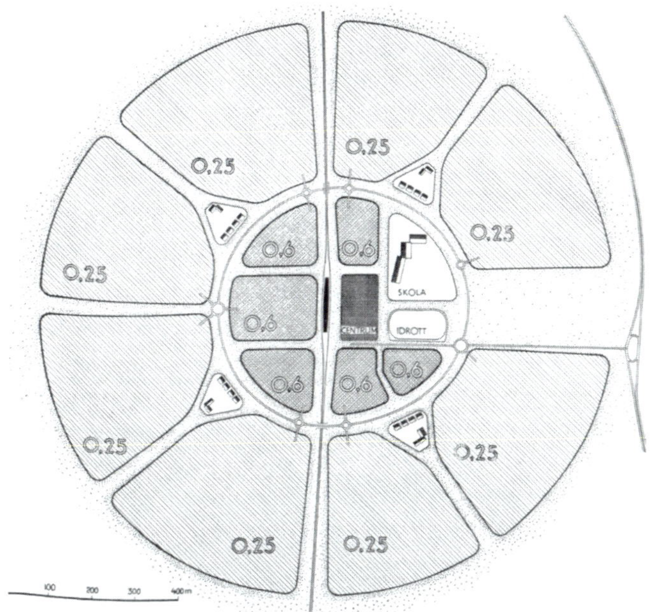

0.25
0.25
0.25
0.25
0.6
0.6
SKOLA
0.6
CENTRUM
IDROTT
0.6
0.6
0.6
0.25
0.25
0.25
0.25
100
200
300
400 m

tional potential for street-life and pedestrian flows. The concept of a 'movement economy' means that certain locations in the city's system of streets will favour a greater intensity of co-present individuals, which can predict where businesses at street-level are more likely to thrive, as Bill Hillier pointed out. Co-presence can also be understood as the extent to which both local and global populations find their way to and use public space. Such spatial reach of the public realm is a performance aspect in which how cities are patterned is a significant factor, as Ann Legeby of Stockholm's KTH Royal Institute of Technology has pointed out. Similarly, the sense of stewardship and ownership of shared yards is set up by how the urban form configures the open space, as alluded to in my work 'Uncommon Ground: Urban Form and Social Territory'.

Jane Jacobs noticed that messy but livable neighbourhoods which were supplanted actually had quite vibrant local economies, but that this vibrancy simply did not find its way back into the more rationally planned and large-scale developments that replaced them. Notably, in promoting small-scale diversity, Jacobs established an economic knowledge of how cities function which the field of urban economics has embraced as 'Jacobean externalities' referring to the innovation and knowledge-spillover which occurs when diverse industries are found in competitive and heterogeneous clusters. Current planning praxis recognises that designing socially sustainable cities means setting the stage for the "exuberant diversity" she advocated. This concept is set out in Jacobs' book, *Cities and the Wealth of Nations*, and later picked up in the urban studies theorist Richard Florida's focus on the so-called knowledge economy.[3]

As Jacobs put it, cities "are not like suburbs, only denser. They differ from towns and suburbs in basic ways, and one of these is that cities are, by definition, full of strangers." The exchange between strangers may be non-verbal, but these encounters in the public realm reflect the norms and boundaries of society in one way or another. There is a potential that friction and conflict will ensue, but also negotiation and resolution.

Regularly encountering one another in the streets, squares and other public spaces of a city means we are confronted on a daily basis with difference. Hence, diversity and density in combination set the stage for tolerance of government and of other people. For instance, as density increases, public transportation becomes crucial to maintain mobility in the settlement. Living in large metropolitan settlements makes one dependent upon government for public transportation, refuse collection, street-cleaning and for zoning ordinances which regulate disturbance. In other words, tolerance may extend not just to other people and to ideas, but also to government regulation. Where low diversity is the norm, clannish behaviour and intolerance of what is deemed 'big government' are more prevalent.

Rather than pursue a more scientific turn, planning today has in some senses abandoned the social ideals which 'norm planning' did actually aspire to, subject to the ideals of the day. Planning is far more market-driven today; construction is lucrative both for construction companies and for cities which can sell land in order to balance budgets. Outwardly speaking, planning is about people, meeting-places and sustainability, according to the dogma of the day. While participatory planning has admittedly come a long way, in the Swedish and Scandinavian planning context especially, one gets a bit of a smoke-and-mirrors sense that the proceedings are somewhat of a show. In many cases, a planning process is considered well-executed when the citizen dialogue ensures a successful end-product – namely an approved plan. The danger is that an emphasis on consensus, i.e. getting all parties on board with a proposal, risks prioritising process over product. If a successful process is all we are after, then how the built form holds up to the demands placed upon it over time are by definition not the primary focus. This risks leaving out important analyses and knowledge production which ultimately have more bearing on how a built environment is received, how attractive it is perceived to be and whether it satisfies the sustainability aims to which we aspire. These are factors which process alone cannot ensure we get right in the end. In the final analysis, it is not the planning process but how the resulting buildings perform for the citizens living and working among them which will be the measure of their success as a design.

Planning dialogue is a process to engage with the public to obtain feedback on design proposals that may inform the end result. However, such feedback must also be subject to professional expertise and not be filtered uncritically into the design. Too much focus on planning as process, without testing the proposal itself against up-to-date knowledge on how architecture performs best at the urban scale risks undermining our legitimacy even further. Residents should rightly be seen as spokespersons for the location or neighbourhood in question, but they should not have the right of veto in a case when substantial research or empirical evidence contradict their views. When advocates for the status quo are deaf to the arguments in favour of new development, whether it is more housing or a new school or a better traffic solution, this runs counter to Jacobs' caution that "cities have the capability of providing something for everybody, only because, and only when, they are *created by everybody*".[4] Jacobs did not mean that total consensus should reign. Rather, thanks to advancements in urbanism research, today we can aspire to a generalisability that Jacobs would likely have welcomed, participatory planning notwithstanding.

What we know today is that urban design is simply too complex an undertaking, operating at too many scales simultaneously, to allow for well-grounded proposals to be modified simply because of what current residents *think* that they want. That is not to say that residents should not be consulted and engaged in the process of production, only that in the likely event of non-consensus, professional opinion in some cases will need to prevail. A recent example of this tendency is when residents oppose proposals which eliminate traffic separation because they see the advantages in terms of traffic safety but cannot envision that streets designed for all road users tend to be more pedestrian-friendly environments, safer at night and better for local businesses. Here, professional expertise must outweigh what in some cases is simply a localised suspicion of the unfamiliar and perhaps a deep-seated mistrust of planners due to past mistakes.

So, returning to the knowledge-critique which Jane Jacobs levelled at architects and planners, this question has made surprisingly limited progress within the practices of urban planning and design. Rather than addressing the critical issues and complexity of urbanism practice and advancing a knowledge base that she advocated, some prefer to copy the quaint small-scale character of traditional cities in the belief that it is in this ambience that the solution lies. Or, in a baffling turn, to bring back neighbourhood unit planning, revamped for the current era with a parametric design but likewise concentrically planned and with each thing in its place, just like in the 1960s.[5]

If planning history has taught us anything, it is that the urban plan that takes a clean slate as its point of departure and incorporates neither local knowledge nor current research is doomed to fail spectacularly.

It would be more in the spirit of Jane Jacobs, now roughly 100 years after her birth, to finally address this issue of the legitimacy of the architectural profession, demanding knowledge-based practice, relevant analyses and design proposals which deliver the urban life that the architectural rendering promises. If there is any doubt as to whether Jacobs considered urbanism to demand a scientific rigour, it is enough to recall that Jacobs herself challenged architects and planners to "constantly and skeptically test her ideas against evidence". Then, let's do it!

1 Ann Legeby, *Patterns of co-presence: Spatial configuration and social segregation*, Diss. (Stockholm: KTH Royal Institute of Technology, Trita-ARK, 2013), and *Dela(d) stad: Stadsbyggande och Segregation*, 1–5, (Stockholm: KTH Royal Institute of Technology, TRITA-ARK, 2013–2015).

2 Stephen Marshall, "Science, Pseudoscience and Urban Design",*Urban Design International*, vol. 17, issue 4, (2012), pp. 257–271.

3 Richard Florida, *The Rise of the Creative Class: Revisited* (New York: Basic Books, 2014).

4 Jane Jacobs, *The Death and Life of Great American Cities* (New York: Random House, 1961), italics added by the author.

5 "Activity Based City 2.0", an urban development concept developed by Skanska, WSP, Scania and MTR presented at the Almedalen Week Conference, Visby, in 2018.

SOS
PARK ASSOCIATION OF NEW YORK CITY
Opposes NYU Library!

CHAPTER XII

Complexities and Contradictions in Jacobs

Tigran Haas

"The Jane Jacobs vision attracts all people of humanistic sense and instinct… Jane Jacobs won ideologically. She did not win in reality. She's lost everywhere in terms of how we build cities."
PROFESSOR NATHAN GLAZER,
Harvard University, American Sociologist

"If you seek authenticity for authenticity's sake you are no longer authentic."
JEAN-PAUL SARTRE
French Philosopher

"Obviously, neither radiance (sunlight), nor gardens, nor spaciousness, nor beauty can have any place in Mrs Jacobs' picture of a great city."
LEWIS MUMFORD
American Cultural Theorist

"This is Sesame Street; a place where people, birds, monsters all live in perfect harmony."
PHIL DONAHUE
Guest Star on *Sesame Street*

Jane Jacobs speaks at an event organised in opposition to the proposed construction of New York University's Elmer Holmes Bobst Library in New York City, 20 June, 1966.

LOOKING THROUGH THE contemporary lenses of ever-transforming cities and changing landscapes but still having in mind the multi-layered urbanism, culture, history, and timeless principles of built environments for people, Jacobs' ideas now seem rooted in the past and outdated in many ways. In trying to understand how cities work, she sometimes could not see the forest for the trees. Despite her deep and natural dialectics and thinking about systems, Jacobs had trouble seeing the bigger picture and structural complexity of the macro-meso-micro foundation of urbanity – such as the city's infrastructure development, the problems of scale, the green areas, race and ethnicity, the booming population, the ever-changing nature and fabric of cities, and the economy.

In the first biography of Jacobs, Alice Sparberg Alexiou argues that one of the rather serious shortcomings in Jacobs' otherwise brilliant discourse on cities (in *The Death and Life of American Cities*) is her failure to include any meaningful discussion of race.[1] Margaret Crawford, the UC Berkeley professor of architecture and urbanism, often brings forward the important issue of race and poverty in relation to Jacobs in her various talks on public realm and urbanism. And this omission in Jacobs' work remains problematic, in the sense of its failure to include race as an important element of urbanism – what the London School of Economics sociologist Fran Tonkiss characterises as the real "social life of urban form".[2] Jacobs was an outspoken advocate of racial equality, but her primary audiences were white Americans and her discourse was therefore very much dependent on that.[3] This was a difficult issue to tackle; nonetheless, it was essential, considering that *Death and Life* is now seen as one of the great treatises and manifestos of architecture, planning and urbanism. The hugely influential Rem Koolhaas declares that hardly any theoretical descriptions of the city have been presented by architects since Jacobs' *Death and Life* (1961), Robert Venturi's *Learning from Las Vegas* (1972), and his own *Delirious New York: A Retroactive Manifesto for Manhattan* (1978), which describes how a city performs and how it should perform.[4] In her book *Naked City: The Death and Life of Authentic Urban Places* (2009), Zukin directs criticism at Jacobs for her representation of two urban quarters – New York's West Village and Boston's North End – as idealised visions of the future for American (and all other) cities. Sharon Zukin posits that Jacobs focused too much on the built character of the street and did not give sufficient attention to the sociological factors affecting cities. Jacobs' overly romanticised notions of the city and neighbourhoods helped attract people back to the city but, in the process, transformed them into "idealised urban playgrounds". A misinterpretation of Jacobs' message has even been used by developers and their political allies to the point where her ideas have been deployed as marketing tools. As Zukin astutely observes, despite Jacobs' intentions, her vision of ideal city life has shaped two important tools that help developers achieve their goals: the politicians' growth theory and media representations of cultural consumption in cities.[5] Her analysis of the mechanics of street life and of the ways in which people use buildings, streets and vacant spaces in such areas is eye-opening. The principles of neighbourhood planning that derive from her observations are far more closely attuned to how people actually live than those of orthodox city planning.[6] Another problem associated with Jacobs' lack of deeper understanding of cities and neighbourhoods is closely connected with the understanding of culture, ethnicity and justice (issues of race and conflict in public space) in relation to the built environment, particularly the public realm that bonds the urban fabric of cities.[7] These issues are well understood by authors and researchers such as Setha Low and Ash Amin, who see the need for socially collective and just public spaces as an absolute necessity.

The celebration of people-centred public spaces, neighbourhoods and cities is at the heart of Jacobs' urbanism; but which people do we mean? Who is doing the celebrating? And what are these spaces really for? Race, equality, ethnicity, justice, poverty, equity and diversity were incredibly difficult terms to define during those times, and they were difficult for Jacobs to handle in the everyday urban discourse. However, places of happiness and relaxation, and places for people to enjoy and thrive in were the hallmark tenets of that era's racial liberals, whereby the celebration of people's similarities was a much easier task – and certainly cozier and safer than a discussion of racism and the differences and inequalities among people. That was simply not Jacobs' focus.

Sidewalks were the essence, the primary public spaces of the city, where Jacobs sees the celebration of 'publicness' and authentic urbanity as the "intricate street ballet outside of her home in Greenwich Village". Here one see parallels with the New Urbanism movement which held the same view, although the movement did manage to produce, in spite of all hurdles, the most important social housing revitalisation initiative of all time in the form of the US housing department's

HOPE VI programme. Omissions and exclusions embedded in Jacobs' urban ideas (and idealism) were understood neither then nor now, as the majority of city planners, urbanism advocates, academics and professionals only see the glorification of her work and blind adaptations of it, ignoring the reality of American and other multicultural and diverse places and cities around the world. The daily life of a city and the evolution of its fabric are among the most complex issues about cities in general. The "perfect urban neighbourhoods" Jacobs identified can therefore at times be seen as a radically disruptive homogenous community, notwithstanding diversity and urban social mix. Jacobs did address the issues of affordability and displacement in her vision of the city, although one finds only fragments of this in obscure places, beyond the realm of her major works. So the ideal of the urban village (a term associated with the sociologist, Herbert Gans and later with the urban planner, David Sucher, and HRH The Prince of Wales) that Jane Jacobs advocates is in danger of becoming a 'gentrification' ideal and can be used as a lever of power to displace long-time residents. But Jacobs herself was not someone who attacked state power or the power of capitalists; she instead went after the planners as she was a communitarian spirit in essence, a free spirit against state control.

Complexities are part of city building. Jacobs' greatest adversary, Robert Moses, or as the Jacobians see him, the "evil planner of New York", had to deal with all of those complexities in parallel.[8] The rivalry between Jacobs and Moses, a struggle for the soul of a city versus the body of a city, is one of the most dramatic and consequential rivalries in modern American history. Roger Starr, who was once the city's housing commissioner, was also in conflict with Jacobs. In his view, there was a contrast between what one can actually do and what would best be done in an ideal world. In the political and economic realities of that time, if you have many poor people who need housing, what could be done was to build public housing. According to Jacobs, doing so was disastrous, but she did not really offer a viable and realistic alternative. During his lifetime, Moses was known as a master builder and a person who could get things done; he did create the dynamic infrastructure that helped New York boom. At the same time, he initiated some of the largest wipeouts of communities in the surrounding area, which had

Robert Moses (1888–1981) led the biggest city planning projects in the New York metropolitan area in the mid-20th century.

catastrophic consequences; nonetheless, the city centre is what it is because of the Moses vision.[9] Jacobs is justifiably renowned for fighting to preserve the West Village community. Her achievements in New York, however, were primarily defensive victories, and not easily compared with Moses' massive public works or even the more human-scale kinds of community improvements she longed for.[10]

The balance can be achieved via a combination of the Jacobian–Moses vision for the city because neither can work alone. Jacobs' vision was overly focused on aesthetics, small streets, and varied sizes of buildings, as in micro-urbanism, which includes small plots and streets that make up a neighbourhood; it therefore tends to omit the economic component. The need to protect cities from gentrification and to ensure that they cater to all its residents, particularly low-income communities, was and always will be among the prime goals of any urbanist; however, sometimes (and often today) those idealised Jacobian neighbourhood schemes can become actively hostile toward low-income neighbourhoods and real integration. Jacobs did study the economy of cities and advocated for diversity, the granular structure of social movements, housing typologies, and tenures, and she wrote about it in her later works; she simply did not unpack urban complexity in an effective manner, only going halfway. Jacobs suggested that "just and diverse streets" reflected the functioning of the city as "a problem of organised complexity", but in that process, she forgot the organised and founding complexity of the city as a living machine. With or without Moses, Jacobs' romanticised social conditions were already becoming obsolete when she wrote about them in the 1960s (the force of money and state power, large-scale projects, hyper-gentrification and the commodification of the public realm).[11] Gans astutely summarised the crux of the matter in Jacobs' urban lens when he addressed the fallacy of physical determinism (something David Harvey addresses in the "Communitarian Trap" in relation to New Urbanists, but in a much smaller and shallower manner than Gans).[12] According to Gans, Jacobs made claims about social cohesion based on architecture, for which she had no evidence. She also refused to acknowledge that the pathologies of American cities in the 1960s were mostly due to issues of racism, not solely urbanism and construction.[13] Her argument is built on three fundamental claims: (1) people desire diversity; (2) diversity is ultimately what makes cities live and the lack of it makes them die; and (3) buildings and streets as well as the planning principles on which they are based shape human behaviour.[14] The first two of these claims were grounded in her observation studies and fact-gathering in the places where she lived and observed, but they still lack the facts and empirical data required for them to be fully accepted. In contrast, the third claim is in the realm of physical fallacy, physical determinism (something modernists were famous for), and leads her to ignore the social, cultural, and economic factors that contribute to vitality or dullness. It also blinds her to the less visible kinds of neighbourhood vitality and the true causes of the city's problems.[15] Her analysis in the "Forces of Decline and Regeneration" section of *Death and Life* is accurate when it talks about the self-destruction of diversity; the problem is that self-destruction of diversity, which is similar to the "gentrification" that we know of today, is not exactly the same thing. Self-destruction of diversity is a concept that is much more over-arching than gentrification, because it also includes the self-destruction of diversity in business districts (and not just by chain stores and office buildings). Nobody is denying that Jacobs often took the long view of urban issues, and "gentrification" (using today's term) was no exception.[16] One of her main points about the self-destruction of diversity was that the best way of preventing the problems generated by self-destruction is to create even more healthy urban neighbourhoods that would be capable of being gentrified (today's term again) in their turn, so that pressure was taken off of those relatively few existing urban neighbourhoods that experienced the self-destruction of diversity (gentrification).[17] Claims similar to these have also been made by New Urbanist proponents, particularly the American architect and urban planner Andres Duany.

Jacobs' work was not distinctly feminist, but in the context of a masculinist urban studies tradition, the adoption of ideas and observations from *Death and Life* and its perspective on the actual lives of women, children and the elderly may create room for a gendered view on re-urbanisation and gendered urban processes such as gentrification.[18] In the late 1960s, discussions about the problem of cities (urban crisis) often centred on issues relating to the black underclass, making much of crime and riots. A deeper understanding of the role of a place within the spatial configuration of meso-macro cities and regions in fostering social mobility with social capital was beyond Jacobs. As previously mentioned, she lacked a deeper economic understanding of micro-urbanism and analysis of race and justice. Jacobs was not oblivious to race, but specifically chose to focus on other issues because for her, race was obscuring the real problems of cities. According to her, cities decline, stagnate, and grow even without racial problems, and in the final analysis this indicates a problem both in her thinking and her writing.

★

In many ways, Jacobs was part of the Kuhnian paradigm shift. Her book's great strength lay in her ability to analyse the interplay and intricacy between structure and society at the block level. Her understanding of the dynamics of the city (at the micro level) came from the inferences she made as she walked around it, observing it closely. As discussed previously, her lack of academic training was problematic when it came to the methods of social science and research in general, but it was probably also a source of strength because her understanding of the street was not distorted by preconceived ideas or the prevailing social scientific methods of the time.

The American economist Edward Glaeser rightly points out that the built legacy of Moses was by no means all bad. His parks and pools added value to the city and were a great blessing to New Yorkers in the years before air conditioning. The transportation infrastructure of his roads and bridges were necessary, enabling millions of Americans to save hours, months, and years through faster journey times.[19] Cities are nothing without their infrastructure, and while Jacobs was right that cities are built for people, they are also built around transportation systems. Jacobs underestimated the true value of new construction, of building up. Today we know that successful, thriving cities need both the human interactions of Jacobs and the enabling infrastructure of Moses.[20]

Jacobs' visionary perspective is evident in the suggestion that, in the 1960s, it was via the street that a society's life and plurality could be better investigated. A street is a place of passage involving circulation, street corners, conversations, violence, understanding, eroticism and diversity; a place of sociability where civilisation is constructed. It is in the street space that contemporary social relations effectively happen.[21] In treating sociology as the study of human relationships and behaviour, the American sociologist Nathan Glazer did not feel restricted to the methods and theories of the discipline, preferring to forge his own. In an autobiographical essay,[22] he wrote: "As a sociologist I have been more interested in specific issues than in the discipline of sociology itself, more in empirical subject matter than in theory, more in substance than in methodology." Glazer had at least partially rejected the sociological method in favour of a more impressionistic portrait, or cultural study, based on a range of sources.[23] Jacobs continued to champion empirical knowledge using observation as her main method of collecting real-life data, which fed her understanding of planning, building, traffic, etc. Her inductive reasoning was the obvious driving force of her vision, and it had richness and validity, but her reasoning should by no means be equated with or mistakenly taken for (as some authors would want us to believe) the conceptualisation and methodology contained in the 1967 work, *The Discovery of Grounded Theory*[24] by the sociologists Barney Glaser and Anselm Strauss. Jacobs had in fact developed, through direct observation rather than utopian theory, a highly personal way of thinking about cities and "researching" them. Decades later, New Urbanists would try to replicate her approach of verifying almost everything with their own eyes. If this was developed into a systematic approach, a research strategy, we could easily call it "observational urbanism". Unfortunately, it is still in the stage of becoming, but it remains a powerful method and stands in direct opposition to academic theorists who put their trust in embedded urban planning and design ideas, approaches, and theories as well as the intellectual fashions of postmodern and poststructuralism, which dominate the field of fundamental sciences today, more than their own field observations and experiences. Jacobs not only saw things differently with her own eyes, but she habitually observed, measured, and walked the city. She took nothing for granted and internalised everything around her. If a theory did not fit with her observation, she trusted her senses. In this regard, the American urbanist William H. Whyte and Jacobs were of a similar mindset. So what is to be made

Next pages: Jane Jacobs at Toronto City Hall in 1986, surrounded by fellow Torontonians architect Barton Myers, one-time Toronto International Film Festival honcho Wayne Clarkson, musician Phil Nimmons, actor Eric Peterson, author Margaret Atwood and artist Michael Snow.

of observational urbanism then, if anything at all, in this case? The "grounded theory" involves a systematic generation of theory from data, an inductive methodology and a process that is systematically executed.[25] Grounded theory has the capability to produce theory from data, theories that are empirically grounded in the data from which they arise.[26] The important thing to remember is that this is not some kind of naïve inductivism but rather a process of sensitive deduction based on carefully developed ideas. This conceptual induction fosters even more deduction. According to Glaser and Strauss, the grounded theory inductively emerges from its data source in accordance with the method of constant comparison, which includes an amalgam of systematic coding, data analysis, and theoretical sampling procedures. These procedures enable the researcher to interpret most of the diverse patterning in the data by developing theoretical ideas at a higher level of abstraction than the initial data descriptions.[27] It is a highly systematic approach, which takes the view that all things are integrated, all actions are integrated with other actions, that nothing is mono-variable, that everything is in motion, and that patterns are systematically recurring over and over again.[28] This approach, certainly then and even today, is a leading method of social science research. Much can be learned from close observation of the rich dynamics of communities and the relationships between people. As far as we know, Jacobs never came into contact with the grounded theory work of Glaser and Strauss, nor did she apply any of their principles or methods. Perhaps due in part to her acknowledged disdain for academia, her empirical methods and observations were never granted much legitimacy in that intellectual realm. Nor did she expect readers to interpret her amateur, inductively generated ideas as in any way founded on academic credentials. She had every opportunity to consult with the leading sociologists, geographers and environmental psychologists of the day but of course she never did. A similar disconnection can be seen with regard to case studies, where data (as in the case of grounded theory) can be acquired from multiple sources, with observations (looking and listening) being just two methods along with reports, documents, theoretical literature, quantitative sources/statistics, interviews, surveys, questionnaires and ethnological approaches, etc.[29] To gain better, more valid and reliable results and more truthful and stable data, more sources are recommended.[30] For example, the work of social scientist Robert Yin in his article, "The Case Study as a Serious Research Strategy" (1981), never entered her realm of interest in her later days, where one expected a certain maturity in her perception toward academia and real social science research (not just the complexity theory that has never really gained proper traction and acceptance in built environment disciplines, except among a few eccentric architects and researchers).

That notwithstanding, the seminal publications of Jacobs (1961),[31] Christopher Alexander (1977),[32] and William Whyte (1980)[33] cannot be construed as empirical science (for example, in the vein of Glaser and Strauss) but are based on detailed observations of cities, neighborhoods, districts, and people. Such "research" as they contain can be fitted into urban design, an applied social science where knowledge is and has to be much broader, spanning both natural and social sciences as well as the arts and humanities. As the Australian academics Kim Dovey and Elek Pafka observe, better metrics than those used by Jacobs need to be developed for understanding density and distinguishing between building and population densities, housing and job densities, and internal versus street life densities, etc.[34] There simply are no typical or universal cities that one might study.[35] Interestingly, these chief protagonists of "observational urbanism" are not sociologists, but, as Nathan Glazer points out, they do have "sociological imagination"; so they cannot be discarded. Jacobs had developed a highly personal way of thinking about and seeing cities, and she explained her ideas and the rationale behind them so effectively that they have since been either adopted or rejected by generations of planners. Research in applied social sciences such as urban planning and urban design is the systematic, rigorous investigation of a situation, problem, or urban phenomenon geared to generate new knowledge or validate existing knowledge within the field. However, another parallel concern in this field has to do with the discovery and definition of problems, rather than with matters of research design, by which the hypotheses derived from these problems may be put to the test. In that spirit, scientific research can be seen as an art, not a science.

William Hollingsworth "Holly" Whyte was an American urbanist, organisational analyst, journalist, and people-watcher, not so very different to Jacobs, who was also an urbanist, a journalist, an author, and an activist. Both were observational urbanists. Whyte was in many ways Jacobs' mentor, and both celebrated the small-scale, the diverse and the mixed, thus they were antagonists of large-scale planning in terms both of housing, commercial or other types of redevelopment. Admittedly their views sprang from the quarters of Greenwich Village and Midtown Manhattan, but for them large-scale development represented the death of the city that they knew and loved: the destruction of the essential ingredient that was diversity. They favoured retaining the old infrastructure and voiced its advantages in creating a diverse social environment (for example, Boston's North End, which was an area that Gans had introduced to Jacobs). But as Nathan Glazer observed in a discussion just before he passed away, based on what was happening in the urban realm of cities – like the redevelopment of Manhattan's west side, the Atlantic Yards in Brooklyn, or the hyper-development of Shanghai and Beijing, coupled with New Delhi and Mumbai – he felt and feared that the true prophet of the future city would not turn out to be Ebenezer Howard or Jane Jacobs (or Holly White for that matter) but rather Le Corbusier.[36]

As for high-rise buildings, Jacobs was either ambivalent about them, or benignly disposed. She does not address them in her work, so it is hard to say what she might have made of modern cities with vast numbers of sky-scraper housing blocks, their density out of all proportion. As Glazer observes, high-rises are seen as a political or economic necessity, in Jacobs' time and even more so now, and their reality overwhelms what you might call a more humane vision, which other political and economic circumstances once made possible. The realities of our time appear to produce another default that is highly unappealing, and we may not know how to deal with it.[37]

★

Since the early 1990s, Lujiazui has been developed specifically as a new financial district of Shanghai.

One of the difficulties in confronting social sciences (or applied social sciences such as urban planning, urban design, and architecture) arises from the fact that human beings frequently modify their habitual modes of social behaviour as a consequence of acquiring new knowledge about the events in which they participate or the society of which they are members. Another difficulty concerns the validity of conclusions reached in social inquiry.[38] A particular problem is located in the tension between individuals and society. The term "human beings" could be accounted as a specific one because it is predicated on individual human beings; but it could also be designated as a collective term on the grounds that it involves reference to forms of activity characterised by the behaviour of groups of human individuals. However, there are no firm principles for deciding between these alternatives or much prospect of developing these rules.[39] An important aspect that one has to keep in mind is the problem confronted by social scientists when they import their own values into the analysis of social phenomena, the so-called "value judgment". We observe something when we become aware of it. We acknowledge what we observe, as in "This is so." We judge when we form an opinion, as in "I think this about that." Observation in the urban arena is a neutral act of taking in information upon which we base our judgments. Such judgment involves rendering an opinion on the relative value or merit of what is being observed. Jacobs gathered and chose facts and empirical information in an unsystematic way that supported her preconceived theoretical standpoints or notions about the city that did not consider random statistical selection or the explicit articulation of sampling methods.[40] Even though this might seem to be case study research, it is not. If she subconsciously followed the logic of scientific discovery and case study research, as some authors naively believe she did,[41] or even used inductive qualitative approaches of grounded theory based on sensitive deduction, the results of her studies are based on her belief that the overpowering strengths of unstructured observation and the validity of the data so generated will simply be sufficient – and the final proof of the grand conclusions she draws.

Peter Laurence points to the fact that Jacobs endorsed and welcomed complexity science, which offered her a way to understand not only the intricacy and interconnectedness of a city's plans and purposes but also the interwoven nature of life itself, as suggested by the word's etymology.[42] This does not condone the fact that Jacobs never performed organised research and inductive studies in the manner of Glaser and

Strauss, or that she never really followed any kind of real social science case study methodology. Her lack of education in planning, urban design, architecture, environmental psychology, aesthetics, urban sociology and human geography etc, is highly problematic and one of the reasons for the lack of any formal research methods in her work. Moreover, she did not like or admire academics or professional planners, indeed she tended to despise them, as was clearly indicated by the complete absence of references or any real bibliography in her work, which may be seen as pretentious and even shocking. Her application of complexity science – and its orthodox proponents even today suggest that this is the only way to study and understand cities (and that she went deeper than any other researcher) – did not bring her the full picture. She would not be forced to go beyond the aestheticised "place-centric" obsessions of her non-scientific observations, yet *Death and Life* was presented as a manifesto and a new universal theory of cities. Her strong belief in the beauty of urban smallness and the sanctity of the so-called human scale would be both her blessing and her curse.

The poet Charles Baudelaire's aesthetic vision of the modern city was framed around the debonair figure of the *flâneur* (Jacobs was certainly one of those, as were William H. Whyte, Alan Jacobs, Christopher Alexander, Georges Perec, Charles R. Wolfe and other observational urbanists) – whose role as an observer of, and commentator on, life in the streets and arcades of Paris was presented as the counterpoint of modern man.[43] The *flâneur* was not only the dweller of the emerging modern metropolis but also its creation.[44] The *flâneur* simultaneously embodied a way of occupying public space and relating to it in a manner that was possible only in the new urban environment, while also being defined in terms of this relationship to space. In addition to providing an aesthetic rendering of the modern world, Baudelaire's vision was therefore, at its core, an urban one which celebrated the spectacle, energy, creativity and cultures of the "street".[45] Jacobs' ethnography of everyday life and urbanity provided us with a picture, scope, and scale of urban life, inviting us to leave our workplaces to mingle in the social relations that give life to a city. Jacobs avoids a broader scale (her critique of the modernists) and ends up concentrating on the other extreme – the scale of the city block (as she did in the North End in

Next pages: Paris Street; Rainy Day (*Rue de Paris, temps de pluie*) is a large 1877 oil painting by Gustave Caillebotte. Art Institute of Chicago.

Boston and Greenwich Village in New York).[46] Michel de Certeau, the cultural theorist, provided a way of analysing how, using city space in a myriad of idiosyncratic ways, people subvert the meanings and values of the powerful, including resisting the totalising notions of the urban. Through the act of walking, cartographic space is transformed into a place of meaning and memory. Thus, multiple places defined through use, imagination, and a range of cultural practices will exist within a single urban landscape.[47] Jacobs was not so much rigorous as intuitive in her observational approach, but she did look with a keen, clear and imaginative eye and she did have a natural (grounded) insight into the built environment around her.[48] The interesting thing, which distinguishes Jacobs from, for example, the most prominent New Urbanist, Andres Duany, or one of the latest "observational urbanists", Charles Wolfe, is the fact that even with her lucid prose and her simple allusion to urban immersion and participation, *Death and Life* contains no illustration that would give us a sense of the city's visual aspects – no movement, snapshots, living diaries, sketches. These are some of the most fundamental elements of sensing and decoding the city for an observational urbanist.[49]

That being said, there has clearly been an overemphasis and focus on Jacobs and her work, while people like the sociologists Louis Wirth and Lewis Mumford have been overshadowed. These scholars and great writers had a great deal to say. In particular, they were able to describe cities based on a scholarly focus on the systematic theory of city building and the complexity of the urban realm. They created a dialogue about everyday city life that was fundamentally different than before; this included straightforward issues such as how cities affect human life, life choices, and everyday conduct. Wirth believed that there were three key characteristics of cities: a large population, social heterogeneity, and population density – and all three have fundamental consequences for social life in the city.[50] Wirth ordered us to avoid identifying urbanism as the way of life that defines a city. In contrast, Mumford, in addition to stressing the importance of cities, believed that cities evolved as a function of their relationship to nature and their spiritual values, followed by their physical design and economic functions in the community. He also portrayed the city as a kind of theatre, with the social drama of the community being the "play".[51] Wirth argued that explaining the nature of urban life and accounting for the differences between cities of various sizes and types was possible using his three key defining characteristics. In contrast, Jacobs saw a living city as a problem of "organised complexity", which involves "dealing simultaneously with a sizeable number of factors which are interrelated into an organic whole."[52] That notwithstanding, Mumford's book, *The Urban Prospect* (1968), was a tour de force collection of essays on nature and the city, at the level of Glazer's *From a Cause to a Style* (2007), written about 40 years later; both works went much deeper into the real complexity of cities than Jacobs could ever do.

Jacobs was known for not participating in discussions within the professions of architecture, urban planning and design, nor did she attend relevant conferences (except for one in Harvard in 1956), contribute to the zeitgeist topics and projects of the day, or publish in professional journals.[53] In other words, she was not part of the contemporary language and discourse; instead, she had her own. Her emphasis lay elsewhere. Jacobs' words and images created a language that embodies our longing for a good place to live.

The fundamental premise of Jacobs' thinking was that planning should be undertaken from the grassroots up, predicated on a measure of self-determination. As the urbanist and historian Thomas Campanella observed: "It was the Jacobian revolution and its elimination of a robust physical-planning focus that led to the diminution of planning's disciplinary identity, professional agency, and speculative courage."[54] The idea, which exists even to this day, that some megaproject or "starchitecture" development could cure all the ills of a city is absurd.[55] But Jacobs' concern was mostly about what the central planners were actually doing, and not their very existence. Campanella's further observations bring us to the first of the three legacies of the Jacobian (planning) turn: it diminished the disciplinary identity of planning. The second legacy of the Jacobian turn was related to the first: granting the grassroots precedence over the authority and expertise of planners led to a loss of professional agency.

The third legacy of the Jacobian turn is perhaps the most troubling of all: the apparent paucity among today's American planners of the speculative courage and vision that once distinguished their profession.[56] Many good ideas – public housing, urban renewal, new-build suburbs – seemed to be turning out bad. All of them the target of Jacobs' profound and hostile criticism. However, planning was connected with the realities of the politics and economics of urban development. And the reality was that the involvement of planners or the planning model seemed unable to improve what would occur as a result of normal economic activity.[57] Jacobs is best-known for her impact on city planning and she was among the most articulate voices against "slum clearance", high-rise development, highways carved through urban neighbourhoods, and big commercial projects. But she did not object to developments simply because they were big; she also advocated an entirely different urban vision.[58]

While the expanded range of scholarship and practice in the post-urban renewal era diversified the field, that diversification came at the expense of an established expertise – strong, centralised physical planning – which had provided professional visibility and identity both within academia and among "place" professions such as architecture and landscape architecture. Yet ultimately, Jacobs, Florida, Sassen, Glaeser, Berger and others are in many respects complementary urban thinkers with very different lenses on the macro-, meso-, and micro-complexity of cities. "Cities are thoroughly physical things", Jacobs once wrote, but as Wirth, Tonkiss, and other urban theorists remark, "Cities are also products of social relationships – they are socially produced." Her ability to influence how cities are perceived remains unrivaled. But Glaeser, Mitchell, Florida and others add a compelling new component to that perception, and go beyond nostalgia and the romanticisation of diverse, child-friendly, dense city neighbourhoods. Their forceful, systematic advocacy of increased complexity of the city beyond Jacobs' aestheticised "place-centric" obsessions, focusing on redevelopment efforts involving people, technology, infrastructure and global flow, should provoke serious discussions among academics, practitioners, and policy makers for years to come. As Campanella observes: "Planners today need not a close-up lens or a wide-angle lens but a wide-angle zoom lens. They need to be able to see the big picture as well as the parts close up; and even if not trained to design the parts themselves, they need to know how all those parts fit together."[59] As Laurence points out, despite Jacobs' well-known antagonism toward the abstract understanding of cities expressed by a plethora of architects and planners, she was at base a theorist. Yet, compared to the "bird's-eye view and arm's-length approach of professional theorists", Laurence notes that her approach is like her activism – at eye level and hands on; her urban theory was the corollary of her activism and vice versa.[60]

What each of us sees and understands depends on our own experience: where we come from, personally and professionally. Observation can often tell more about the observer than about the environment being observed. It reflects the values, beliefs, and worldview of the witness. We see through the lenses of our interests and understanding. We recognise patterns that match what we have seen before. Urban observation is also aimed at informing better, more equitable, plans, policies, and political decisions. A historical, interdisciplinary tradition of urban observation, with the modern-day 'urban diary', is an experiential method of documenting city life and form. Through evocative photography, use of smartphone apps, and other cutting-edge tools, we can explore and document the urban spaces as well as the structures and human activities around them. According to Merriam Webster's Dictionary, to observe is to watch carefully, especially with attention to details or behaviour for the purpose of arriving at a judgment; to make a scientific observation is an act or instance of observing a custom, rule, or law and an act of recognising and noting a fact or occurrence, often involving measurement with instruments. Public life studies have been useful for documenting the relationships between environmental design and behaviour so that informed decision-making and design processes can improve places for people. They enrich our understanding of city life, particularly the quality, performance, and success of a place as well as the needs of inhabitants. Such studies assist with documenting existing conditions, identifying issues, developing solutions, and evaluating the impacts of design interventions. Observing people in public space is complex. City life is transitory, with people moving and conditions constantly changing. There are extensive variables such as architecture and design, weather, noise, smell, light, and shade as

Next pages: Shooting the documentary *City Limits* with director Laurence Hyde in 1971.

CF-SJD

well as the number, location, and types of people using the space. Proponents of New Urbanism, for example, chose to visit the cities, towns, neighbourhoods and streets that they liked – not only to observe but also to measure them in detail. That has been the New Urbanism method ever since – dealing with every kind of community plan, from hamlets to big-city downtown zones. New Urbanists verify everything with their own eyes, again and again, as Jacobs did. This is what can truly be called "observational urbanism". It is a powerful method that does not oppose academic theorists who trust ideas and intellectual fashion more than their own observations and experiences, rather it complements them. This approach, whereby New Urbanists diligently work to ground their ideas by testing them with the empirical data of observation and experience, was championed by Jacobs and by the architect and theorist Christopher Alexander. But the ultimate challenge for all urbanists involved in influencing and practising urban planning and urban design is to translate, apply, and further develop the best ideas to promote the types of urban environments that can encourage and nurture the full potential of our social creativity, targeted at sustainable and open-ended human development.[61] Much more congenial to Jacobs' way of thinking, when it comes to the above issues, were the design theories of Kevin Lynch,[62] Alexander,[63] Whyte,[64] and Jan Gehl[65] as well as the novel traffic policies of "shared space" that are spreading across Northern and Western Europe today. All of these pay careful attention to what real people do and how they interact with each other and with the built environment. Each of these researchers, to some degree, shared Jacobs' understanding of the city as a spontaneous entity.

1 Alice Sparberg Alexiou, *Jane Jacobs: Urban Visionary (*New Brunswick: Rutgers University Press, 2006).

2 Fran Tonkiss, *Cities by Design: The Social Life of Urban Form* (Cambridge: Polity Press, 2014); Sonia Hirt (ed.) with Diane Zahm, *The Urban Wisdom of Jane Jacobs* (London: Routledge, 2012), pp. 37–48.

3 Margaret Crawford, *From the Feel Good City to the Just City* (Event Transcription, USC Bedrosian Center, 2 October, 2015), USC Bedrosian Center |SLAB |UCLA Department of Chicana/o Studies 1–7.

4 Rem Koolhaas, "In Search of Authenticity", in Ricky Burdett and Deyjan Sudjic (ed.), *The Endless City* (London: Phaidon, 2007), pp. 320–323.

5 Sharon Zukin, "Changing Landscapes of Power: Opulence and the Urge for Authenticity", in *International Journal of Urban and Regional Research*, vol. 33, issue 2 (June 2009).

6 Herbert J. Gans, "A Review of The Death and Life of Great American Cities by Janc Jacobs", in *Commentary Magazine*, (February 1962).

7 Setha Low and Kurt Iveson, "Propositions for more just urban public spaces", in *City Journal*, vol. 20, issue 1 (2016), pp. 10–31; Ash Amin, "Collective Culture and Urban Public Space", in *City Journal*, vol. 12, issue 1 (2008), pp. 5–24.

8 Anthony Flint, *Wrestling with Moses: How Jane Jacobs Took on New York's Master Builder and Transformed the American City* (New York: Random House Trade, 2011).

9 Hillary Ballon and Kenneth T. Jackson (ed.), *Robert Moses and the Modern City: The Transformation of New York* (New York: W. W. Norton & Company, 2008).

10 Christopher Klemek, "Jane Jacobs's Urban Village: Well Preserved or Cast Adrift?", in *Journal of the Society of Architectural Historians*, vol. 66, issue 1 (March 2007), pp. 20–23.

11 Zukin (2009).

12 David Harvey, "The New Urbanism and the Communitarian Trap", *Harvard Design Magazine*, issue 1, Winter/Spring 1997, pp. 1–3.

13 Herbert J. Gans, *People, Plans, and Policies: Essays on Poverty, Racism, and Other National Urban Problems* (New York: Columbia University Press, 1991).

14 Gans (1962) and Gans (1991).

15 Gans (1991).

16 Nathan Storring, "Jane Jacobs on Gentrification", 2015, electronic resource [http://www.nathanstorring.com/2014/10/29/jane-jacobs-on-gentrification/]. Accessed on 21 January 2019.

17 Michael Powell, "An Urban Theorist Questions the Gospel of St. Jane", *New York Times*, 19 February 2010, electronic resource [https://cityroom.

blogs.nytimes.com/2010/02/19/an-urban-theorist-questions-the-gospel-of-st-jane/]. Accessed on 20 July 2019.

18 Marguerite van den Berg, "The discursive uses of Jane Jacobs for the genderfying city: Understanding the productions of space for post-Fordist gender notions", in *Urban Studies*, vol. 55, issue 4 (2018), pp. 751–766.

19 Edward L. Glaeser, "What a City Needs; Comment on Wrestling with Moses: How Jane Jacobs Took on New York's Master Builder and Transformed the American City, By Anthony Flint", *New* Republic, 4 September, 2009, electronic resource [https://newrepublic.com/article/68989/what-city-needs]. Accessed on 15 March 2019.

20 Edward L. Glaeser, *Triumph of the City: How Our Greatest Invention Makes Us Richer, Smarter, Greener, Healthier and Happier* (New York: Pan Macmillan, 2011); Anthony Flint (2011).

21 Jane Jacobs, *The Economy of Cities* (New York: Vintage, 1969).

22 Nathan Glazer, "From Socialism to Sociology", in Bennett M. Berger (ed.), *Authors of Their Own Lives: Intellectual Autobiographies by Twenty American Sociologists* (Berkeley: University of California Press, 1990), p. 207.

23 David Riesman, Nathan Glazer and Reuel Denney, *The Lonely Crowd: A Study of the Changing American Culture* (New Haven: Yale University Press, 1950).

24 Hirt and Zahm (2012).

25 Barney G. Glaser and Anselm L. Strauss, *The Discovery of Grounded Theory: Strategies for Qualitative Research* (New York: Aldine de Gruyter, 1967).

26 Barney G. Glaser, *Doing Grounded Theory: Issues and Discussions* (Mill Valley: Sociology Press, 1998).

27 Barney G. Glaser and Anselm L. Strauss (1967).

28 Glaser (1998).

29 Bill Gillham, *Case Study Research Methods* (London: Continuum, 2000).

30 Robert K. Yin, "The case study as a serious research strategy", in *Science Communication*, vol. 3, issue 1 (1981), pp. 97–114; Robert K. Yin, *Case Study Research: Design and Methods* (Thousand Oaks: Sage Publications, 2003).

31 Jane Jacobs, *The Death and Life of Great American Cities* (New York: Random House, 1961/1992).

32 Christopher Alexander, Sara Ishikawa, Murray Silverstein with Max Jacobson, *A Pattern Language: Towns, Buildings, Construction* (New York: Oxford University Press, 1977).

33 William H. Whyte, *The Social Life of Small Urban Spaces* (Washington, D.C.: The Conservation Foundation, 1980).

34 Kim Dovey and Elek Pafka, "The Urban Density Assemblage", in *Urban Design International*, vol. 19, issue 1 (2014), pp. 66–76.

35 Kim Dovey and Elek Pafka, "The science of urban design?", in *Urban Design International*, vol. 21, issue 1 (2016), pp. 1–10.

36 Nathan Glazer, "History's Angel", in Timothy Mennel, Jo Steffens and Christopher Klemek (ed.) *Block by Block: Jane Jacobs and the Future of New York* (New York: Municipal Art of Society New York, 2007); Nathan Glazer, *From a Cause to a Style: Modernist Architecture's Encounter with the American City* (Princeton: Princeton University Press, 2007).

37 Howard Husock, "The Urban Crisis After 40 Years: An interview with Nathan Glazer", in *Cities Journal*, Summer 2011.

38 Ernest Nagel,*The Structure of Science: Problems in the Logic of Scientific Explanation (*Cambridge: Hackett Publishing Company, 1979); Marx W. Wartofsky, *Conceptual Foundations of Scientific Thought: An Introduction to the Philosophy of Science* (New York: Macmillan, 1968).

39 Nagel (1979).

40 Sonia Hirt, "Jane Jacobs, Modernity and Knowledge", in Sonia Hirt with Diane Zahm (2012).

41 Ibid.

42 Peter L. Laurence, "Jane Jacobs Before Death and Life", in *Journal of the Society of Architectural Historians*, vol. 66, issue 1 (March 2007), pp. 5–15.

43 Michel Foucault, "What is Enlightenment?", in Paul Rabinow (ed.), *The Foucault Reader: An Introduction to Foucault's Thought* (Harmondsworth: Penguin Books, 1986).

44 Marshall Berman, *All that is Solid Melts into Air: The Experience of Modernity* (New York: Viking Penguin, 1988); Deborah Talbot, *Who the Hell is Jane Jacobs? And what are her theories all about?* (Ipswich: Bowden & Brazil, 2019).

45 Ibid.

46 Andrei Mikhail Zaiatz Crestani and Brenda Brandão Pontes, "The Public Space (In)visible to the Eyes of Jane Jacobs", in Roberto Rocco (ed.), *Jane Jacobs is still here: Jane Jacobs 100. Her legacy and relevance in the 21st Century* (Delft: TU Delft, 2018). Available as an electronic resource [https://issuu.com/robertorocco/docs/jane_jacobs_report]. Accessed on 1 May 2019.

47 Michel de Certeau, *The Practice of Everyday Life* (Berkeley: University of California Press, 1984).

48 Elizabeth Lynne and Stephen A. Goldsmith (ed.), *What We See: Advancing the Observations of Jane Jacobs* (Oakland: New Village Press, 2010).

49 Charles R. Wolfe, *Seeing the Better City* (Washington, D.C.: Island Press, 2016).

50 Louis Wirth, "Urbanism as a way of life", in *The American Journal of Sociology*, vol. 44, issue 1, 1938, pp. 1–24.

51 Lewis Mumford, *The Culture of Cities* (New York: Harcourt Brace, 1938).

52 Jacobs (1961).

53 Dirk Schubert, "Jane Jacobs's Perception and Impact on City Planning and Urban Renewal in Germany", in Dirk Schubert (ed.), *Contemporary Perspectives on Jane Jacobs: Reassessing the Impacts of an Urban Visionary* (Farnham: Ashgate, 2014), pp. 137–170.

54 Thomas J. Campanella, "Jane Jacobs and the Death and Life of American Planning", in *Places Journal*, April 2011. Electronic resource [https://placesjournal.org/article/jane-jacobs-and-the-death-and-life-of-american-planning/?cn-reloaded=1]. Accessed on 3 April 2012.

55 Michael W. Mehaffy and Tigran Haas, "Poststructuralist fiddling while the world burns: Exiting the self made crisis of 'architectural culture'", in *Urbani Izziv Journal* [Urban Challenges Journal], vol. 23, issue 1, 2012, pp. 80–90.

56 Campanella (2011).

57 Husock (2011).

58 Peter Dreier, "Jane Jacobs's Legacy", in *City & Community*, vol. 5, issue 3, September 2006, pp. 227–231.

59 Campanella (2011).

60 Laurence (2007)

61 Dirk Schubert (2014); Michael W. Mehaffy, *Cities Alive: Jane Jacobs, Christopher Alexander, and the Roots of the New Urban Renaissance* (Portland: Sustasis Press, 2017).

62 Kevin Lynch, *The Image of the City* (Cambridge: MIT Press, 1960); Kevin Lynch, *Good City Form* (Cambridge: MIT Press, 1981).

63 Alexander et al. (1977).

64 Whyte (1980).

65 Jan Gehl, *Life Between Buildings* (New York: Van Nostrand Reinhold, 1987); Jan Gehl, *Cities for People* (Washington, D.C.: Island Press, 2010).

MANHATTAN AND BROOKLYN
ENTRANC
ENTRA

CHAPTER XIII

What Makes Society Sustainable?

Jesper Meijling

SINCE THE BEGINNING of the 1990s, the idea that only one kind of thinking promises efficiency has become widespread. In recent years it has become better known in debate under the name New Public Management, but it also has other names and manifestations. In particular it has been applied to activities in the public sector, ranging from education and healthcare to infrastructure. In short, the idea has taken hold that public institutions and services are incomplete, or even wrong in their structure, and that they would be more "efficient" if they were run as companies or converted to markets.

One example might be the Swedish railway system, which underwent pioneering reform of this kind that became a model for deregulation in the UK among other places. There was a news story about a young Swedish philosopher who, in the early 1990s, pulled the emergency brake on the then-new high speed train, stopping it in the middle of nowhere. It was meant as a symbolic action in a "campaign for a slower society" and generated enormous excitement with banner headlines and astonished interviewers in all the news media. Today that philosopher's action would not have made even a small announcement in the papers. The incident and the effect it had would have been no different from what has nowadays come to be exactly what we expect, namely that rail traffic is by and large at a standstill. The trend towards ever more delays and disruptions in traffic of this type began not long after that "slowness" philosopher's intervention, and it seems his prayer has been answered. Trains in Sweden have the worst punctuality rate in Europe today, according to several comparisons.[1]

Fighting crime or delivering arrests? Police officers in the 179th St station, New York subway, 1982.

Next pages: Signal box and train management centre for a railway system.

This seems contradictory and so it is. The purpose of railway reform was greater efficiency, but the road taken to achieve it was to organise

the Swedish railways in a previously untried way, with aims such as 'businesslike' and 'market governance'.[2] And it has led us to where we are now. Through reforms and government decisions, a large number of players have been deliberately created to operate within the railway system independently of one another. It is in essence a whole new reality for rail traffic, which starts with the idea that the system should operate 'like a market'. The tracks are managed separately, as are traffic control and traffic information. Driving the trains themselves constitutes yet another activity, shared between a growing number of players. Control of the trains and on-board service are handled by separate companies, as is the maintenance of rolling stock. Station buildings, waiting rooms and platforms all have different bosses. Certain types of stoppages and breakdowns recur almost daily, as does the lack of clarity about how they should be dealt with. The diversity of players creates blurred demarcation lines and responsibilities. When a stoppage or a serious delay occurs, who should you as a traveller turn to? If you are stuck on a train that is not moving, who is supposed to provide information, come to the rescue, resolve the situation? In what order? Who is responsible? This is what nobody really knows any more. The clear, hierarchical chain of responsibility has gone. The market players do not want to lose advantages to one another or release information that might be counted against them. At the same time they have the political blessing that tells them their actions are correct according to the new norms that have been established.[3]

In 1992, Jane Jacobs published an analysis that seems as though it might provide some important clues to a better understanding of this development, where a new norm for what is considered to be the right way of doing things enters areas where it was previously unknown. If you take Jacobs' point of view, the confusion in the railway system is a consequence of the fact that those in charge have started mixing different sorts of rules and priorities without realising it. This results in a fragmentation of the system not just into different parts and players, but also between a number of views on how things should be managed: what it is best to do and gives good results, in other words what is 'efficient'. What seems to one player to be the right thing to do can be considered entirely the wrong thing for another. The people who devised the new order wanted to stimulate competition and to avoid cooperation between different lines and companies. But that doesn't work for the traveller. The company that now owns the carriage workshops wants to sell them and build offices on the land. That won't work for the train traffic. The party that owns the rails wants to allow as many trains as possible to run. That won't work for railway maintenance and stability. And so on, right through the whole system.[4]

The origin of the present situation on the rail network can be described as a divergent logic that has crept into the established logic of an existing system. Like Jacobs, we could say that a different kind of set of rules, establishing what it is best to do, has been applied to tell players what their motivation should be and how they are to treat one another. It is a regulatory system that is not capable of creating the better order that was perhaps intended, but instead leads to confusion and inefficiency. Where politicians, civil servants and investigators have endeavoured since the early 1990s to transform the railway system into a kind of level playing field for market players, they have in fact been trying to establish a new kind of norms for right and wrong: players are supposed to be able to arrange matters with one another if they so wish, or not bother to do so if they thought they would not make anything out of it. They are to work freely and in competition, but not to collaborate. They are to be inventive and entrepreneurial, and at the same time make a profit for their owners. They are not to take on any senior responsibility yet are not to see themselves as subordinate parts of a system.[5]

But this quest for a new type of norm comes up against the problem just mentioned, that what is right in one situation or within a certain type of system is not necessarily right in another situation or within another system. The idea that the people involved in operating the railways should act as "free players in a free market" cannot simply disregard the railway's intrinsic functional logic, which is complicated and unwieldy because the railway is what is called a "tightly coupled" large technical system. (This means that all the parts are tightly connected and need to be controlled centrally, and that the effects of faults – such as delays and fallen power lines – proliferate rapidly through the system.) Train traffic is a sensitive system with narrow margins, even in terms of space: all trains are confined in the same strictly limited traffic machine where inventiveness and improvisation are impossible. Things that are both possible and desirable in a market – the notion that players can come, go and move around as they please – become a problem in a system like the railways. Thus standards taken from a free market and applied directly to a technical system cannot fulfil the aim of achieving stability and efficiency. The same action that is right in a free market situation turns out to be wrong in the railway situation.

The book by Jacobs that throws an explanatory light on this phenomenon is *Systems of Survival*, which takes a broad-brush approach to the issue of the market as an ideal model for public sector businesses, among other things. Jacobs does not come down for or against different systems but wants the reader to see the wider context around the various situations that we as people come across in society, and how we act within it. Jacobs' basic idea is that industrial businesses, occupational contexts and institutions of different kinds constitute situations that are different from one another, with different conditions and norms. One cannot therefore assume that what is logical and desirable in one situation (in a certain occupational context, in a certain public institution and so on) is the same in another. A norm for how to act correctly can be wrong when the context is changed. And that is precisely what was happening increasingly frequently, according to Jacobs, in the 1980s. Norms and organisational principles that came from one context were "imported" into another because, for some reason, they were seen to be better or more attractive, but which then proved to fit badly with the requirements for obtaining desirable results. Jacobs' conclusion is that this can lead to very serious problems, even corruption and criminality.

It was primarily the public sphere that was deemed to need reforms and new ideals. It is there too that Jacobs sets a large part of her investigation. She starts by making a distinction between public and private operations and critically examines the idea of the market as an overarching ideal for both spheres. But the big question she poses in the book is not about the details that emerge in the investigation. Through discussion she enters a realm that can almost be called a mystery: what makes society sustainable? The concept of sustainability is to be understood here at a basic level, as a prerequisite for a society to exist and function day after day, even in the future. Jacobs' handling of the subject is unlike anything she had attempted in earlier books: the discussion is conducted in the form of a dialogue between a group of friends in an apartment in New York. The conversation ranges across a wide variety of observations about what guides people in their actions in different public and economic spheres and situations, and how we can judge what is right and wrong.

One example is an event in New York related by one of the friends and brought into the discussion. According to newspaper articles, the subway police in New York had turned to a consultant specialising in productivity. The consultant clearly saw all different kinds of work as commercial, based on production results per unit of time. He reached the conclusion that the best measure of good and efficient police work was the number of arrests made per hour. The police force's practised hunting instinct was duly activated, but was not now directed at criminality per se but at "pegs" on a board, in other words the number of fines handed out. The police who achieved the best production results were rewarded and promoted. The police managers were highly impressed by the consultant's model. But the consequences were not long in coming: it led to many wrongful arrests and false accusations. Also, the accused, often from disadvantaged minorities, were implicated in the lying because they were induced to make false confessions. With an anthropological eye, Jacobs goes over a lot of material concerning real events that can, in a similar way, tell us about what is rewarded or disapproved of in a certain situation, what behaviour typically raises esteem in one context but lowers it in another – all with an eye on how behaviour is deemed to lead to a result that is perceived to be good, worthy of imitation, effective and so on.

Jacobs seeks a historically evolved ethic for working life and life in society. We can call it "the moral foundations of public life", which corresponds to the term she uses in the book's subtitle, *A Dialogue on the Moral Foundations of Commerce and Politics.* In the context Jacobs describes in the book, "moral foundations" should be understood more on the basis of their primary meaning of "manners and customs", how one behaves sensibly in different situations. The dialogue in the book can be described as an ethical discussion, in other words an exploratory conversation about moral judgment and what defines an action as good, appropriate and exemplary. Jacobs leaves the questions of private life to one side, the aim of the discussions is to understand what norms for social relations do not undermine welfare and development but rather help us to earn our livelihood and survival in the long term. A concept that was not yet current when Jacobs wrote the book is "social sustainability", which is surely not far removed from what she was getting at. On the other hand, a term that Jacobs did like to use was "civilisation", as another word for actually maintaining useful norms and behaviours in the different spheres of a society – and thus pointing to the risks that exist for a society which loses important concepts of what behaviour will serve its survival.

Jacobs' conclusion from her friends' conversations and their many examples is that we do not live with one general norm but two separate sets of norms, which influence our actions in a way that will ensure the survival and welfare of society and its citizens. They correspond to (and describe) two different ways of satisfying the human need to survive, each calling for a different ethic. The two norm systems are actually developed clusters of characteristics, values and norms – Jacobs uses another word for such clusters or bundles, namely "syndrome". The fact that there are two, not just one, is something that distinguishes the human race's transactions with strangers from those of other animal races. One can be called "territorial" and has been built up around survival actions such as gathering, hunting, conquering and defending territories and groups. The other (and this is the one that is entirely specific to human beings) is based on actions like exchanging and trading, to satisfy the same material needs as the first one. Thus Jacobs believes that these patterns developed historically over a long period of time and hence are not always immediately intelligible in a modern context. Jacobs calls them (taking her inspiration from Plato) "the guardian" and the "commercial" moral syndrome respectively.[6]

As guiding rules and regulatory systems, the two are mutually exclusive if you compare them on individual points. According to the guardian ethic, it is deemed wrong to bargain with what one has been made responsible for, while it may be acceptable to use force. From the commercial ethic point of view, it is deemed wrong to use force but right to bargain. There is not always a crystal clear demarcation between these spheres, notes Jacobs, since many situations and areas in society may have elements of both. Most areas and most types of business do however have ethics clearly characterised by one or the other syndrome, and their practice and separation are primarily based on cultural knowledge we acquire when we live in society.

Jacobs notes that a civil servant in an administration is a "guardian" who should not sell his services at the market price, just as a tradesman should not use force but rely on the principle of free will. The tradesman (shopkeeper, business owner, entrepreneur) should be inventive and innovative. The representative of an administration or system should not invent or change things from day to day, since expediency in such a business depends primarily on its functioning according to clear and established principles. In the course of history the act of following established principles has become an expression of a code of honour for institutions. It can mean loyalty to a public institution or a system and as well as to a group, such as one's own profession, but also to a whole society. In the longer historical perspective, the guardian ethic seems to be compatible with phenomena that have territorial extensions such as land and states, latterly also with hierarchical orders such as universities and state offices and, in modern times, things like big technical systems on whose stable functioning many are dependent: all of these require loyalty, observation of rules, continuity and, not least, the assumption of responsibility. I think it can also be described as the morality of responsibility, rewarding the acceptance of comprehensive responsibility – something which is not compatible with a commercial ethic, where responsibility must be clearly restricted for anyone involved to avoid an outcome that is unreasonable or wrong.

Jacobs' point in *Systems of Survival* is clear: we will create serious problems if we mix together the norms of different spheres without critical thinking. In the best case, anomalies and strange contradictions are the result, and in the worst case systemic corruption, where what would normally be a right is transformed into a wrong (such as the subway police who arrest innocent people in order to 'increase profits'). The consequence is a kind of moral monster of contradictory and destructive confusions, or "monstrous hybrids" as Jacobs calls them. Her most classic example is the Italian-American mafia that mixes norms of loyalty, force and revenge from the guardian ethic with norms of bargaining and deal-making from the commercial ethic. Another monstrous hybrid was the Soviet society, where in place of the freedom, inventiveness and initiative of the commercial ethic, the entirety of economic life was controlled (towards its extinction) through the hierarchy, obedience and loyalty of the guardian ethic. Both these hybrids have proven to be destructive for society – but the mafia can continue because it is a parasite flourishing on the viability of the surrounding society. In New York's subway, in the hands of the guardians, the trade ethic view of production results was transformed into a deprivation of liberty: suddenly the business-inspired and incentive-driven were transferred to a quite different moral landscape that was characterised by coercive measures and the questioning of people's honour. The consultant who had designed the model was only aware of a single ethical norm system, unaware that he had crashed right into another. In this way he (it was probably a man) did not achieve good results but a systemic breakdown.

It is useful that Jacobs manages to pursue her investigation at a more overarching level, beyond ideologies and opinions. In that way she creates the possibility of bypassing the problem of some people saying that they are "for" private enterprise and market solutions, with others saying they are "against" them. Rather than believing that society's different spheres and functions can be moulded according to one or the other package of opinions or ideas without major difficulties, Jacobs wants to drive the discussion as practically as possible, from the basis of what can be shown to work, without creating awkward conflicts of purpose, in order to achieve such objectives as we can agree on. Thus Jacobs' point is not to present a ready answer on what works, but to run analyses from that kind of starting point.

The idea that was gaining ground when the book was written at the end of the 1980s and the beginning of the 1990s is today known by the name of New Public Management (NPM). It had begun to penetrate public service organisations with the idea that the public sector should be made more efficient by working in a "business-inspired" way or being organised "like a market". Specific forms of this transfer of norms entailed setting up quantified "targets" in place of the professional's assessment and responsibility (for example how many people could be arrested in the subway, the number of patient visits that could be carried out by the healthcare system or the crimes that the police could log as completed investigations), along with notions of competing for "customers", and reorganising public sector departments into "purchasers" and "providers" and so on. In that way it was possible to reduce, step by step, the tangible connection between the tasks of employees and their overarching purpose, which in name at least could remain the same as before[7] – the subway police would still be called subway police, but they would be "more efficient" and "work in a new way".

A Bible for the NPM was the book *Reinventing Government* by David Osborne and Ted Gaebler that came out in 1993.[8] Several of Jacobs' examples of monstrous hybrids (for example the "profit-driven" subway police) could have come straight from that book. But of course the difference is that this book (like many other books in the same genre that came out during the 1990s and the first decade of the 21st century) presented such examples and stories as desirable policy models: they were said to be fool-proof recipes for successful efficiency. If you introduced market thinking into public services, the assumption ran, better results would automatically follow. In relation to this, Jacobs' *Systems of Survival* could be described as an anti-NPM manifesto.

Where individual business interests are mixed with public interests, inefficiency and corruption may be the result. A better known example, which Jacobs also cites, is the relationship between the public sector and companies in the so-called military-industrial complex, where companies in the defence industry acquire the power to set aside the mechanisms of competition through their size and a mutual interdependence with their own client, namely the state. This phenomenon is most marked in the US, but it also occurs in other countries with big defence industries, like France and Sweden. And it is the citizens and taxpayers who suffer the consequences. In Sweden today, for example, we can also talk about a "welfare industry complex", in which big private healthcare companies make their profits from public contracts only, and run their business entirely within the framework of the public healthcare system's finances and budget. Here a type of systemic corruption is emerging, where people are committed to high political assignments of trust and at the same time hold leading posts in healthcare companies – where the issue of companies' profit motives may conflict with the interests and purposes of healthcare. The most comprehensive example of this in Sweden so far is the Nya Karolinska hospital project in Stockholm, which has merged the public sector and private business spheres in all parts of the project, from planning and construction to how healthcare is operated. A large number of conflicts in different situations associated with activities at the hospital have arisen in the wake of the project, which at the end of the day are about right or wrong in relation to public responsibility and the function and purpose of healthcare.[9]

One variant of the dilemma – namely two norm systems with the risk of misconceptions – is described already in Jacobs' breakthrough work of 1961, *The Death and Life of Great American Cities*. One might say that it takes the form of a projection – perhaps a "monstrous projection" to put a further spin on Jacobs' terminology. The book is about how cities live, function and are built, but her analysis is focused on how best to understand the intrinsic logic and functionality of the city: what a certain town planning model can or cannot achieve in the matter of desirable results, starting from its own spatial, social and economic logic. The criticism that Jacobs directs in her book at the modernist town planners of the Sixties comprises, among other things, the fact that they did not analyse at all or even attempt to describe the actual conditions and problems in the city, but projected completely different ideals and norms on to it. Hence they were doomed to achieve unwanted results and conflicts.

The overall lesson that can be taken from *Systems of Survival* and *Death and Life* is not least the importance of looking at the conditions of a situation, of trying to describe them and identify their decisive characteristics and differences. The problem with the unthinking mixing and projection of norms begins precisely with the fact that it does not address the conditions for what is appropriate in a given situation. That is what happened with the Swedish rail system: the function and objectives were never specified before people started applying the new "market" ideas.[10] In the present day the same phenomenon can be seen in healthcare, where it is not its own resources, strengths and weaknesses that form the starting point for reform and change, but ideas that originate from economic theory. Healthcare is consequently beginning to be seen as "deliveries of treated diagnoses".[11] It rewards the healthcare company to confine itself to increasingly specialised treatments for easily managed cases, but in the long term this does no favours to the patient, the healthcare system itself, medical knowledge or society if healthcare is organised and operated just like any other market.

With Jacobs' help we can see this more specifically and practically. New Public Management and similar models do not merely represent ideas and ideals that trigger discussions and divided opinions. They create confusion and inefficiency, rolling out activities and practices that are wrongly programmed on the basis of indiscriminately borrowed and applied standards. When these models are superimposed onto activities and institutions that are important to society, the long-term consequences are worrying and possibly downright threatening.

1 Cf. *The European Railway Performance* Index (BCG 2017); cf. also the Traffic Authority's own international comparisons plus punctuality statistics May 2017–May 2018.

2 See for instance *En öppen järnvägsmarknad i Sverige* (Communications Department, Ds. 1993:63).

3 Concerning the new market order, see e.g. Gunnar Alexandersson, *Den svenska buss- och tågtrafiken: 20 år av avregleringar* (Stockholm: Handelshögskolan, 2011); concerning the problems in defining responsibilities, cf. Jesper Meijling, *Marknad på villovägar* (Stockholm: Premiss, 2014), and Jesper Meijling, "Slutstation", *Arkitektur*, issue 4 (2014).

4 Competition as an objective and collaboration as a problem for the railways are described in a number of railway investigations during the 1990s and the beginning of the 21st century, well described for example in SOU 2003:104.

5 Gunnar Alexandersson, *The accidental deregulation: essays on reforms in the Swedish bus and railway industries* 1979–2009, Diss. (Stockholm: Handelshögskolan, 2010).

6 For a summary compilation of the characteristics see Jane Jacobs, *Systems of Survival. A Dialogue on the Moral Foundations of Commerce and Politics* (New York: Random House, 1992), p. 215.

7 There is plenty of literature. For a real textbook example see Anders Jarefors & Bengt Jäderholm, *Beställare/utförare: Den svåra uppdelningen mellan politiker, tjänstemän och leverantörer* (Uppsala: Konsultförlaget, 1998).

8 David Osborne & Ted Gaebler, *Sluta ro, börja styra!* (Stockholm: Tiden, 1993).

9 The daily *Dagens Nyheter* reporters Anna Gustavsson and Lisa Röstlund's investigation of Nya Karolinska brings together a good deal of evidence for this, see e.g. *DN* 24 Sept. 2018, 8 Aug. 2018, 31 May 2018, 11 Apr. 2018, 11 Feb. 2018, 13 Dec. 2017, to name but a few. See also Henrik Ennart & Fredrik Mellgren, *Sjukt hus* (Stockholm: Ordfront, 2016); Jan Öhrming. *Allt görs liksom baklänges: verksamheten vid Nya Karolinska Solna* (Huddinge: Södertörns högskola, 2017); Jesper Meijling, *Nya Karolinska – ett pilotprojekt för marknadsstyrd vård?* (Stockholm: Arena Idé, 2018).

10 The SOU series of railway studies from 1991 to 2008, beginning with *Ökad konkurrens på järnvägen,* SOU 1993:13.

11 An influential writer and consultant in Swedish healthcare – particularly for the Nya Karolinska Hospital – with these ideas is the economist Michael E. Porter. See Michael E. Porter & Elizabeth Olmsted Teisberg, *Redefining Health Care: Creating Value-Based Competition on Results* (Boston: Harvard Business School Press, 2006).

STOP KILLING OUR LOVED ONES
JUST
for Eric
Michael
Akai
Trayvon
Ramarley
Sean
too many
1199
CLIFFORD GLOVER
NOV 1 1962
DAY CARE CENTER

CHAPTER XIV

America's Dark Age

Peter L. Laurence

IN 1972, A reporter from *The Village Voice* went to Toronto to visit Jane Jacobs, who had left New York with her family four years earlier. Echoing a feeling shared by other New Yorkers, as well as other Americans, about the absence of one of Greenwich Village's most famous residents, he titled his piece "Won't you come home, Jane Jacobs?"[1] Jacobs' unequivocal answer was "no". She would not be returning to New York.

When asked if she had any feelings of guilt about leaving, she replied:

> None at all. I did the best I could for 20 years. I fought as long as I could, but I've had enough. There's no virtue in fighting battles and losing. In Toronto you have a chance of winning. No, I have no regrets about leaving. One of my great-great uncles left Bavaria in 1828 because he saw the coming Prussianisation of Germany. And you know, I'm glad he did.

Thousands taking part in the "Day of Outrage", protesting police brutality and killings, New York City, 13 December 2014.

Next pages: Sharp contrasts in Toronto. A new skyline took shape in Toronto's business district in the Sixties and Seventies. Picture from 1971.

Had the reporter asked Jacobs if she felt any regret or sadness, perhaps she would have had a different answer. However, by 1972, her feelings about leaving New York were offset by the weariness of nearly two decades of non-stop fighting against 'improvement' schemes that would only make New York and, by extension, other American cities, less livable. She fought to save her West Village neighbourhood first from a street-widening/sidewalk-narrowing plan, and later wholesale reconstruction in an urban renewal scheme to build middle-income apartment blocks. She had fought the Urban Renewal Administration to improve project housing in East Harlem – unsuccessfully –and then fought for ten years to build an alternative housing model in the West

ONTARIO

NATIONAL
LUXFER PRIS
LIMITED
162 PARLIAME

Village, facing financial and bureaucratic obstacles at every turn, only to find the highly compromised design of the West Village Houses to be physical evidence of the difficulties of overcoming the income-segregated, developer-driven, tower-model of housing construction. She fought the plan to bisect Greenwich Village's Washington Square Park with an extension of Fifth Avenue, and a few years later, helped lead the fight to stop the Lower Manhattan Expressway, which would have cut a wide swathe of destruction through the Lower East Side, Chinatown, Little Italy, SoHo, and other neighbourhoods. That fight lasted some six years, with two campaigns leading to false victories where Jacobs and her fellow activists saw the project revived with new bureaucratic tactics. The third and final campaign was successful, but it culminated in her arrest for inciting a riot and the obstruction of public administration.

By the late 1960s, Jacobs was fed up. In an interview she said:

> I resent, to tell you the truth, the time I've had to spend on these civic battles. The new book [*The Economy of Cities*] was begun two years later than it should have been because of that expressway and the urban renewal fight in New York's West Village. It's a terrible imposition when the city threatens its citizens in such a way that they can't finish their work. Why, I know artists who aren't getting their pictures painted because of an expressway, poets who aren't getting their poems done.[2]

To the reporter from *The Village Voice*, she put it this way: "It's absurd to make your life absurd in response to absurd governments." By this time, moreover, Jacobs was disgusted by the war in Vietnam and resented being forced to help fund it with her tax dollars, let alone assist it with her sons' lives. In 1967, she was arrested twice for civil disobedience, first at the October 'March on the Pentagon', and then at a December action at a New York City military induction centre. In 1968, when her sons decided that they would choose jail over conscription, the family moved to Canada. This was not a fight that Jacobs otherwise knew how to win. And, in the previous two decades, having been extensively investigated by the Federal Bureau of Investigation for communist sympathies, having lost her State Department job due to McCarthyism, and having battled, in writing and on the street, the Urban Renewal regime and its corrupting influences, which sought to take her own home, Jacobs increasingly saw the United States losing sight of its democratic ideals – and becoming increasingly imperialistic. Being threatened by soldiers in gas masks at the Pentagon had a profound impact on her, as she told *The Boston Globe* in an edition of November 14, 1993: "They looked like some big horrible insect, the whole bunch of them together, not human beings at all. And I was also not only appalled at how they looked, but I was outraged that they should be marching on me, on me, an American!" The empire, it seemed, had occupied its own cities and turned on its own citizens. Going into exile did not bring a feeling of loss – quite the opposite.

In Toronto, Jacobs and her family found a city like the New York of earlier decades. "It's as if we've found the city we used to love", she remarked. And as she wrote in a 1969 editorial against the proposed Spadina Expressway soon after arriving: "Here is the most hopeful and healthy city in North America, still unmangled, still with options." In particular, Toronto was a city where immigrants were welcomed. "The city government, and many other city institutions", she noted later, "continually celebrate the ethnic differences among the citizens, and tirelessly emphasise that this diversity is a source of social and economic richness."[3] Moreover, community battles, such as stopping the construction of the Spadina, were more easily fought – and more likely won. In that *Village Voice* article, Jacobs described the municipal board hearings as "orderly, dignified, honest, no displays of ego, no phonies, just a real exchange of information. Nothing like New York at all. Even the politicians here are different. In fact there is only one Toronto politician who scares me and that's because he's just like a New York politician: sneaky, devious, dangerous."

Asked whether Toronto, with all of its high-rise construction, was turning into another New York, she responded with hope that Torontonians, and other Canadians, would look to the US as an object lesson of what not to do. She observed:

> The builders and highway people are tearing it [Toronto] down as fast as they can, but they're being fought before things get as bad as they are in New York. We're lucky here, you know. The States

> serves as a sort of early warning system for Canada. We can look down and see what's going wrong in New York and Cleveland and then try to avoid the same thing happening here. But it's not easy, because the same destructive forces are at work in Canada.

In Canada, Jacobs also found a less militaristic and imperial nation. As she told the *Toronto Star* in October, 1970, referring to the United States: "I hate spending money for taxes that go to war goods, expressways, and secret police." In 1974, she gave up her US citizenship to become a Canadian. Of the naturalisation process, she recalled in a letter to her mother written in September of that year, that "in a paper we had been given, upon applying, about the duties of Canadian citizens, I was very pleased to see that one of our duties is 'to get along well with our neighbours'. This really is a remarkably nice, sane country."[4] Moreover, having already settled into her new community and soon become involved in local affairs – the activities of "self-government" – she wanted the right to vote, especially in the local elections, which she considered the most important.

However, as much as Jacobs admired Canada as a nation, she was not keen on the trappings of nationalism, whether economic or bureaucratic, or remote and bureaucratic control over local matters. By 1969, having finished *The Economy of Cities*, she was already contemplating *Cities and the Wealth of Nations* (1984) – in which she questioned the aggrandising concept of gross domestic product and the large nation-state. And in an interview with the *New York Times magazine*, published in May, 1969, she observed:

> I think it is also questionable that large nations are really viable governmental units any longer. They may be obsolete – like dinosaurs. The viable nations of the future may be on the scale of Sweden or Holland, rather than on the scale of the United States, China, or the Soviet Union.[5]

This sentiment was not new for Jacobs. Early in her career, in the 1940s, she rejected President Franklin Delano Roosevelt's federalism, not to mention his unprecedented third and fourth terms in office, fearing the eclipse of local self-determination. Decades later, she similarly rejected Canadian federalism. In *The Question of Separatism: Quebec and the Struggle over Sovereignty* (1980), she made the case for Quebec's independence. In *Toronto: Considering Self-Government* (2000, with Mary W. Rowe), she made the argument for greater independence for Toronto from its provincial and national governments.

Perhaps a surprising sentiment for an advocate of "great cities", Jacobs even believed that some cities could be too large – at least from the point of view of their governance. In 1969, echoing arguments she made in *The Death and Life of Great American Cities* for the decentralisation, or re-localisation, of city government, she observed: "Take New York. Back before the turn of the century, it was five cities. It was probably a mistake to consolidate them into one. Five autonomous city governments are probably not enough for New York now. Just because a city is a huge economic unit, it does not follow that it must be a huge governmental unit."

The great difficulty was how to organise local self-government – a topic of particular concern in *Death and Life* – while simultaneously arranging a system that could handle problems of large scales and indeterminate geographies, such as transit and pollution. As Jacobs observed in 1957, in an essay titled "Metropolitan Government" for the *Architectural Forum*, the United States' 174 metropolitan areas were a "weird melange of 16,210 separate units of government". This frequently irrational and sometimes hostile patchwork of overlapping jurisdictions made municipal and regional planning and governing challenging, if not impossible. For example, Cleveland's "jigsaw government", with its 60 or more municipalities, "cannot plan its waterfront rationally, nor can it distribute the rest of its services fairly". By contrast, Jacobs observed that Toronto was "the only metropolitan federation in operation thus far in North America" with its federation of the city and 12 suburban satellites, all of which were located in a single county.[6] This structure allowed for comprehensive planning and avoided the rivalries and hostilities between cities and the counties in which they were located. Politically, the result was something closer to a city-state. Economically, Jacobs would later go so far as to entertain the idea – set out in *Cities and the Wealth of Nations* – of replacing national currencies with individual city currencies.[7]

As Jacobs settled into life in Toronto, she continued fighting large-scale developments that were destroying the diverse fabric of the city. In 1973, she protested against a plan to demolish and replace 20 old houses with six identical apartment buildings. To stop the demolition, she, her sons, and other protestors tore down the fences surrounding the houses, temporarily halting the wrecking machinery. The action prompted Toronto's mayor to negotiate with the provincial authorities about the idea of renovating the homes and building the remaining (affordable) housing in the backyards and spaces between the old homes. As opposed to the original scheme, the variety of resulting buildings suited the various needs of the residents – singles, families, elderly couples, and widowers – and municipal support for the infill concept took hold. Although high-rise construction came to dominate parts of the city, in 1981, Jacobs observed that "Some of the infill building has been tall; most of it is low; but high or low these little plans have all been used to knit together again pieces of the city fabric that had become frayed or unraveled."[8]

Meanwhile, Jacobs returned to writing. *The Question of Separatism*, written in the late 1970s, was immediately concerned with the relatively local question of Quebec's sovereignty, but continued her overarching inquiry into the balance of cities' self-governance and nations' federal powers. When it came to federal powers, Jacobs worried about growing imperialism, as manifested both domestically and internationally. Having read Edward Gibbon's *The History of the Decline and Fall of the Roman Empire* years earlier, the nature of empire was not a new line of inquiry for her; already in *The Economy of Cities*, she observed, for example, that the great capitals of modern Europe "did not become great cities because they were the capitals. Cause and effect ran the other way." Of the Roman Empire specifically, she noted that once Roman "cities were no longer centres of economic opportunity (as they once had been) in the western empire... their inhabitants had become so oppressed by the official taskmasters that they had to be prohibited from fleeing into the country." And these were "*free* inhabitants, not slaves". Drawing the point home, she opined that the economy of the United States – in part because of the "economic conflicts" created by "racists and paternalists" – was in the process of stagnating, and that if the situation "proves to be profound and unremitting, it could be comparable to that of the later Roman Empire."

In *The Question of Separatism*, Jacobs reiterated her association of empire with oppression and inevitable decline. She observed that with centralised control oppression increased, stating: "The biggest and most thoroughly centralised governments have always, finally, required the special environment of oppression to continue to maintain themselves. And some could never have attained their great size at all had they not grown in that environment."[9]

And she observed that, throughout history, empires and very large nations – in part through oppression, sheer scale, complications, and the aggrandisements of bureaucracies and the powerful – "invariably reached a point when they behaved like decaying and disintegrating organisms, from ancient Persia to modern Britain."

So, was decline inevitable? Jacobs pondered the question. "Must the people of large sovereignties always be doomed to helplessness in the face of intractable problems, and to the eventual certainty of irreversible decline with all its hardships, waste and loss?" she asked.

Her answer, which was fully consistent with her arguments for self-government in *Death and Life*, was to pursue local self-determination, the decentralisation of power, and even to accept political separation, succession, or independence. She offered the independence of Canada, Australia, New Zealand, Iceland, and Norway as some examples of peaceful secessions from an empire, while also noting a long list of secessions or secession attempts that emerged from foreign or civil wars and sometimes bloody separatist movements. The separation of Norway from Sweden, to which she devoted a chapter, was of particular interest to her as one where a split was achieved without terrorism or warfare, an outcome she felt "did honour not only to both [countries] but also to civilisation". Of Sweden, the more powerful nation, Jacobs remarked: "In striking contrast to so many nations of 19th-century Europe, Sweden did not embark upon seizures of empire abroad; quite as strikingly, its government did not behave imperialistically at home. The behaviour was all of a piece, both at home and abroad, as nations' behaviour so frequently is."[10]

In *Cities and the Wealth of Nations*, an argument for the key role of urban economies and city-based innovations, Jacobs' thinking about the fall of empires – the United States in particular – continued. She observed: "Today the Soviet Union and the United States each predicts and anticipates the economic decline of the other. Neither will be disappointed." She believed that these countries' prolonged militarism, and the other costs necessary to maintain their empires, would be their ultimate downfall. She argued that "imperial decline is built right into imperial success" because "the very policies and transactions that are necessary to win, hold, and exploit an empire are destructive to an imperial power's own cities and cannot but help lead to their stagnation and decay."

As Jacobs had long maintained, without vital cities, a nation or empire lacked its economic and cultural engines. Looking at the history of empires including Persia, Rome, Byzantium, Turkey, Spain, Portugal, France, Britain, and others, she noted: "The longer an empire holds together, the poorer and more economically backward it tends to become." For its part, Jacobs observed, the United States "has been milking its cities and city regions even more prodigiously [than the Soviet Union], a feat possible because, being more numerous, more highly developed, and richer, American cities have had more to yield than Soviet cities". The result of the arms race and its economic emphasis on military production was that city economies were subsidising "transplant regions" through "transactions of decline", undermining "the contexts in which Americans can expand" and causing "economic life" to constrict.

Jacobs wrote *Cities and the Wealth of Nations* early in the Reagan and Thatcher regimes, as the post-war Keynesian economic paradigm gave way to 'neoconservatism' and 'neoliberalism' in the US and UK respectively. Indeed, her book was in part prompted by the failure of Keynesian and Chicago School monetarist economic theories to account for, or relieve, 'stagflation' – the combination of rising prices and unemployment – in those and other advanced countries. Jacobs' economic analysis was relatively simple: the condition of high prices and too little work was a "normal and ordinary condition to be found in poor and backward economies the world over". Moreover, it was commonplace in poor and backward parts of the US and other countries. What was new about 'stagflation' was that the twin afflictions had begun to victimise the country as a whole. Ultimately, the problem was emotional as much as economic: it was hard to admit that these countries were "sliding into profound economic decline".

Since the 1950s, the reaction of neoconservatives and neoliberals has been to promote military spending, privatisation, and deregulation to support corporations, and to cut public spending and social programmes. But as Jacobs indicated, reactions to economic problems were, and are, emotional – and ideological. Historian Nancy MacLean has documented the rise and spread of Hayekian neoliberalism and Chicago School economic ideology in *Democracy in Chains: The Deep History of the Radical Right's Stealth Plan for America* (2017). While focused on the emblematic career of the economist James McGill Buchanan, "a zealous advocate of the market order", MacLean reveals the sweeping, often racist, social agenda of a growing cadre of neoliberal/libertarian economists and their wealthy and super-wealthy backers. With a fear of 'socialism' bordering on psychosis, these pioneering conservatives became fervently hostile not only to the state, but to government, the public sphere, and ultimately democracy itself. Like their contemporary followers, these libertarians believed that the individual good of the wealthy and powerful was more noble and important than the good, and even the humanity, of those lacking wealth and power. Capitalism trumped democracy. In an effort to sell this idea, in 1962, Buchanan argued that democracy, as majority rule, violated "the liberty" of the elite. Such ideas drew directly on those of John C. Calhoun, whose support for slavery and hostility to the federal government, and the democratic processes that might abolish slavery, led to the Civil War. In the contemporary context, this philosophy was, and is, used not only to rationalise and promote racist segregation and discrimination, and general hostility to government and the public realm, but also to the closure of public schools, regressive tax reform, deregulation of industry, anti-city policies, ideas of personhood for corporations and "running government like a business", gerrymandering, and voter suppression. In the Trump era, partisans will go so far as to make excuses for executive corruption and even collusion with anti-democratic enemies of the state.

In *Becoming Jane Jacobs*, I addressed claims that Jacobs herself was a libertarian and that her ideas were aligned with, and even influenced by, the pioneering neoliberal economist Friedrich Hayek. I explained that Jacobs explicitly rejected libertarian ideology when she stated, in 1985, that "Margaret Thatcher's government *appalls* me." She added:

"As for not wanting to help the poor or saying 'let everyone stand on their own feet,' no, I don't believe that at all."[11] Although both Jacobs and Hayek were interested in complex systems and the phenomena of self-organisation, she did not share Hayek's belief in the market, self-interest, and the price mechanism as the best tools for organising a society. Unlike Hayek, who abhorred the concept of "social justice", she was not a social Darwinist, quite the opposite. Jacobs regarded cooperation and mutual support as the most important forces in shaping civilised human societies, and, of course, cities.

Ignoring Jacobs' radical politics of neighbourhood organisation, among other aspects of her thinking, conservatives and libertarians have long confused her communitarianism and localism for atomistic individualism and the anti-government positions of neoliberals. They have assumed that someone who does not subscribe wholesale to the left politics of the day must be right-wing. Meanwhile, self-described libertarians ignore the use of police or military force on protestors; indeed, many welcome it, as Naomi Klein observed (in *The Shock Doctrine: the rise of disaster capitalism*), as part of a domestic "shock doctrine" aspiring to criminalise political opposition. Yet it was such use of force against the Vietnam protests, and in imperialistic wars, that led Jacobs to her most outspoken criticisms of the government. In *Systems of Survival* (1992), Jacobs, speaking through one of her characters, observed:

> I used to think of government – meaning good government – as the major force at work in the civilising process. Now I'm inclined to think of government as being essentially barbaric – barbaric in its origins and forever susceptible to barbaric actions and aims. But don't get me wrong. We need it.

Nevertheless, as Jacobs explained in *Systems*, a countervailing force was needed to keep the "guardian" role of government in check, and vice versa. "Some other civilising agent must therefore be necessary", she wrote, calling this the "commercial moral system", which included voluntary trading and exchange of all kinds, cultural and economic. Together, the cooperative dynamic of the two moral systems, not one of them independently, was the basis of flourishing civilisations. She continued:

> This, I now think, is the guardian-commercial symbiosis that combats force, fraud, and unconscionable greed in commercial life – and simultaneously impels guardians to respect private plans, private property, and personal rights. Mutual support of morally contradictory trading and taking [by government, through taxation, police powers etc]; it tames both activities and their derivatives. So perhaps we have a useful definition of civilisation: reasonably workable guardian-commercial symbiosis.

As with *Cities and the Wealth of Nations*, it is no coincidence that Jacobs wrote *Systems of Survival* in the wake of the Reagan/Thatcher era. As an analysis of the "moral foundations of commerce and politics", *Systems* rejected the idea that government should be run like a business. Inspired by Plato's *Republic*, Jacobs sought to show that commerce and governance required two completely different moral systems and that the idea of applying the moral system appropriate for business to government was, at best, deeply misguided. At worst, it was an invitation to the systemic corruption that resulted from the inappropriate mixing of moral systems' values and activities in inappropriate contexts. For example, while trading and selling are appropriate in the marketplace, government officials are expected not to sell votes, collude with corporate interests and serve private donors, or profit from office or the markets that they are charged with regulating. For these reasons, she wrote, "officials are forbidden to take a job in a business they have regulated, or a job lobbying former guardian colleagues, until a year or two has elapsed after they have left government service".

Similarly, the Thatcher/Reagan era calls for deregulation and privatisation typically benefited corporate interests. Jacobs agreed, stating: "Where governments have unadvisedly taken on commercial functions, privatisation of those enterprises makes sense morally and financially." However, this did not alter the fact that "Government agencies are entangled in commerce, the more complex a society, the more so. It's simple-minded to suppose privatisation can eliminate that."

When it came to the corruption of commercial culture, Jacobs noted: "The eighties [1980s] were very educational." The ideology of these years was not subtle. Looking, for example, at the language used in the *Wall Street Journal* to report on the activities of investment bankers and their clients in the mid-1980s, she observed that their rhetoric was drawn from war reporting. "No guns and axes, to be sure", she wrote. "But to find words for the aggression, conquest, mayhem, and defences being reported it was necessary to resort to war imagery. Commercial imagery can't supply them. The protagonists invented and named such weaponry as poison pills, white knights, and greenmail." As represented by the catchphrase "Greed is good" – popularised by the semi-fictional corporate raider protagonist of the film *Wall Street* (1987) – basic standards of commercial morality and business ethics were corrupted in these years.

Following her study of morality and corruption, Jacobs' sequel to *Systems, The Nature of Economies* (2000), was a hopeful book. Drawing, among other scientific and economic sources, on *Gaia: A New Look at Life on Earth* (1979/95) by James Lovelock, *The Next Economy* (1983) by Paul Hawken, *Biomimicry* (1997) by Janine Benyus, *Symbiotic Planet: A New View of Evolution* (1998) by Lynn Margulis, and the research that led to *Cradle to Cradle: Remaking the Way We Make Things* (2008) by William McDonough, Jacobs sought to revive the harmonious classical relationship between ecology (*oecology*) and economics (*oikonomia*). As the "green revolution" and a growing public consciousness of environmentalism at a global scale seemed to be finally taking hold, she was hopeful that the time was ripe for a paradigmatic shift in thinking about natural resources, economic production, and material flows. Nevertheless, underlying the positive message of her second-to-last book, *The Nature of Economies*, was nothing less than the question of "the ability of the human race to rescue itself from collapse as a species".

Appearing approximately 15 years later, *Dark Age Ahead* (2004), Jacobs' final book, was far less optimistic. The post-9/11 world was gripped by xenophobia, war, and imperialism. The moralities of both guardian and commercial institutions remained in doubt. Not one to be Pollyannaish, Jacobs returned to thinking about the collapse of the Roman Empire, and, greatly taken by evolutionary biologist and cultural anthropologist Jared Diamond's writing about the collapse of other civilisations, she speculated on systemic threats to "North American culture". The reasons she had left the US seemed to have caught up, at least in part, with Canada.

Dark Age Ahead focused on five essential cultural pillars that Jacobs saw as under threat of collapse: community and family; higher education; science and fact-based thinking; taxation and government; the self-regulation of professions. The threat came from neoconservative (or neoliberal) ideology, particularly as related to public investments, but also the systemic corruption of the kind she warned against in *Systems of Survival*, as it destroyed the foundational institutions and traditions built on trust. At the outset, Jacobs explained that she focused on these five areas as compared to another list of five critical failures – racism; profligate environmental destruction; crime; voters' mistrust of politicians and resulting lack of democratic participation; and the growing gulf between the rich and poor – because she felt that the latter five were often symptoms of the first. Crime, for example, was related to breakdowns in community as well as neoliberal "austerity" economics. Environmental destruction was related to the decline of fact-based thinking. Private prisons were a product of both neoliberal ideas of "reinvented government" and an example of the "monstrous moral hybrids" she described in *Systems*. Racism and sexism, meanwhile, were profligate.

To be sure, Jacobs covered many areas of concern with greater or lesser attention in her final book. Written in a hurry in her 80s, shortly before her death in 2006, it was regarded by some critics as either poorly edited or too gloomy, or both. In retrospect, however, Jacobs accurately predicted the cultural decline represented by the Trump regime. Indeed, she could well have been speaking of 2017 when she wrote:

> Legions of hired liars labour to disconnect reality from all manner of images – images of personalities, of legislation, of corporations, of places, and of activities. Spin-doctors, virtuosos of deceptive image-making and damage control, have become authoritative spokespersons in political campaigns and troubled institutions, able not only to disconnect reality but to construct new reality.

Next pages: Donald Trump as a guest of the talk-show host Jay Leno in *The Tonight Show* on NBC, 7 September 2004.

Jacobs concluded *Dark Age Ahead* by observing that the United States "has often been equated with Rome by historians and social commentators seeking modern lessons from Rome's mistakes." But she was not hopeful that the nation would recover from its spiral of decline. She observed: "History has repeatedly demonstrated that

empires seldom seem to retain sufficient cultural self-awareness to prevent them from overreaching and overgrasping." Moreover, she added: "They have neglected to recognise that the true power of successful culture resides in its example." Lastly, she noted: "Any culture that jettisons the values that have given it competence, adaptability, and identity becomes weak and hollow. A culture can avoid that hazard only by tenaciously retaining the underlying values responsible for the culture's nature and success." It is only too easy now to pair events of the past couple of years with Jacobs' observations. She ended *Dark Age Ahead* by quoting Lincoln's expression of "government of the people, by the people, and for the people" as among the most important "core values" of the nation. She would be very sad to see how tarnished that value – and the example to the world built upon it – has become. She would be shocked by the extent to which American democracy has been undermined by career politicians and the corporate donors that fund them.

Jacobs could not predict the future. She did not know how things would turn out. While she read history and referred to complexity science and non-linear dynamics, she turned to metaphors of pendulums and spirals to describe the drama of civilisation, writing:

> Some people think optimistically that if things get bad enough, they will get better because of the reaction of beneficent pendulums. When a culture is working wholesomely, beneficent pendulum swings – effective feedback – do occur. Corrective stabilisation is one of the great services of democracy, with its feedback to rulers from the protesting and voting public... But powerful persons and groups that find it in their interest to prevent adaptive corrections have many ways of thwarting self-organising stabilisers.

Between the protesting, voting public and the powerful, she did not know who would win. But, no, she would not be coming home.

1 Clark Whelton, "Won't you come home, Jane Jacobs?", *The Village Voice* (6 July, 1972).

2 Susan Brownmiller, "Jane Jacobs", *Vogue* (May 1969); Max Allen (ed.), *Ideas That Matter: The Worlds of Jane Jacobs* (Owen Sound: Ginger Press, 1997), p. 22.

3 Jane Jacobs, "The Responsibility of Cities", in Samuel Zipp & Nathan Storring, *Vital Little Plans* (London: Short Books 2017), pp. 197–210.

4 Jane Jacobs in a letter to her mother (Sept. 21, 1974), cited in Allen (ed., 1997), p. 143.

5 Leticia Kent, "Jane Jacobs: Against Urban Renewal", in Allen (ed., 1997), p. 22.

6 Peter L. Laurence, *Becoming Jane Jacobs* (Philadelphia: University of Pennsylvania Press, 2016); Jane Jacobs, "Metropolitan Government", *Architectural Forum*, vol. 107 (August 1957), p. 124 and p. 204.

7 Jane Jacobs, *Cities and the Wealth of Nations* (New York: Vintage Books, 1984), p. 158.

8 Jane Jacobs, "Big Plans and Little Plans", in Allen (ed., 1997), pp. 124–125.

9 Jane Jacobs, *The Question of Separatism: Quebec and the Struggle over Sovereignty* (New York: Random House, 1980), p. 77.

10 Today, Norway and Sweden are respectively ranked 1 and 3 in the world "Democracy Index", a fact that probably correlates with their amicable relationship. See *The Economist Intelligence Unit*, "Democracy Index 2016", *The Economist*, http://www.eiu.com/topic/democracy-index.

11 Thatcher's and Reagan's social and economic policies were significantly influenced by Hayek. See https://www.margaretthatcher.org/archive/Hayek.asp.

CHAPTER XV

Interview: The Trouble We're In, and The Changes to Come

Blake Harris

THROUGHOUT HER WRITING, Jacobs took a special interest in concepts such as growth and innovation and what she achieved has in turn influenced eminent economists such as Robert Lucas and Paul Krugman. Lucas used her arguments in *The Economy of Cities* and *Cities and the Wealth of Nations* to revise his understanding of the significance of the social environment for economic development, and also the economic effects of an ongoing exchange of knowledge in that environment.[1] Her analysis of the growth phenomenon drew attention to the need for room for unpredictability and open paths in the companies' surroundings. In *The Nature of Economies* she made an effort to situate our understanding of the economy within the domain of Nature and to clarify the links between nature's resource and feedback flows and man-made economic processes.

Late in her life, Jacobs had an ambition to summarise all of her economic thinking in a single book which had the working title *Uncovering the Economy: A New Hypothesis*, though she never managed to finish it.[2] In this interview, published in 2002, Jacobs gives her own words about where she was standing in her last years on economic questions: What is the role of cities for future innovation? What risks are our economies facing today if they can't change? How can we create a balance between growth and the use of natural resources?

JESPER MEIJLING AND TIGRAN HAAS

Jane Jacobs outside her home in Toronto, 1995.

Q. *Apart from the many other professions that have been listening to you, now economists, according to press reports, are also beginning to take you seriously. Which particular ideas would you want them to pay attention to in terms of how we view cities?*

A. How important innovation is to us. How we cannot, and in fact we never could, just continue to do the same thing without courting utter disaster, because you can't exploit the same resources too long. You can't do the same thing monotonously too long. If there is one thing that will save us, it is innovating in time. We have reached a stage when we must mimic nature and how nature does things, not in a superficial way, but very deeply.

Q. *There are some who say that cities are losing their capacity to be the crucibles of value-creation. It is a very dark view, that cities are ceasing to be the intellectual engines.*

A. We are in trouble. Anyone who thinks about it and looks at life knows that we are in a lot of trouble.

Q. *What happens if cities become these sterile, non-listened-to places?*

A. This has happened historically quite a few times. When we say the Dark Ages, we mean a particular time in European history when that happened. But the more prehistory and the more histories other than Europe that have been looked into, the more clear it becomes that there have been quite a few dark ages.

Q. *Do you have any sense that creativity is fleeing the cities, going off somewhere else where it feels safer, where schools are better? Are the bright, creative people leaving the cities?*

A. Nothing goes on forever; the same thing doesn't go on forever. For people who want to project trends, the one trend you know won't happen is a continuation of what is happening now. It may be higher, it may be lower, but nothing stays that much the same. So we have all these problems of sprawl. It is very expensive in land, it is very expensive in energy, very expensive in time and money. And those are good reasons why it won't go on. But that is not why it won't go on. It is because every few generations comes along a generation that just despises what the generations before it did. That happened at the end of Victorianism. It also happened at the beginning of Victorianism, when the whole classic form of architecture and site planning that was derived from it – and even furnishings – were jettisoned.

When this happens, the generation that experiences this big change in taste – I don't know a better word for it, but it is more than taste – they get absolutely ruthless about what the previous generations did. They build what would have been considered very inappropriate. They tear down what they want, they drive through what they want. That's going to happen with the present suburbs. Some generation is going to come along that just despises them and is going to treat them that way and do something else with them. What will they do? I don't know and nobody knows. You can see some germs of some possibilities now – the new urbanism. There is already a revulsion against modern architecture. And I think we are probably very near the brink of one of these big changes in taste again. And that always means big changes in function, too.

Q. *There are communities where there is a very real choice between development or the preservation of the land, the water, the landscape, sometimes people's health. If you put that decision into the hands of the people, the community, they will almost inevitably choose the jobs and the development. How do you balance that with your thoughts that if you put it into the hands of the people, it will work?*

A. Well, take Oregon, for example. They would go to where the logging was, set up their saw mill, do the logging, cut all the trees, and leave. And the town collapses. That kind of exploitation, not only with logging, but mines and all sorts of resource places, even farms – anything that is built on that kind of exploitation – is very insecure. Anything which is overexploited is going to end up in economic disaster for everybody concerned.

Q. *So you have to regulate.*

A. No, you have to do it differently. You don't just exploit but do it more slowly. That's no answer. It is a way of using the land differently so it is sustainable, not just so that you can lengthen the moment you can exploit it. The way you make things sustainable is largely by diversification, adding things that haven't been done. You know, nature itself is not simple. It is very, very complicated. And any eco-system is an extremely complicated thing. The moment we try to simplify it and exploit one thing, or make some sort of a mono-culture, we are going to be in trouble. The way to deal with nature in an harmonious way is to recognize that it is diverse, not just in terms of the whole globe, but also in any single place. In one logging town, for instance, one solution to getting jobs was to put up cranberries, and there is now a nice mail-order business of cranberry products that didn't exist before. And the wood that they cut, instead of just shipping it all out, if you can create jobs making products from that wood, you don't need to cut as much wood and you still have good jobs, there are more of them and it is more sustainable. That's the idea in general, you diversify.

Q. *But who makes the decision about the diversification?*

A. You can't make people creative by telling them, "Be creative". It has to be economically sound for them to be creative, and feasible both for the area itself and for what they can do. You can, however, look to see what is missing. You can't just say to people, "Don't do that". You have to say, "Hey, you are able to do this". You have to be positive, not just negative. The trouble with regulations is they are always telling you what you can't do. You can show people what they can do, but not necessarily tell them they have to do it. You know there are so many bright people, so many good ideas, so much concern. You find this in lots and lots of localities. It's there. It often just needs a little encouragement to show how to use resources to better advantage and that you don't always have to do what you were always doing in the past, what your parents did or your grandparents did, if indeed the town lasted long enough for that.

Q. *What are the limits of regulation? Is it possible to make a generalization about what we should regulate?*

A. You have to be careful and not get abstract about this. You have to look at specific things, and they change over time. For instance, a few decades ago in Toronto, there was not a single outdoor café. Regulation against these had been made when the streets were full of horses and horseflies – when it really was not sanitary to sell food on the sidewalk and so on. The times have changed but the regulation had not.

In Toronto, as well, there were regulations about how many square feet of windows had to be with so many square feet of floor and the distance of buildings from each other [which prevented the conversion of a lot of downtown spaces into living spaces]. These regulations had all been made at a time when the tuberculosis rate was terribly high. These regulations about distance of buildings, width of courtyards, amount of windows, were all calculated to combat tuberculosis. We got at tuberculosis in other ways, but these regulations lived on.

So what is a good regulation? Well, for one thing, knowing why it is in there and when it is no longer necessary. Knowing when a different regulation is necessary. But these are things that governments and bureaucracies are generally very bad at. There are planning departments which have learned to do a lot of things but they often have not learned to do away with useless regulations. Canada and the United States are just full of architects who just break their hearts fighting regulations that are destructive. They have wonderful ideas, beautiful ideas about what they can do.

Q. *When you first moved to Toronto from New York, were there elements in Toronto, because it was a smaller city, that made you more optimistic that you could make more of a difference there compared to New York, where everything had become so politicized, so big?*

A. No. I thought it was an adventure, how nice and so on. And then we heard about this expressway that was coming through right where we lived, and my husband said, "Oh my God, another expressway". And we had to get into that. There are responsibilities you can't evade if you find yourself in an expressway path. You have to do something about it. But, you know, I'm like most people in this. I have other things to do. I don't like getting in these fights. I hate the government making my life absurd. I don't want the government to set an agenda for what I have to be doing by it being so stupid that I have to devote myself to that. I have other things to do. And this is true of most people. It is really an outrage when you come to think of it. Here are all these people who get paid for government jobs, and we the taxpayers are paying them. And how are they spending their time? Making life miserable for us so we can hardly earn the money to pay their wages because we are so busy fighting them. That's what I mean by making our lives absurd.

Q. *When you start talking about the big role of government and that it messes around too much in people's lives sometimes, is there a danger that one can become too free-enterprise, that one is forgetting the social network that government can provide?*

A. You are putting words in my mouth. I never said that government was messing around too much in our lives. I said it was doing stupid things. That's not the same thing at all. It may be doing too little in our lives and still be doing stupid things. It's not an ideological thing.

Q. *Ideological labels don't stick too well to you.*

A. You try, if you can, to get people to look at the specific thing that is happening and not try to generalize it as an ideology. Ideologies, no matter what kind, are one of the greatest afflictions, because they blind us to seeing what is going on or to what is being done.

Q. *But you have lived and been civically active first in New York and then in Toronto. Can you describe the difference you found between the two cities?*

A. I know very well what people are struggling to do in New York. In the old community I used to live in, I know how hard people worked all the time, harder than practically anyone in Toronto works on civic things. Because they were so much more under the gun in New York, so much more desperate. And I get that community – the West Village community – newsletter still once a month and see what they are going through. And every time I read it, I almost weep for them, how hard they are working on things. So, no, people in Toronto don't work harder at it than New Yorkers. I think the thing is that they are institutionally so different. It is just so much more feasible here in Toronto for citizens to make a decent difference.

Q. *Why? What is the different culture? Is it an individualistic as opposed to a more collective approach?*

A. No. No. The minute you get into all these loose abstractions – I think it is much more concrete. I think it is the size of the bureaucracies in New York. It's the huge amounts of money for certain things that became available to New York and other American cities from the federal government. And one attitude that does make a difference – I think that the American melting pot compared to the Canadian mosaic has been very destructive to the United States. But mostly, it's the way their institutions work.

Q. *You have talked about self-organizing states. Today, there are these twin pulls of globalization one way and national identities going the other way.*

A. Everything in nature is self-organized, and a whole lot of what human beings do is self-organized. And there are all sorts of states that were self-organized. But as soon as you get above a certain size, and I don't know what that size is, but we could easily find out by looking at the some 200 sovereign states in the world today. But as soon as you get above a certain size, it is not self-organized at all. It has gotten that size by conquest. And that is the very opposite of being self-organized.

Q. *What does self-organized mean?*

A. Well, it means there wasn't a plan and command structure that made the thing, that decreed it and then shaped it. A great many things now which are done by command are not self-organized any more. They started as self-organized, because that is the way that creativity usually happens. For example, our postal service. People got documents and messages around to each other before there were any postal services.

And finally, when there was enough of this and enough custom and systems had grown up about who paid and how much you paid and how you sent these things, finally governments took them over and had institutional postal services. But it was a self-organized system before that. Commercial law was that way. There was no such thing as commercial law under feudalism, and the merchants themselves made their courts and supported them and abided by the rules. And they set them up wherever it was convenient for the merchants and ship owners. All of these were taken over by governments after they were established. Governments are very uninventive. That is one difference between something that is self-organized. It grows what you might call organically. Some things always remain self-organized and self-regulated.

Q. *Lately, you have been fighting the amalgamation of a number of cities around Toronto into the new megacity of Toronto.*

A. Well, I think this is so ill-conceived, the Toronto megacity, from so many directions, that there is not going to be much reason to think that we can work it tolerably. It is something that is going to have to be wiggled out of somehow, probably by transformation rather than reversal. One thing is, of the expenditures this megacity is going to have to make – responsibility and the funds are not combined. And the city won't have the power, and yet is going to have to pay 80 percent of the funds for various programs, if I have it correctly. It is all out of balance. And that will be quite a disaster, as it always is when you get responsibility and power uncoupled from each other. The other thing is we are going to have much bigger municipal bureaucracies than we have ever had to contend with. And coming from a big city which amalgamated its boroughs and then began running downhill, I understand how awful it is working with great big bureaucracies.

Big bureaucracies have to go on the premise that one size fits all. I have always thought [that] they work to the lowest common denominator. It wouldn't be any different if it was the highest common denominator. The idea that they have to put as much as possible into a common denominator – Toronto had escaped that with its different municipalities, not only because they were separate, but because they are small enough to make these distinctions if they wanted and do a better job. And a big one can't. The idea that big bureaucracies are efficient, is that ever a laugh! If anybody has ever tried to deal with a great big bureaucracy, in comparison to a small one, which one do you think is more efficient?

But I also don't want to sound too negative. Quite often, our governments have done good things. If the government is doing something good, support it. But you have to have a point of view that nobody is going to swat you and make you lie down just because there is a great big thing – not being intimidated by the size and difficulties of something. And keeping the idea that if the government is doing something wrong, you never give up on it.

Q. *Without even trying to pretend to get a little sense of your ideas, but whether it is economics, how energy can overflow into other areas, or whether it is in terms of neighborhood activities and the creative things that make a neighborhood, where will the core of change and innovation be in this new megacity? Will they be destroyed? Will they still be there?*

A. You know, you can't predict these things. They are self-organizing. They are surprising. By cores, I take it you mean incubation modes and things like that – they happen where they will. In hindsight, you can often see why. But it is quite futile to try to predict it. And it is also futile to attempt to control it. That is mostly suppressing. These things come out of human creativity. You can just rejoice at it and try not to stop it.

Q. *What do you do when you can't predict? You don't just sit there and wait for these wonderful things to start bubbling up.*

A. Oh no, you are part of the bubble.

Q. *So much of what you have talked about and thought about over the years in terms of neighborhoods, so much of it is about people going outward, whether it is on the street, whether it's their neighbor, whether it is in their community. Yet there is a new concern that we might start turning inward with our computers, in our little nests at home. Are you concerned that this computerized world is also going to change the focus of the neighborhood?*

A city in transition: The ongoing building of the fourth tower in the Toronto Dominion Centre 1984.

A. [There is] a very persuasive argument that the computer, in the form of things like the World Wide Web and the Internet, is actually [giving] people firsthand experience with use of a Web and making virtual changes in a Web-like way. This is not real. But after all, quirks and quarks and atoms are not real, for all we know. But thinking of them, picturing them and seeing the world with these things, really illuminates our understanding. It may be untruthful and it may be wrong, but usually, each of these things gets a little nearer the truth. So this Web-thinking in the place of the mechanical, cause/effect kind of thinking is certainly closer to the truth. The use of the computer [may be] indispensable to this, both for the complications we have to understand and have begun to understand and also because of a different notion this gives people. You know it's always been available to people that they be hermits. But think of how few of them have been. So, no, I don't think the human race will suddenly be smitten with an overwhelming urge to become hermits because of a new machine.

Q. *Do you see a more exciting time today, with these new technologies? Or have we become more cynical?*

A. I think that the world is getting more exciting. I think the end of the Cold War, which made the whole world in many ways absurd.... Think of how many idiotic things were done, on both sides, everywhere, because of the exigencies of that cold war. It has been a great liberation to have that off us. But also, we are living, I am convinced, in one of the most intellectually exciting times the human race has ever gone through. We are emerging from this linear cause-and-effect way of seeing the world into a way that has really been led by the ecologists, into a Web world, beginning to understand relationships in quite a different way. And it is affecting everything. And no end of people have grasped this and are seeing the world differently and analyzing things differently and seeing possibilities differently – basically in a very hopeful way. And I think this is awfully exciting. People who are younger than I am, you are lucky. You can play a part in what I think can be an extremely hopeful stage.

Q. *Are people puzzled that you are now into economic theories and even biology? Many people thought you were just into city planning and building neighborhoods. Do people shake their heads and not get it?*

A. No, people seem to get it. They don't really find it outlandish that one would also bring in biology. Lots of people have been thinking, in some ways, along the same lines. You know, I think we are misled by universities and other formal intellectual places into thinking that there are actually separate fields of knowledge. And most people know that there aren't. But they are always getting victimized somehow by the idea that there are. And they are delighted when in some respectable way it becomes clear that there are not separate fields of knowledge, that they link up. That life and the Earth and everything in it really is a seamless web, and that's not merely a poetic expression. It is a very functional thing, that it is a seamless web, and that it is possible to understand something about these webs.

Reprinted with permission from Blake Harris and Steve Towns, Editor of Government Technology Magazine, 2010

Next pages: Jane Jacobs, here in the twilight of her days in front of the high-rise silhouette of Toronto's business district.

1 Robert E. Lucas, "On the mechanics of economic development", *Journal of Monetary Economics*, no. 22 (1988), p. 13, pp. 37–39. See also Paul Krugman, *Development, Geography and Economic Theory* (Cambridge: The MIT Press, 1995).

2 See: Samuel Zipp & Nathan Storring (ed.), *Vital Little Plans: The Short Works of Jane Jacobs* (London: Short Books, 2016), pp. 317–337.

Bibliography – The Books of Jane Jacobs

Constitutional Chaff: Rejected Suggestions of the Constitutional Convention of 1787 (1941)
Jacobs' first book, published by Columbia University Press under her maiden name of Jane Butzner, came out when she was 25 years old and had been studying economic geography, among other things, at Columbia University in New York. *Constitutional Chaff* looks into the debate surrounding the first constitution of the United States, the most central document in the country's political history. Jacobs traces an 'archaeology' of each of the seven articles of the constitution adopted in 1788, and sets out the draft alternatives that were considered and rejected – and the discussions that led to the compromise that was finally reached. In this book, Jacobs establishes a sort of a first draft of the topics that would run throughout her writing: the connections between public debate, thought systems, civilisation and the construct of Society, as well as the idea of self-determination in relation to a common order.

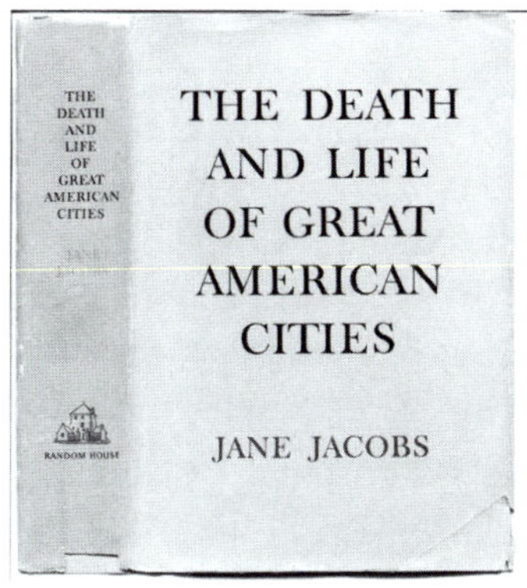

The Death and Life of Great American Cities (1961)
Arguably the most influential book ever published about town planning, and Jacobs' big breakthrough work. After beginning in freelance journalism in the 1930s writing about the work, life and economies of the city, based on explorations in New York's various industrial districts, and work-

ing herself into an editorial career specialised in town planning and urban development at a high professional level in the 1950s, she had eventually collected the material and analysis that resulted in this 450-page text. Using the meticulous observations and conclusions she made of her home quarter in New York's Greenwich Village, among other places, Jacobs breaks down the intentions of modernist town planning and shows how it is not capable of delivering what it promised in terms of safety, health and neighbourliness when new high-rise projects are built. In contrast, this is what the existing, gradually developed city can fulfill. In the second and third sections of the book Jacobs takes her argument further, focusing on what modernist planners appeared to have forgotten: the city's economic vitality. Jacobs' central formula for this revolves around diversity, which she illustrates with reference to Manhattan's changing urban environments, in contrast to the modernist view of the city as a sharply defined and completed work of art. Town planning that aims for accessibility, close connections and diversity in a living city produces more transactions between different players, more opportunities for businesses and better social and economic sustainability. Jacobs' criticism of what she sees as poor pseudoscience in planning finds support in the emerging systems theories at that time, for example cybernetics and complexity theory, which influence her own analysis of people's behaviour in cities and cities' economic behaviour. Her books *The Economy of Cities* and *Cities and the Wealth of Nations* are a direct continuation of the first work.

The Economy of Cities (1969)
In this book, Jacobs progresses from the make-up of the individual city to cities as a wider phenomenon. She discusses the historical origins of city societies and enquires why some cities grow but others do not. With her analysis in *Death and Life* as a starting point she develops a theory about growth, with a characteristically generous measure of

empiricism. New products and services do not emerge from nowhere but from existing products and services already found in cities – among the examples are 3M's office supplies products that derived from a mineral business and an outfit that developed brassieres which had their origins in other items of clothing in New York's garment district. They multiply by dividing, but not in the limited way that Adam Smith described but by branching out and creating new processes that emerge in specific work situations. The richer in content these situations are and the more there are of them, the more new work can develop – the greater the diversity, the greater the possibilities for growth. Jacobs uses this interpretation to explain what lies behind cities that exhibit strong growth. She calls it "import replacing" (not to be confused with what is known as import substitution): with sufficient diversity and knowledge in a city, businesses begin to produce the sort of things that they previously imported. One example she gives of this is the manufacture of spares for imported bicycles and mopeds in a city in East Asia which gradually developed into the manufacture of whole vehicles. Through refinement and making the process more effective, new products and services are created which in turn can be exported. Jacobs' analysis resembles the concept of innovative milieux, but she places more emphasis on the cities' broader and more mixed production environments and man's imitative tendency.

The Question of Separatism: Quebec and the Struggle Over Sovereignty (1980)
Canada's constitutional crisis and the struggle for independence in the province of Quebec are the subject of this book, but it is also develops a discussion about cities and the role of their economies within nations, and about the scope of smaller nations for self-determination and economic viability. Jacobs argues for the advantages of the province's independence to both Quebec and Canada and to their main

economic centres, Montreal and Toronto. Both sides would have the most welfare progress to gain from independence for Quebec – by using their own currencies and the driving force of each metropolitan area, the exchange between them would create greater prosperity than with just one unit. The most important comparison in the book is that of Norway and Sweden, the two new, smaller states enjoying peaceful development and economic success as a result of the dissolution of their union in 1905. Jacobs' point is that diversity is a potential economic strength, against the idea that uniformity, standardisation and bigger units are better by definition.

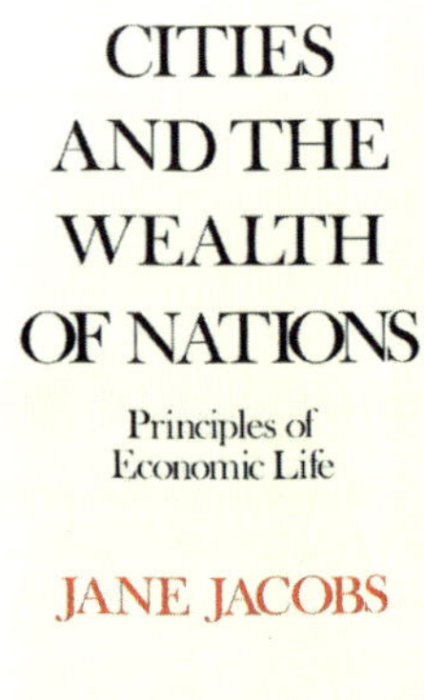

Cities and the Wealth of Nations: Principles of Economic Life (1984)
A direct sequel to *The Economy of Cities*, this book looks at how cities relate to regions and states. Contrary to what economics would have us believe, it is cities and not countries that drive economies in Jacobs' opinion. The cities *are* the economies. She investigates stagnating regions in order to understand what creates growth and what stifles it. The immediate background is the economic crisis of the 1970s in the West, and the concomitant stalling of development in the Third World, which triggered support measures. Did it work? How to create economic dynamics? Jacobs sees differences in the patterns between regions that have dynamic urban economies and those that do not. She argues that development cannot be "air-dropped in", nor can it be driven solely from a starting point of agriculture or a few selected industries. It needs to grow from within an exchange between cities, with the help of diversity and diversification built on skills and competitiveness. Cities and city regions in crisis can help one another. The opposite scenario, of diminishing exchange and severed connections, can lead to skills being lost and a downward spiral of decline. In the most striking example in the book, a destitute and culturally impoverished but previously flourishing mountain village in

rural Appalachia, Jacobs connects her detailed observations with a larger topic of civilisation's cohesive forces and possible decay, which also points the way to her last book, *Dark Age Ahead.*

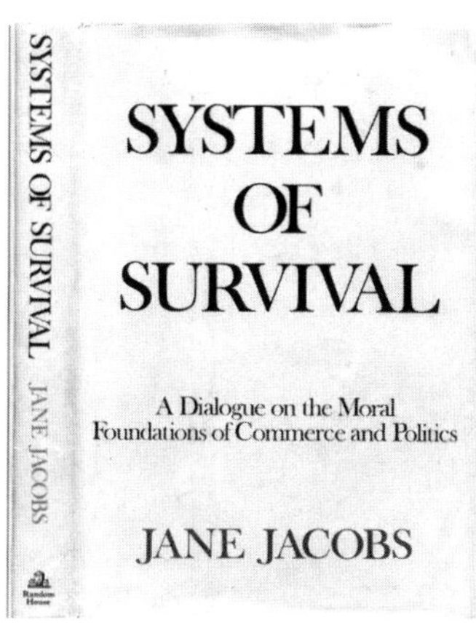

Systems of Survival: A Dialogue on the Moral Foundations of Commerce and Politics (1992)
What makes a society sustainable? In *Systems of Survival* Jacobs seeks a historically developed ethic for work and social life. Here it is not the physical and spatial structure of society that concerns her, nor is it yet private morality, but wider social sustainability and civilisation. What norms for our dealings in society help us to achieve our livelihood and survival in the long term? Through a Plato-inspired dialogue with a few friends in an apartment in New York, the analysis emerges around a wide variety of observations of what guides people in their dealings in different public and economic spheres – and how we work out right and wrong. The conclusion of this conversation is that we humans act with not one but two norm systems, which are very different from one another, and which we shift between depending on situations. Jacobs highlights the serious problems that arise if we mix the norms of these different spheres together without a real understanding. The book was written when the idea of New Public Management was beginning to penetrate public institutions at the beginning of the 1990s, the central idea being that the public sector would work better if it were organised like a market. One of the examples relates to New York's subway police who were supposed to be made more efficient by a model that saw officers being paid according to how many fare dodgers they arrested, and what the consequences of that were.

The Nature of Economies (2000)
An examination of the relationship between human economies and nature's system properties. The dialogue continues in the same New York apartment. Through the friends' conversations, Jacobs develops the idea that the first premise for understanding economic life is that it exists within nature, as a part of it, and cannot be understood outside it. Economies do not obey abstract laws, as both the neoclassical and the neoliberal understanding would have had us believe. The germ of the idea Jacobs develops in this book is already there in *Death and Life* in 1961: her interest in complex, adaptable systems and in self-organisation. Here she follows that through, testing comparisons with the growth processes and feed-back flows in nature's own "economy". Her conclusion is that the same underlying system is present in both ecosystems and economies: their development takes place through differentiation and new combinations, and expansion through diverse and many-sided uses of given energy resources – regardless of whether it is the sunlight necessary for photosynthesis, natural resources or human creativity.

Dark Age Ahead (2004)
About the present age and near future in North America. In her last book Jacobs develops a truly long-term perspective and returns to the phenomenon of cultural decline. She links back to her own analysis of social sustainability and civilisation in, for example, *Systems of Survival*, with a dark survey of contemporary tendencies. Jacobs describes – in the very early years of this century, that is – how the United States appear to be heading

for a cultural collapse that bears similarities to earlier periods of decline in world history: involving a collective loss of memory, in which people no longer remember even what they have forgotten of skills, values and the purpose of institutions. She highlights a number of the most important foundations of society which she thinks are being eroded: science and public faith in it; higher education that has been emptied of purpose; politics that have been run without responsibility and used, in spite of prosperity, to break down public life; even social life itself among citizens, which is withering away because of the increased difficulties people face in establishing their own lives and supporting their families. The risk, according to Jacobs, is that things have gone so far already that the US can no longer expect the pendulum to swing back: it is no longer a matter of swinging but of a downward spiral.

ABOUT THE AUTHORS

Ola Andersson is an architect and a partner in the firm, Andersson Arfwedson Arkitekter AB in Stockholm. He also writes about architecture and town planning in the daily press and specialist journals, including the newspaper *Dagens Nyheter.* Andersson has published books entitled *Vykort från utopia* ("A Postcard from Utopia", 2012); *Hitta hem* ("Finding the Way Home", 2014); and *Texter om Stockholm och andra städer* ("Texts about Stockholm and Other Cities", 2017).

Vania Ceccato is a professor at the Department of Urban Planning and Environment, School of Architecture and the Built Environment, KTH Royal Institute of Technology, Stockholm, Sweden. She coordinates the national network *Säkra platser* (Safe Places). Supported by The Swedish National Crime Prevention Council (BRÅ), Ceccato has initiated a series of projects about the development of local skills and information exchange around the context of crime and crime prevention. Among other things she has written *Rural Crime and Community Safety* (2014), and *Retail Crime: International evidence and prevention* (2018) in cooperation with Rachel Armitage.

Peter Elmlund has a Bachelor of Science in economics and specialises in urban development. Since 2002 he has led the Urban City Research programme as a director at Ax:son Johnson Foundation, a project that among other things provides support to a Masters course in sustainable urban design at the Faculty of Architecture School in Lund University – LTH (*Lunds Tekniska Högskola*) – and a research project about public space at the Royal Institute of Technology, Stockholm, where he is a guest researcher in residence. The project, "The Future of Places", which has developed into the Centre for the Future of Places at KTH, began as a collaboration between that foundation and UN Habitat, and its work has contributed to the content in "The New Urban Agenda", which the member countries signed at the Habitat III meeting in 2016. Among other things, Elmlund has written *Den välsignade tillväxten – tankelinjer kring ett århundrade av kapitalism, teknik, kultur och vetenskap* ("Blessed Growth: Thoughts on a century of capitalism, technology, culture and science", 1998), in cooperation with Kay Glans.

Jill L. Grant is a professor emerita in planning at Dalhousie University in Halifax, Canada. Among other things she has written about power and participation in town planning, sustainability issues and creative cities, with the emphasis on local factors and perspectives. Her writings include: *The Drama of Democracy: Contention and Dispute in Community Planning* (1994), and *Planning the Good Community: New Urbanism in theory and practice* (2006).

Tigran Haas is an associate professor focusing on urban planning and design, and sustainable city development at the School of Architecture and the Built Environment, at KTH. He is currently the director of the Centre for the Future of Places at KTH, and the programme director for urbanism studies at KTH. Dr Haas also heads the research programme for the project "Urban Form and Human Behaviour". Haas has published over 60 articles and eight books, of which the latest is the anthology *In the Post-Urban World: Innovative transformations in global city regions* (2018), in cooperation with Hans Westlund.

Blake J. Harris is the bestselling author of *Console Wars: Sega, Nintendo and the Battle that Defined a Generation* (2014), later adapted for television. Harris has written for *ESPN, IGN, Fast Company, /Film* and *The A.V. Club* and appears regularly on *Paul Scheer's How Did This Get Made?* podcast. In 2019, Harris published his second book, *The History of the Future,* which tells the story of Oculus, the virtual reality company that was ultimately acquired by Facebook.

Ebba Högström is a researcher, teacher and architect. She is senior lecturer in urban studies at the Swedish School of Planning at Blekinge Institute of Technology, Karlskrona, Sweden, where she is also director of the Masters programme in urban planning. Her research is geared towards planning, design and experience of built environments and landscapes. She focuses on societal institutions and has a special interest in ethnographic methods for capturing subjective experiences and analysing spatial experience. Among other things she has published *Caring Architecture: Institutions and relational practices* (2017), in cooperation with Catharina Nord.

Peter L. Laurence is an associate professor of architecture at the Clemson University School of Architecture in Clemson, South Carolina. As an architectural historian, Laurence specialises in 20th century American architectural and urban history, and is internationally recognised as an expert on the life and writing of Jane Jacobs. Laurence is the author of the renowned biography *Becoming Jane Jacobs* (2016), and is also a partner in "The Urbanism Project".

Michael W. Mehaffy is a guest researcher at the Centre for the Future of Places (CFP) of KTH. He is the head of the Sustasis Foundation, a think-tank dealing with urban sustainability, having its head office in Portland, Oregon. Mehaffy is active internationally as a researcher, educator and practitioner in urban design and strategic city development. He is a member of the editing panel of two international journals and the author or co-author of over 20 books, the latest being *Cities Alive: Jane Jacobs, Christopher Alexander, and the roots of the New Urban renaissance* (2017).

Jesper Meijling is a researcher, writer and architect. He is affiliated to the departments of historical studies and urban and regional studies at KTH. Meijling often studies the phenomenon of marketisation of public services and spaces, as in his book *Marknad på villovägar* ("Markets astray", 2014). His report on the new Karolinska hospital, "Nya Karolinska – ett pilotprojekt för marknadsstyrd vård?" ("Nya Karolinska – a pilot project for the marketisation of health care?", 2018), has attracted much attention. Meijling has also written about Jane Jacobs for Swedish readers, for example in his book *Påståenden om framtiden* ("Claims on the Future", 2008).

Eva Minoura is doctor of technology in town planning, a consultant for town planning projects in the early stages, and she leads the unit of professional skills at the Swedish architects' association (SA). On the basis of her field of research she lectures on how urban design and architecture promote social processes. She develops courses for working architects and is a specialist in shaping the interfaces between public and private interests in the built environment, for example in the design of gardens in residential settings.

Saskia Sassen is professor of sociology at Columbia University in New York. Her research covers migration, urban conditions and the state in the globalised economy, with a particular focus on inequality, gender and digitalisation. She has had a wide-ranging international influence on modern urban sociology and on a new understanding of globalisation. Among other things she has written *The Global City: New York, London, Tokyo* (1991), and *Territory, Authority, Rights: from medieval to global assemblages* (2006). Her latest book is *Expulsions: Brutality and complexity in the global economy* (2014), a detailed examination of the systems logic that enables deep economic divides and the destruction of natural resources.

Per Svensson is a political editor for the Swedish daily *Dagens Nyheter* and a writer. He was previously a senior columnist at *Sydsvenskan* and before that the editor-in-chief for culture at the evening paper *Expressen*. He grew up in the post-war suburb of Täby outside Stockholm and moved to Malmö in 1980. In books such as *Storstugan* ("The Living Room", 1996), *Svenska hem* ("Swedish Homes", 2002) and *Malmö – världens svenskaste stad* ("Malmö – the world's most Swedish of cities", 2011), Svensson has homed in on the interplay between ideology, politics and town planning, and Jane Jacobs is a very present source of inspiration in his work.

Catharina Thörn is a sociologist and lecturer in cultural studies at the University of Gothenburg. She carries out research into urban development, public spaces and gentrification and among other things she has written *Gentrifiering* ("Gentrification", 2014) in cooperation with Helena Holgersson; *Den urbana fronten – en dokumentation av makten över staden* ("The Urban Front: a documentation of the power over the city", 2015) in collaboration with Katarina Despotovic; and *Stad till salu – entreprenörs-urbanismen och det offentliga rummets värde* ("City for Sale: Entrepreneurial urbanism and the value of the public space", 2016) in collaboration with Mats Frantzén and Nils Hertting.

SOURCES OF ILLUSTRATIONS

The editors and publishers are grateful for kind permission to reproduce the illustrations listed below. Every effort has been made to trace copyright holders, but we would be glad to hear if any have been inadvertently overlooked.

Cover: Elliott Erwitt/Magnum for *Vogue* magazine, 1960. Jane Jacobs papers, John L. Burns Library, Boston College.
Back cover: Walter Daran/Hulton Archive. Getty Images.
4–5: Jane Jacobs organised protests against the planned highways through Washington Square Park, New York City, 1963. Fred W. McDarrah. Getty Images.
14: Ron Bull/*Toronto Star*. Getty Images.
19: Reproduction from *Architectural Forum*, April 1956, pp. 50–51.
23: Hank Walker/The LIFE Picture Collection. Getty Images.
26: Bettmann Archive. Getty Images.
32: Ralph Morse/The LIFE Picture Collection. Getty Images.
38: Ed Molinari/*NY Daily News* Archive. Getty Images.
42: Reproduction of frontispiece from *Constitutional Chaff: Rejected Suggestions of the Constitutional Convention of 1787.*
46: Reproduction from *Architectural Forum*, May 1956, p. 149.
50: Bettmann Archive. Getty Images.
54–55: Sam Falk/*New York Times*. Getty Images.
62–63: Ernst Haas. Getty Images.
72: Phil Preston/*The Boston Globe*. Getty Images.
78–79: Frank O'Brien/*The Boston Globe*. Getty Images.
83: Michael Lipack/*NY Daily News* Archive. Getty Images.
86–87: pxl.store, Shutterstock.
92: Fred W. McDarrah. Getty Images.
94–95: Bettmann Archive. Getty Images.
102–103: Fred W. McDarrah. Getty Images.
106: Michael S. Williamson/*The Washington Post*. Getty Images.
110–111: BusinessCollection, Shutterstock.
117: Wikimedia Commons.
120: S. Ziese/Blickwinkel. Alamy Stock Photo.
126: Chris Ratcliffe/Bloomberg. Getty Images.
130: Reproduction from *The Economy of Cities*, 1969, p. 58.
133: Walter Daran/Hulton Archive. Getty Images.
136: Watford/Mirrorpix. Getty Images.
138: Reproduction from *Architectural Forum*, July 1955, p. 125.
144: Art Kowalsky. Alamy Stock Photo.
146: Heather Ainsworth/Bloomberg. Getty Images.
148: Bettmann Archive. Getty Images.
154–155: Richard Levine/Corbis. Getty Images.
158: Mirrorpix. Getty Images.
162: Tom Gallagher/*New York Daily News*. Getty Images.
166–167: Magnus Hartman. TT Nyhetsbyrån.
174: Andreas Feininger. Getty Images.
178–179: NASA.
190: Reproduction from *The Death and Life of Great American Cities*, pp. 178 and 182.
194–195: Steven Pisano.
197 (top): Reproduction from the lobby project Activity Based City (ABC).
197 (bottom): Reproduction from Sven Markelius (editor), *Det framtida Stockholm: riktlinjer för Stockholms generalplan* [The future Stockholm: guidelines for Stockholm's general plan], 1945, page 57.
202: Fred W. McDarrah. Getty Images.
207: Bettman Archive. Getty Images.
212–213: Ron Bull/*Toronto Star*. Getty Images.
216: Xiaodong Qiu. Getty Images.
220–221: Fine Art Images. Getty Images.
226–227: Jane Jacobs papers, John J. Burns Library, Boston College.
234: Dan Neville/Newsday RM. Getty Images.
236–237: Kennet Ruona.
250: Tony Savino/Corbis. Getty Images.
252–253: Boris Spremo/*Toronto Star*. Getty Images.
266–267: Kevin Winter. Getty Images.
270: Richard Lautens/*Toronto Star*. Getty Images.
280–281: Ken Faught/*Toronto Star*. Getty Images.
284: Keith Beaty/*Toronto Star*. Getty Images.
298–299: Penn Station: "Action!". Jane Jacobs picketing against the demolition of the original Pennsylvania Station, New York City, 1963. Fred W. McDarrah. Getty Images.

INDEX

A
ACTION !
AGBANY

ESSAYS ON JANE JACOBS

In association with Axel and Margaret Ax:son Johnson Foundation
This edition is based on *Samhällsbyggandet som mysterium. Jane Jacobs idéer om människor, städer och ekonomier* (Lund: Nordic Academic Press, 2018)

Editors: Jesper Meijling, Tigran Haas
Translation: Julie Martin
Text editor: Andrew Mackenzie
Image editors: Jesper Meijling, Nils Johan Tjärnlund
Design: Patric Leo
Original: Petra Ashton Inkapööl, Patric Leo
Repro: Italgraf Media, Stockholm, Sweden
Print: TMG Sthlm 2020 via Italgraf Media, Stockholm, Sweden
First edition, second printing

ISBN: 978-91-985236-9-0

AXEL AND MARGARET AX:SON JOHNSON FOUNDATION
FOR PUBLIC BENEFIT